The Ubiquitous Interne

T0251058

Understanding the role of the future internet requires addressing both the users' experiences and the industry's approaches to capitalizing on their users. Combining these two perspectives, this book provides an important contribution to developing a coherent view of the social consequences of the ubiquitous internet.

—*Tanja Storsul, University of Oslo, Norway*

This book presents state of the art theoretical and empirical research on the ubiquitous internet: its everyday users and its economic stakeholders. The book offers a 360-degree media analysis of the contemporary terrain of the internet by examining both user and industry perspectives and their relation to one another. Contributors consider user practices in terms of internet at your fingertips—the abundance, free flow, and interconnectivity of data. They then consider industry's use of user data and standards in commodification and value-creation.

Anja Bechmann is Associate Professor, Head of Digital Footprints Research Group at Aarhus University and board member of the National Council for Digital Security in Denmark. She is the initiator and co-developer of the Digital Footprints software and has published extensively on cross-media, internet economy, privacy regulation, and social media.

Stine Lomborg is Associate Professor of Communication and IT at the University of Copenhagen in Denmark. She has published extensively on user studies, focusing on the role of social media in everyday life. She is the author of *Social Media – Social Genres: Making Sense of the Ordinary* (with Routledge).

Routledge Studies in New Media and Cyberculture

The Ubiquitous Internet

User and Industry Perspectives

**Edited by Anja Bechmann
and Stine Lomborg**

Routledge
Taylor & Francis Group

LONDON AND NEW YORK

First published 2015
by Routledge

2 Park Square, Milton Park, Abingdon, Oxfordshire OX14 4RN
711 Third Avenue, New York, NY 10017

*Routledge is an imprint of the Taylor & Francis Group,
an informa business*

First issued in paperback 2018

Library of Congress Cataloging-in-Publication Data
The ubiquitous Internet : user and industry perspectives / edited by Anja
    Bechmann and Stine Lomborg.
      pages cm. — (Routledge studies in new media and cyberculture ; 25)
    Includes bibliographical references and index.
  1. Information technology—Social aspects.   2. Internet—Social
aspects.   3. Internet industry.   4. Ubiquitous computing—Social
aspects.   I. Bechmann, Anja, 1976–   II. Lomborg, Stine, 1982–
    HM851.U25 2015
    303.48′33—dc23
    2014030120

ISBN: 978-0-415-72574-3 (hbk)
ISBN: 978-1-138-54853-4 (pbk)

Typeset in Sabon
by Apex CoVantage, LLC

Contents

Figures and Tables

FIGURES

TABLES

Acknowledgements

We are grateful to all contributors for their dedication and high expertise. Our thanks also go to the anonymous reviewers of the original book proposal for insightful comments and to the many anonymous reviewers who have helped improve the chapters included in the book. Finally, we thank the Routledge team for their support and confidence in the book and the Digital Humanities Lab, Aarhus University, and the University of Copenhagen for funding our work on this book.

Introduction
The Ubiquitous Internet: Introduction and Conceptualization

Stine Lomborg and Anja Bechmann

Over the past twenty years, personal computers wired to the internet have become a natural part, for some even the backbone, of how people across the globe plan and execute work and leisure activities in everyday life. The lived experience with and monetization of the internet is still taking shape, partly owing to the fact that technology does not stand still. With the advent and rapid growth of platforms for mobile internet use, internet services have become platform independent with optional digital access devices such as smartphones, laptops, and PDAs. At the same time, internet services are increasingly made interoperable through APIs (Application Programming Interfaces), so that users experience seamless interfaces from one service to another through single logins, and companies and public organizations alike increasingly come to rely on digital data in their modeling of services and business innovation. Under the heading 'the ubiquitous internet,' this mobile, platform-independent, and interoperable character of the internet is the focus of this book. We examine the ubiquitous internet as a multisided and complex phenomenon. It manifests itself in diffusion patterns of ubiquitous internet devices, a diverse set of cultural practices of digital media use, and a whole range of sociopolitical issues across domains, including data protection, business innovation, and standardization processes.

In their seminal history on ubiquitous computing, Dourish and Bell (2011) sketch a fast development since the 1970s: from mainframe computers to desktop PCs to what they consider to be the third wave of computing technology—ubiquitous computing. This third wave is characterized by computing devices that are powerful, yet small enough to be carried around by people or embedded in other objects that inhabit daily life. Indeed, the ubiquitous internet extends itself across a wide variety of digital technologies. 'Wearables' such as the Fitbit Tracker and Google Glass which log, accumulate, and organize sensory, biometric, geo-locational, and other types of personal data are introduced to users in pursuit of, among other things, self-monitoring and augmentation of lived experience. 'The internet of things,' or what Greenfield (2006) has labeled 'everyware,' looms with intelligent devices applied for sustainable living, smart cities, and task relief (e.g., driverless cars, intelligent clothing, and robotic health care services). Many of these phenomena are still at an early stage of development and diffusion and thus have yet to assume a stable form. Yet, one specific class of technologies appears to have made the ubiquitous internet enter the mainstream: portable communication devices such as tablets and smartphones with dedicated apps for all imaginable purposes are carried around by ordinary individuals around the world and used in the course of daily life. This book centers on such technologies as they offer the first glimpse into what ubiquitous internet might involve for users, as well as for the technology and data industries.

Whereas the technological development of ubiquitous computing devices provides a necessary condition for the internet becoming ubiquitous, the ubiquitous internet is a much more complex, yet also more fuzzy phenomenon, loosely defined and often implicitly addressed in the scholarly literature. Arguably, the ubiquity of the internet encompasses not only technological platforms, but also the networked communications these platforms facilitate with services (i.e., apps, websites, etc.) and with people, including the massive data trails that are generated by these communications. In this book, we frame and discuss the ubiquitous internet not as a unitary phenomenon, but as a multi-dimensional concept that can be roughly defined and analyzed along four basic parameters:

1. the *accessibility* of multiple digital platforms and devices and the existence of—and convergence between—multiple standards in an integrated communication infrastructure;
2. the *mobility* of digital devices and services as means of facilitating seamlessly integrated communication practices throughout the individual users' everyday trajectories;
3. the *interoperability* of digital devices and services, multiple services in one device, multiple interfaces of one service, etc.; and
4. the *openness* of data, and by extension, the potential to integrate databases to make fine-grained profiling of users to create personalized, customized services and marketing.

Together, these parameters form the working definition of the ubiquitous internet that has informed the chapters of this book. To clarify and substantiate the ubiquitous internet further requires detailed research on not only the accessibility and potential invasiveness of internet on users, but also on the datafication of industries and the political responses to this process. Each dimension of the ubiquitous internet highlights new social dynamics, for instance, new kinds of divides between user groups, new types of global regulatory response, blurring distinctions between human and machine, and a tight interlocking of market logics and new forms of participation and personalization (Bechmann & Lomborg, 2013). Through a set of state-of-the-art empirical and historical studies of these social dynamics, this book aims to advance empirical as well as theoretical insights on the ubiquitous internet.

Studies of digital media use have shown how ordinary users have become increasingly tethered to their digital media in everyday life to the extent that the very media become taken for granted (Ling, 2012; also Deuze, 2012; Foth, 2011). Some have described how users willingly or blindly share their data with companies who thrive on datafication through social media platforms and raised critical questions about the commodification of users (Elmer, 2004; Fuchs, Boersma, Albrechtslund, & Sandoval, 2012; van Dijck, 2013), and the consequences of tethering for social life (Turkle, 2011). The user convenience of internet at your fingertips from any device near you and information that floats 'freely' and follows you around on the internet through interoperable cloud services potentially set new standards for user behavior and strategies on the internet in terms of sharing and data connecting that we know very little about (Taddicken, 2012). From a user perspective, Baron (2008) has pointed to the notion of being 'always on' as a central experiential quality of mobile media, but we lack a nuanced understanding of how being always on maps onto the practices through which users move seamlessly across services and media platforms in everyday life.

Another strand of research, on the digital media industries, has addressed datafication from the point of view of business innovation, for instance described through the empirical lens of the currently hyped 'big data' revolution (e.g., Mayer-Schonberger & Cukier, 2013), or the critical theoretical perspectives of surveillance (e.g., Gandy, 2006; Lyon, 2001) and the political economy of algorithmic filtering and personalization (e.g., Gillespie, 2010; Pariser, 2011). From a business perspective, the data generated and shared by users on the ubiquitous internet create new opportunities for monetization, through monitoring, data mining, and profiling techniques. However, despite the frequently voiced concern for user exploitation and commodification, we still know quite little about how exactly cloud companies like Facebook, Google, and Amazon, let alone the traditional retailing industry, aggregate and mine user data to generate value. Such knowledge is particularly critical, because the ubiquitous internet challenges institutional concepts of privacy, law, and economics of the internet.

Yet another strand of research has discussed the political and regulatory implications of interoperability as a key systemic factor of ubiquitous internet, both in terms of technological standardization and data consolidation (DeNardis, 2011; Lessig, 2006; Palfrey & Gasser, 2012). A key concern here is with the degree of 'openness' and 'neutrality' of the internet as it evolves over time. More and more information on the internet flows only within industry-owned domains such as Facebook and Google and across platforms that have their own internet standards (e.g., apps and browsers for mobile platforms). Business analysts have called this fenced-off internet the 'splinternet' (Bernoff & VanBoskirk, 2010; Thomson, 2010) to describe the movement from open shared standards such as the World Wide Web to different competitive clusters of standards and internet control.

While distinct in their focus, it is remarkable that these bodies of litera-ture are sparsely interconnected. This book presents a first step towards dia-logue between them, by bringing user and industry perspectives together in the theoretical grounding and empirical analysis of the ubiquitous internet. Thus, the book presents a set of four empirical studies on users, focusing on the communicative affordances and usage patterns of ubiquitous internet (Part I), and a set of four analyses approaching the ubiquitous internet from an industry perspective, focusing on its social implications for ordinary users as well as economic and institutional stakeholders (Part II).

The integrative meta-frame of the book is media sociology, particu-larly the sociology of digital media. All the contributions to this volume are derived from media sociology, understood very broadly as a subfield of media and communication studies interested in the social consequences and societal embedding of media. As such, media sociology builds on a long tra-jectory in mass media research of empirical studies and theorizing on media audiences and uses as well as media institutions, policy, and regulation. We contend that this line of research offers a particularly ready platform for dialogue and possible cross-fertilizing of user and industry studies of the ubiquitous internet. Part of the exercise in this book is therefore to explore how far established frameworks of media sociology shed light on the ubiq-uitous internet. This exploration is based in the eight individual chapters detailing the user and industry perspectives, respectively.

The second step, initiating the dialogue between user and industry analy-ses, is accomplished by the book as a whole. Firstly, the combination of user and industry perspectives in this compilation serves the idea of viewing the two perspectives as *context for one another* to elicit deep analysis of how user productivity and behavioral patterns may add to the value chain of online businesses while at the same time offering significant personal reward and pleasure for the users. Secondly, by combining user and industry per-spectives, the book concludes by clarifying the cross-fertilizing potentials of the user and industry perspectives and sketching what could become a stronger integration of the perspectives in what we label a *360-degree media analysis* of the contemporary terrain of the ubiquitous internet (Bechmann & Lomborg, 2013). We hope this in turn will inspire future scholars to a stron-ger integration in ubiquitous internet studies.

REFERENCES

Baron, N. S. (2008). *Always on: Language in an online and mobile world*. Oxford, UK: Oxford University Press.

Bechmann, A., & Lomborg, S. (2013). Mapping actor roles in social media: Differ-ent perspectives on value creation in theories of user participation. *New Media & Society*, 15(5), 765–781.

Bernoff, J., & VanBoskirk, S. (2010). *The splinternet: Preparing for an internet fragmented by devices and passwords*. Cambridge, MA. Forrester Research.

DeNardis, L. (2011). *Opening standards: The global politics of interoperability*. Cambridge, MA: MIT Press.

Deuze, M. (2012). *Media life*. Cambridge, UK: Polity Press.

Dourish, P., & Bell, G. (2011). *Divining a digital future: Mess and mythology in ubiquitous computing*. Cambridge, MA: MIT Press.

Elmer, G. (2004). *Profiling machines*. Cambridge, MA: MIT Press.

Foth, M. (Ed.). (2011). *From social butterfly to engaged citizen*. Cambridge, MA: MIT Press.

Fuchs, C., Boersma, K., Albrechtslund, A., & Sandoval, M. (Eds.). (2012). *Internet and surveillance: The challenges of Web 2.0 and social media*. London: Routledge.

Gandy, O. H. (2006). Data mining, surveillance, and discrimination in the post-9/11 environment. In R. V. Ericson & K. D. Haggerty (Eds.), *The new politics of surveillance and visibility* (pp. vi, 386). Toronto: University of Toronto Press.

Gillespie, T. (2010). The politics of 'platforms'. *New Media & Society, 12*(3), 347–364.

Greenfield, A. (2006). *Everyware: The dawning age of ubiquitous computing*. Berkeley, CA: New Riders.

Lessig, L. (2006). *Code: And other laws of cyberspace, version 2.0*. New York: Basic Books.

Ling, R. (2012). *Taken for grantedness. The embedding of mobile communication into society*. Cambridge, MA: MIT Press.

Lyon, D. (2001). *Surveillance society: Monitoring everyday life*. Philadelphia: Open University Press.

Mayer-Schonberger, V., & Cukier, K. (2013). *Big data: A revolution that will transform how we live, work, and think*. New York: Houghton Mifflin Hardback Publishing.

Palfrey, J., & Gasser, U. (2012). *Interop: The promise and perils of highly interconnected systems*. New York: Basic Books.

Pariser, E. (2011). *The filter bubble: What the internet is hiding from you*. New York: Penguin Press.

Taddicken, M. (2012). Privacy, surveillance, and self-disclosure in the social web: Exploring the user's perspective via focus groups. In C. Fuchs, K. Boersma, A. Albrechtslund, & M. Sandoval (Eds.), *Internet and surveillance: The challenges of Web 2.0 and social media* (pp. 255–272). New York: Routledge.

Thomson, D. (2010, March 8). The fall of the internet and the rise of the splinternet. *The Atlantic*. Retrieved from http://www.theatlantic.com/business/archive/2010/03/the-fall-of-the-internet-and-the-rise-of-the-splinternet/37181/. Accessed 2 October 2014.

Turkle, S. (2011). *Alone together. Why we expect more from technology and less from each other*. New York: Basic Books.

van Dijck, J. (2013). *The culture of connectivity. A critical history of social media*. Oxford, UK: Oxford University Press.

Part I

Users and Usage Patterns

This section examines the ubiquitous internet from the users' perspective. The four chapters in this section explore the (new) communicative practices and modes of engagement that arise with the increasingly multi-device, portable, interoperable, and open internet. In what ways does it change or reify existing patterns of internet usage? How do users experience and manage the ubiquitous internet, and with what consequences for their privacy and empowerment? The chapters address the ubiquitous internet both in terms of cross-device and within-device uses, as well as in terms of the interconnectedness of specific services such as apps and social media.

Common for the four chapters is a reliance on empirical user studies, drawing on a diverse set of methods, including surveys, interviews, behavioral API data, and documents. Moreover, the questions of ubiquitous internet use, forms of user engagement, and empowerment that form the basis of the chapters are classic questions posed to all kinds of media in various strands of media audience research (Jensen & Rosengren, 1990).

The internet is itself a dynamic technology that is constantly evolving as users adopt and reject new features and applications and use them in ways that are often unanticipated. The first chapter of this volume, by Grant Blank and William H. Dutton, is anchored primarily in longitudinal survey data on how Britons use the internet, which illuminates the emergence of new patterns of accessing the internet over multiple devices—some of which are portable. Hence, in this first empirical analysis, ubiquity is addressed as the interconnected use of devices for communication that forms a basic condition for internet use. Blank and Dutton specifically investigate the rising use of mobile devices among a range of devices used to access the Internet, and label those who adopt this new approach to internet use 'Next Generation Users.' Next Generation Users are defined as Internet users who access the Internet (1) on mobile and (2) on multiple devices. In contrast, first generation users remain anchored to one or more personal computers in the household or workplace for accessing the internet. Their analysis further shows how the emerging pattern of access is reshaping the use and impact of the internet. Next Generation Users are disproportionately likely to use the internet for entertainment, content production, and information-seeking, even with controls for demographic factors. Blank and Dutton conclude that mobility and multiple devices are reconfiguring access to information, people, and services in ways that are likely to empower Next Generation Users in relation to other users. This, the authors suggest, may herald the beginning of a new digital divide, or be a transitional phase to an un-tethered internet age.

Complementing Blank and Dutton's focus on the patterns of access to and communication on ubiquitous, (mobile) internet devices, in chapter two of this volume Stine Lomborg discusses how ordinary users make sense of these devices as pocket-size, portable entry-points for going online in everyday life. In the scholarly literature, the ubiquity of digital media and communications has been framed, very broadly, as nurturing an experiential sense of being 'always on,' of 'ambient intimacy,' and so on. But what does it mean, in a qualitative sense, for individuals to be 'always on' the internet, for instance by carrying the internet with them on their mobile devices as they go about their everyday business? Lomborg combines an affordance-based analysis of smartphones with an empirical study, based on qualitative interviews with a sample of twelve Danish smartphone users, on the meanings and significance that they ascribe to their smartphones as ubiquitous internet devices in everyday life, with a particular focus on social media. The study argues that the experiential qualities of ubiquitous internet arise not merely from the constant and convenient availability of the internet, but are negotiated in the concrete situations of use.

Continuing the exploration of social media use in the context of the ubiquitous internet, in chapter three of this volume Anja Bechmann presents an analysis of the largest, most interoperable, and diversified social media data company on the internet. Facebook collects personal and sensitive data about its users across devices and services in various contexts ranging from self-reported information on religion and politics, everyday whereabouts and check-ins to pictures from Instagram, playlists from Spotify, and running routes in Runkeeper. The users share these data paths with their network of friends, Facebook administrators, external companies, advertising agencies, and app developers, but how do users navigate in this seamless service? How do they manage interoperability, what is considered to be sensitive data which should not be shared, and why? And what are the user strategies of personal data sharing in the seamless and ubiquitous environment of Facebook? Bechmann focuses on interoperable and potentially seamless communication as one of the main characteristics of the mobile and ubiquitous internet. Drawing on API (Application Programming Interface) data retrieval from Facebook and interviews with high-school students, she presents an ethno-mining inspired study of interoperability and data sharing in the setting of Facebook, showing how participants use Facebook groups as a privacy filter. The high-school students choose not to use the built-in potential for interoperability in the service. The chapter further demonstrates that, in using groups as a privacy filter, the students have a common understanding of personal data and personal data handling, along with a high degree of experienced control when designing their own code of conduct, practices, and uses of the Facebook interface and functions in the quest to socialize with their friends.

Completing the user studies section, and pointing beyond the mundane usage patterns described in the first three chapters, in chapter four of this volume Jun Liu explores the interrelationship between the ubiquity of information and communication technologies and contentious politics. Specifically, Liu looks at how ubiquitous internet generates new dynamics of contentious politics and empowerment by taking information and communication technologies (ICT)-mediated contentions in China as the case. The study investigates two cases in rural and urban China in which Chinese people employed their digital devices for protests, based on analyses of documents and accounts from eleven in-depth interviews with participants in these protests. Liu demonstrates how ubiquitous internet enables and facilitates the emergence of real-time contentious politics, in which it acts not only as means of overcoming censorship but also as means of organizing and mobilizing. Ubiquitous internet thus integrates the dynamics of real-time politics into the process of contentious activities and transforms contentious politics in contemporary China.

REFERENCE

Jensen, K. B., & Rosengren, K. E. (1990). Five traditions in search of the audience. *European Journal of Communication*, 5(2), 207–238.

1 Next Generation Users
Changing Access to the Internet

Grant Blank and William H. Dutton

Many claim that we have entered a 'post-PC' era. The basis for this perception are arguments like 'more and more consumers are using their mobile devices as their "default gateway" for accessing the Internet' (King, 2012), or

> as soon as 3 to 5 years from now, the average business professional will be transitioning from 'Heavy' clients such as desktop PCs and business laptops with large amounts of localized storage and localized applications . . . to very small and extremely power efficient . . . systems . . . which will function mostly as cache for applications that run remotely.
>
> (Perlow, 2012)

Hewlett-Packard's September 2012 announcement that it would lay off 29,000 employees seemed to support this argument with hard data on the decline of the personal computer and subsequent shifts of investment away from desktop computers to the mobile internet. There is no question that the phenomenal growth of smartphones, tablets, and readers is having a major impact on how people access the internet. However, the arguments favoring the 'post-PC' era are based on the assumption that PCs are being supplanted by lightweight, mobile devices. Although PC sales are slowing as the market matures (BBC News, 2013) the assumption that PCs are being superseded lacks systematic evidence based on trends in how users access the internet.

The movement to mobile devices is one element in the larger movement that includes platform-independence and interoperability of services and applications on the internet. All these contribute to the ubiquitous internet, where we no longer 'go to' the internet. Instead the internet is available at all times, in all circumstances—anytime, anywhere. Mobile devices facilitate this move by making the internet accessible when no wired connection is available. Mobile devices offer new kinds of access to the internet but, as our analysis indicates, the relationship between PCs and mobile devices is a great deal more complex than simple replacement of one device by another. We examine mobile use by defining Next Generation Users (NGUs) as internet users who access the internet (1) on mobile and (2) on multiple devices.

We use data from the Oxford Internet Survey (OxIS) to describe the rise, extent and characteristics of NGUs. As we describe the relationship between PCs and mobile devices through the lens of NGUs we will answer several questions: Who uses these devices? What differences might they make in relation to how people use the internet, such as for various entertainment or information services? Are they closing down the internet by making it harder for users to access new content, or are they opening up the internet to new users and uses? If they are valuable new channels for access, are they more widely accessible, enabling new users, or does access on new devices reinforce existing digital divides?

THEORETICAL PERSPECTIVES

Most generally, three competing theoretical perspectives on the social role of the internet may offer useful insights into this shift and its consequences. They are all qualitative explanations of how people relate to the internet, rather than operationally defined models, but they capture the major competing perspectives on the role of the internet in everyday life, which we can compare and contrast with our empirical survey findings.

Technical Rationality

One dominant perspective is a technical rationality that draws on major features of new technologies to reason about the likely implications of adoption. Although many social scientists view this as a technological determinist perspective, it characterizes some of the most prominent scholars of the internet and new technology, such as Lawrence Lessig (1999) and his view that 'code is law.'[1] The view from this perspective is that the move towards 'appliances' is bound up with adoption of closed applications or 'apps' that have a limited set of functions. These appliances restrict the openness, and 'generativity' of the internet, compared to general-purpose personal computers, which enable users to program, write code, and not be limited by a secured set of applications and sites (Zittrain, 2010). Because those who adopt the new appliance devices, such as tablets, are satisfied with the closed applications, they are likely to be less sophisticated than those who remain anchored to personal computing, and less creative in their use and application of the internet. Will they move users toward a role as more passive browsers of information and consumers of entertainment?

Domestication: A Social Rationality

In contrast, there is a more socially deterministic perspective on the role of the internet and related information and communication technologies (ICTs) in the household that is best captured by work on the 'domestication' of the internet. Domestication (Haddon, 2006, 2007, 2011; Silverstone et al., 1992) emphasizes the influence of households or work places on shaping, taming, or domesticating technologies as users fit them into the values and interests of their particular social context. People adopt and integrate technologies into their everyday routines in ways that follow and reinforce existing practices, which differ across households. The concept of domestication was developed as a way to elaborate a conceptual model for exploring the role of information and communication technologies (ICTs) in life within the household (Silverstone et al., 1992; Livingstone, 1992; Silverstone, 1996). The formulation entails four 'non-discrete elements' that enable the domestication process, which have been called: appropriation, objectification, incorporation, and conversion (Silverstone et al., 1992, p. 20). *Appropriation* occurs when the technology is purchased and its entry into a household must be managed. *Objectification* refers to how consumers locate a technology in the household, both physically and symbolically. *Incorporation* occurs when the technology is fitted into everyday routines of a household. Finally, *conversion* designates the ways in which technologies are displayed to others for impression management.[2] These elements do not have a strict order. Although appropriation is clearly prior, the other three elements interact and shape each other.

This chapter is particularly interested in the incorporation of the internet into daily routines of people as they appropriate an array of internet technologies into their everyday routines. Characteristic of the internet is that it is not a single new technology. Rather it gives access to a variety of innovations, including web browsers, location and direction services, email, and social networking. This presents a large menu of items to be incorporated into people's day-to-day life. It will not be done all at once; for many the internet is a continuing, multi-year exploration of new possibilities across multiple artifacts. In such respects, this domestication model is in line with earlier conceptions of the social shaping of technology in organizations, such as the notion of 'reinforcement politics,' which argued that organizations adopt and shape information technologies to follow and reinforce the prevailing structures of power and influence within the adopting organizations (Danziger et al., 1982). Because domestication suggests people shape the internet to their pre-existing interests and values, we would not expect the adoption of new technologies to make much difference in how people use the internet, nor have a significant, transformative impact on the social role of the internet in their lives as it is 'domesticated.'[3]

Reconfiguring Access

A different theoretical perspective revolves around the concept of 'reconfiguring access' (Dutton, 1999, 2005). From this perspective, it is impossible to determine the implications of technologies in advance, either by rationally extrapolating from the technical features of the innovations or by assessing the interests and values of users. This distinguishes this perspective from both a more technologically deterministic view and a socially determinist position. Reconfiguring access takes note of the fact that users often reinvent technologies, employing them in ways not expected by their developers. In addition, the social role of a technology can be influenced by the actions of many actors other than users, and from choices far outside the household, which distinguishes this perspective from the notion of domestication. Control of new technologies, particularly a networked technology such as the internet, is distributed across a wide array of actors, including users, Internet Service Providers, hardware manufacturers, search engine providers, and social networking companies. Rather than expecting the impacts to be determined by features of the technology, or the values and interests of the household, reconfiguring access places a central emphasis on observing the actual use and impact across a diversity of users to discern emergent patterns of use and impact.

However, like a more technologically deterministic model, the concept of reconfiguring access is based on the expectation that technologies do matter—they have social implications—in two major respects. They reconfigure (1) how people do things, as well as (2) the outcome of these activities. People adopt and use technologies, such as the internet, more or less intentionally to reconfigure access in multiple ways, including their access to people, information, services and technologies, and access to themselves. From this perspective, the technology does not simply fit into existing practices, but it changes them. If a person enjoys reading the newspaper, they might decide to use the internet to get access to the news. However, this changes how they get the news and how much news they can get, as well as what news they obtain and how easily they obtain it. It reconfigures their access to the news, in this case.

The internet can change the outcome of information and communication activities by virtue of changing cost structures, creating or eliminating gatekeepers, redistributing power between senders and receivers, making a task easier or more difficult, changing the circumstances under which a task can be performed, restructuring the architecture of networks (many to one versus one to many), and changing the geography of access (Dutton, 1999). By changing costs, or eliminating gatekeepers, for example, the internet can reconfigure access to information, people, services, and technologies, such as by making millions of computers accessible to a user of a smartphone. The role of the internet for users in reconfiguring their access can be used to reinforce existing social arrangements, like helping friends stay in touch, or to reconfigure social relations, such as helping a person to meet new people. It can be used to reinforce a person's interest in the news, but also open up new channels and sources for news.

These approaches have been analyzed by several empirical literatures: the digital divide and the shift to mobile devices. The digital divide literature has focused, first, on access to the internet and then, as more people have gone online, to the study of other inequities in access to use of the internet (DiMaggio et al., 2004; van Deursen & van Dijk, 2013). There now seems to be a consensus in the literature that '. . . the actual use of the Internet is a more prevalent source of inequality than the plain access to the Internet' (Wei, 2012, p. 304). In this context mobile use is only the latest in a series of technologies that emphasize how people use the internet over simple access. Mobile phones were the earliest manifestation of a widely adopted mobile device. They have been tools for expanding and enhancing personal relationships (Ling & Campbell, 2009). The mobile internet adds capabilities for entertainment, information, and other tools that expand the value of mobile use. Our question is, how are people using their new mobile internet capabilities and what theoretical lens best helps us understand?

APPROACH

Diverse methodologies have been used in studies of the internet and its associated tools. The main methodologies used to study domestication, for example, have been qualitative, usually ethnographic (Silverstone, 2005). This chapter uses survey data, which has certain disadvantages because it cannot address questions of meaning in the ways than an ethnographic approach seeks to do. However, others have used surveys to study domestication (e.g., Punie, 1997), and a sample survey has the major advantage that the results can be generalized to a population. In this case, we can generalize to the population of Britain and by reflecting on other World Internet Project research (see http://www.worldinternetproject.org), speculate on the wider applicability of our findings.

This chapter addresses these issues around new patterns of internet access by focusing on the analysis of survey data gathered in Britain as part of the Oxford Internet Survey (OxIS), which is one component of the World Internet Project (WIP), a consortium of over two dozen national partners. OxIS began in 2003 and has been organized around a number of themes that allow us to analyze the dataset for specific trends and topics, including: digital and social inclusion and exclusion; shaping, regulating, and governing the internet; safety, trust, and privacy online; social networking and entertainment; and online transactions and commerce. Based on the demographic and attitudinal questions asked in the survey it is possible to construct profiles of the survey participants, which include users and non-users of the internet. Our analyses relate these profiles to the data about use and non-use to allow us to draw detailed conclusions about who uses the internet, in which way, and to what extent.

Unless otherwise noted all data cited in this chapter are from the Oxford Internet Survey (OxIS).[4] Interviews are conducted face-to-face in people's homes by professionally trained field survey staff. OxIS is a biennial sample survey of adult (fourteen years of age and older) internet use in Britain, including England, Wales, and Scotland. The first survey was conducted in 2003 and subsequent surveys followed in 2005, 2007, 2009, 2011, and 2013. Each survey has followed an identical sampling methodology. The respondents are selected for face-to-face interviews based on a three-stage random sample of the population. The data are then weighted based on gender, age, socio-economic grade, and region. Response rates using this sampling strategy have been high: 60% in 2003, 66% (2005), 68% (2007), 53% (2009), 47% in 2011, and 52% in 2013.[5] Although questions have been added as new issues have emerged, many questions have remained consistent to facilitate comparisons between years.

An important strength of OxIS is that it is not a convenience sample. This distinguishes it from many otherwise excellent datasets. This has both methodological and theoretical implications. Methodologically, as a representative sample, OxIS allows us to project to the adult (fourteen and over) population of Britain. This is not possible for a convenience sample. Theoretically a random sample of adults allows us to explore a number of interesting variables. The convenience samples are often composed of those residing in a particular locale, or college students, for example, who have limited variation in age, social status, and income compared to the general population of internet users. We can explore the effects of these demographic variables where convenience samples cannot.

In most of the analyses below we use the 2013 survey, which completed interviews with 2,657 people. Our analyses are based either on the full sample of 2,657 or on the subset of current internet users, 2,082 respondents, 78.4% of the full sample.[6] However, although the focus of our analysis is on a snapshot of one nation, as part of longitudinal set of surveys and the WIP we are able to compare our findings overtime and with the results in nations around the world to determine of our findings are more or less consistent. Our analysis was innovative within the WIP collaboration, so our exact analysis has not been replicated, but we have found no reports from our partner countries that would suggest the UK findings are unique in the patterns we have discussed at international meetings of the WIP. The main differences are in levels, such as the level of internet adoption, but not in the basic patterns of relationships that we report.

DEFINING THE NEXT GENERATION USER

Are Next Generation Users domesticating two recent developments in the internet, or is their access to the internet and wider world being constrained by new appliances, or reconfigured in other ways by these new technical devices? In contrast to the first generation of internet users the Next Generation User is defined by the emergence of two separate but related trends: portability and access through multiple devices.

First, there has been a continuing increase in the proportion of users with portable devices, using the internet over one or another mobile device, such as a smartphone. In 2003 this was a small proportion. At that time, 85% of British people had a mobile phone but only 11% of mobile phone users said they accessed email or the internet over their mobile phone. By 2009, 97% of British people owned a mobile phone, and the proportion of users accessing email or the internet over their phone doubled to 24%—albeit still a minority of users. In 2011, this increased to nearly half (49%) of all users, and by 2013 to over 66% of all users. Similarly, tablet use grew from 6% of the British population in 2005 to 37% in 2013. Reader use showed an even faster rise: from 7% in 2011 to 27% in 2013. By 2013, a number of portable devices could be used to access the internet both within and outside the household.

Secondly, internet users often have more devices, such as multiple computers, as well as readers and tablets, in addition to mobile phones, to access the internet. In 2005, only 5% of households had three or more computers, but by 2011, this proportion had risen to 18%. It remained at 18% in 2013. Likewise, in 2009, only 19% had a PDA (Personal Digital Assistant). Since then, the development of readers and tablets has boomed, such as with Apple's successful introduction of the iPad in 2010. The very notion of a PDA has become antiquated. In 2013, 53% of internet users had either a reader or a tablet, 25% used both.

Most observers have treated these developments as separate trends. There are even academics who focus only on use of the internet in the household, others only on mobile communication, and others who focus on the use of tablets or the use of smartphones.[7] We will argue, however, these trends across multiple devices are not just related but are also synergistic. The evidence below shows that those who use multiple devices are also more likely to use the internet on the move and from multiple locations—anytime, anywhere.

We therefore define the Next Generation User as someone who accesses the internet from multiple locations and devices. Operationally, we define the Next Generation User as someone who uses at least two of four internet applications on their mobile or who fits two or more of the following criteria: they own a tablet, own a reader, own three or more computers. The four mobile applications are: browsing the internet, using email, updating a social networking site, or finding directions. By this definition, in 2013, over half of Britons, and 66.7% of internet users in Britain, were Next Generation Users (see further on, Table 1.1 and Figure 1.1). The remainder are, by definition, First Generation Users; that is, First Generation Users do not make the intensive use of multiple devices, some of which are mobile, that characterizes Next Generation Users.

Table 1.1   Next Generation Users (%)

	Percent of British population	Percent of internet users
2007	13	20
2009	22	32
2011	32	44
2013	52	67

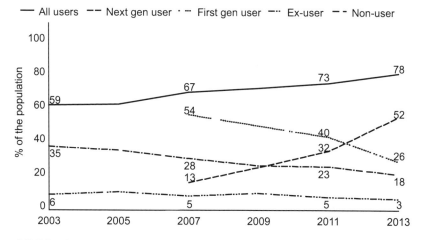

OxIS 2003 N=2,029; 2005 N=2,185; 2007 N=2,350; 2009 N=2,013; 2011 N=2,057; 2013 N=2,657

Figure 1.1   Next Generation Users: 2007–2013.

THE EMERGENCE OF NEXT GENERATION USERS

In 2013, NGUs comprised 67% of internet users in Britain. Next Generation Users are not just teenagers: As a consequence of long-term trends in patterns of use they emerged across all age groups. They did not appear overnight: With the benefit of hindsight, we can look back and see that the proportion of Next Generation Users grew from 20% in 2007, to 32% in 2009, to 44% in 2011, to 67% in 2013 (Table 1.1).

From the Oxford Internet Institute's (OII) first survey of internet use in 2003, and in line with most other developed nations, access has been based primarily on the use of a personal computer in one's household, linked to the internet through a modem or broadband connection. For many, this was complemented by similar access at work or school. The major change in access since 2003 was the move from narrowband dial-up to broadband always-on internet connections, leading observers to speak of 'broadband users.' By 2009, nearly all internet users had a broadband connection, increasingly including wireless connections within the household, such as over a WiFi router. Although speeds will continue to increase through initiatives such as 'superfast' broadband, and wireless connections will expand, this pattern of internet access characterizes the First Generation User in Britain.

How can we explain the rise of the Next Generation User and its significance in the context of the study of the internet, and what difference does it make?

WHY DOES THIS MATTER?

Theoretically, as discussed above, changes in technologies of the internet could reshape access to information and other online resources. The following pages show how this transformation in internet access is indeed linked to important changes in patterns of use, and in the social implications of use. We then show that Next Generation Users are not evenly distributed, but have higher incomes, indicating a new digital divide in Britain and most certainly in other nations. We conclude by showing that the characteristics of NGUs do not explain changing patterns of use and impact, as NGU has a direct relationship with how users access and create information, even when controlling for demographic characteristics.

Figure 1.1 shows that the rapid growth of Next Generation Users has taken place amid a more gradual rise in overall internet use. Internet use in Britain grew from just over 60% in 2003 to 78% in 2013, leaving more than a fifth of the British population without access to the internet. There has been a steady but slow decline in the proportion of people who have never used the internet (non-users), and relative stability in the proportion of those who have used the internet at one time but who no longer do so (ex-users). Despite multiple government and private initiatives aimed at bringing people online, digital divides remain in access to the internet.

At one level, there is apparent stability, particularly visible in the proportion of British people with access to the internet. At a deeper level, a dramatic transition is occurring among users. The proportion of First Generation Users has been declining, whereas the proportion of Next Generation Users has been rising (Figure 1.1). Clearly, the promotion of new technical devices, such as the tablet, has changed the way households access the internet. It is hard to see this as simply a process of domestication, rather than a consequence of new product and service offerings.

How individual users access the internet shapes the ways in which they use the technology, and how people wish to use the internet is shaping the technologies they adopt. This is illustrated by the contrast between First and Next Generation use of the internet in three areas: content production, entertainment and leisure, and information seeking. In each case, a technical rationality might see innovations reducing the openness and generativity of users, whereas from a domestication perspective, you would expect to see little change in patterns of use between Next and First Generation Users. Neither conforms to the pattern of our findings, as shown below.

CONTENT PRODUCTION

In contrast to the technical rationality perspective, with its focus on how the limited openness of new devices restricts users, Next Generation Users are more likely to be producers of content than are First Generation Users, who concentrate more on consumption rather than production (such as by posting material on the internet). For many types of content, Next Generation Users are as much as 40% more likely to be producers. Specifically, Next Generation Users are more likely to update or create a profile on a social networking site (Figure 1.2). They are also more likely than First Generation Users to post pictures and videos, post messages on discussion

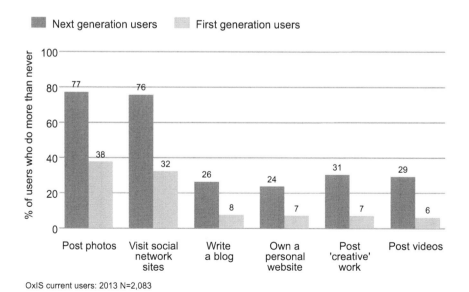

Figure 1.2   Next Generation Users by content production.

boards or forums, and post stories, poetry, or other creative work (Figure 1.2). For more demanding types of content, such as maintaining a personal website or writing a blog, Next Generation Users are over three times as likely to be producers than are First Generation Users. Innovations are reconfiguring access by simplifying production of content and Next Generation Users are taking advantage of these new possibilities, but in a direction opposite to that expected on the basis of the more limited features of appliances.

Entertainment and Leisure

Compared with First Generation Users, the NGU is much more likely to listen to music online, play games, download music, watch videos online, and download, as well as upload, videos or music files (Figure 1.3). As with content production, these are large differences, often exceeding 30% to 40%. To a lesser degree, NGUs bet or gamble online. Next Generation Users seem to have integrated the internet more extensively into their entertainment and leisure activities. In this respect, the association with listening to more music or watching more video content is in line with the technical rationality of appliances, but it shows how the internet is reconfiguring access to entertainment, which would not be anticipated from the perspective of domestication.

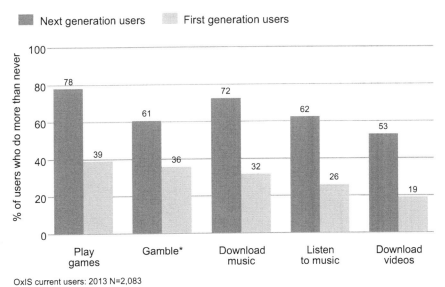

OxIS current users: 2013 N=2,083

Figure 1.3 Next Generation Users by entertainment.

The Essential Importance of the Internet

Next Generation Users are much more likely to agree that the internet is 'essential' in meeting the information and entertainment needs of users. Figure 1.4 reports the percentage that considers various media essential for information, Figure 1.5 reports for entertainment. Both figures tell a consistent story about

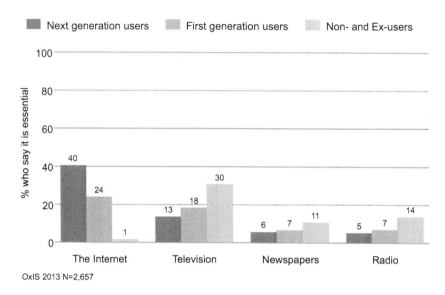

Figure 1.4　Importance of media for information.

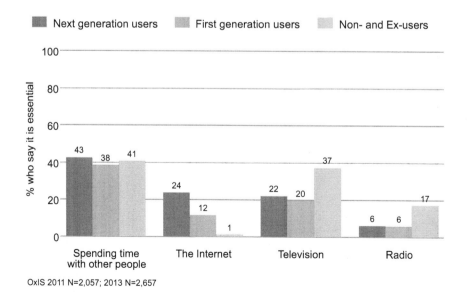

Figure 1.5　Importance of media for entertainment.

Next Generation Users. For information, they are 17% more likely to consider the internet essential; for entertainment, they exceed First Generation Users by 12%. Also notable is that the internet is the only medium where Next Generation and First Generation Users differ, except for spending time with other people for entertainment. These figures underline the disproportionate value that Next Generation Users place on the internet (for further exploration of the meanings attached to the ubiquitous internet, see Lomborg, this volume).

Information Seeking

As interesting as how Next Generation Users differ from First Generation Users is how they are similar. One of the major changes over the past decade has been the growing use of the internet as a source of information, particularly with the rise of powerful and usable search engines such as Google. All internet users increasingly go to the internet for information. It is their first port of call. However, even for this purpose, Next Generation Users are more likely than First Generation Users to go to the internet for all kinds of information (Figure 1.6).

For example, 84% of Next Generation Users go online for news, compared with 75% of First Generation Users. Given the high proportion of all users who rely on the internet for information, these differences are smaller than the differences observed above for content production and entertainment, only 7%–17%, but statistically and substantively significant. The largest difference is looking for sports information. Because sports are an entertainment activity, they have much in common with entertainment uses (cf. Figure 1.3). Sport is the exception that proves the rule. Given that Next Generation Users can

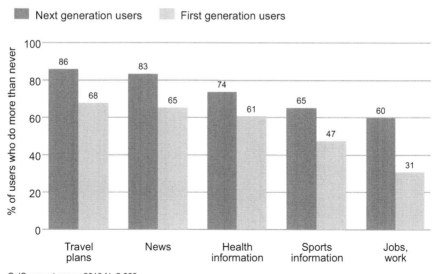

OxIS current users: 2013 N=2,083

Figure 1.6 Next Generation Users by information seeking.

access the internet from more locations on more devices at more times of the day, their use of the internet for information is more extensive, but to a lesser extent because information seeking has become so common for all users.

Portability and Mobility

Do Next Generation Users access the internet from more locations? Figure 1.7 shows that this is indeed the case. NGUs are no more likely than First Generation Users to access the internet from their home, but—importantly—they are no less likely to do so. This underscores the continuing centrality of the household across the generations of users. However, NGUs are far more likely to access the internet on the move and from all other locations, including another person's home, at work, at school or at university, at a library, or at an internet café (Figure 1.7).

This finding might suggest the flaw in a technically rational argument that appliances would undermine the generativity of the internet (Zittrain, 2010). Appliances do not appear to be substituting for personal computers and other more general-purpose devices, but complementing these technologies, and extending them in time and place. Whether this is a transitional phase, where more substitution will occur remains to be seen, but in 2013, nearly everyone with a reader or tablet tends to use these technologies to augment rather than replace their other modes for accessing the internet.

More generally, and in contrast the technical argument, or the domestication thesis, Next Generation Users appear to be empowered, relative

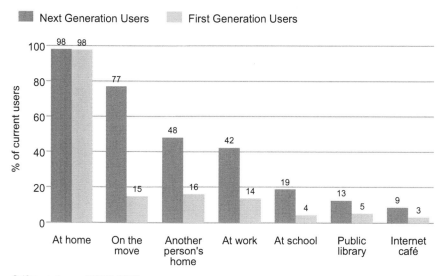

OxIS current users: 2013 N=2,083

Figure 1.7 Next Generation Users by locations.

to the First Generation Users, in creating content, enjoying entertainment online, and accessing information in ways and at times and locations that fit into their everyday life and work in a more integrated way. Of course, those who want to create content and embed the internet in more aspects of their everyday life are more likely to adopt next generation technologies, so in that sense, a domestication process could be relevant, but domestication does not lead to the expectation that new devices will change patterns of access, as shown in our data. Through the social shaping of adoption and the empowerment of users, it is clear that the Next Generation User has a more advantageous relationship with the internet and the resources it can provide for accessing information, people, services, and other technologies.

This leads to the question, who are the Next Generation Users? Who is empowered by next generation access, and who is not?

WHO ARE NEXT GENERATION USERS?

Are Next Generation Users simply the youth of the internet age? Not really. Age and life stage are related to Next Generation use, but primarily to the degree that people who are retired or of retirement age are much less likely to be Next Generation Users. Those who are unemployed are also somewhat less likely to be part of the next generation, whereas students and the employed are equally likely to be Next Generation Users. It is not simply a function of youth or age cohorts. For example, only 52% of students are Next Generation Users (Figure 1.8). In short, domestication does not

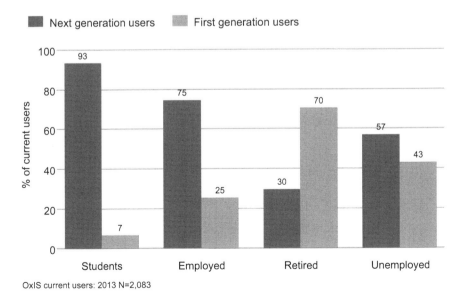

OxIS current users: 2013 N=2,083

Figure 1.8 Next Generation Users by lifestage.

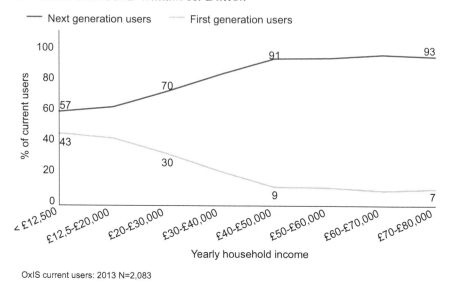

Figure 1.9 Next Generation Users by income.

adequately predict how new technologies are incorporated into peoples' lives, as some are more capable of bending new technologies to serve their needs and interests than are others. In this way, innovations are reconfiguring access by creating a new digital divide across people at different stages of life.

Another major factor related to Next Generation Users is household income. There are Next Generation Users at every income level, but there are clearly a greater proportion of Next Generation Users among the higher income groups in Britain (Figure 1.9). It helps to have more money when buying a variety of devices, many of which remain expensive. The Next Generation User is creating a new level of access to the internet and the Web that supports active patterns of information production and the integration of the internet into everyday life and work. It creates a new cost for the internet and is more accessible to the more well-to-do, suggesting that there is a new digital divide developing in Britain, and probably other nations, between the First Generation Users and the Next Generation Users identified in this report.

MULTIVARIATE PREDICTION OF NEXT GENERATION USERS

These bivariate plots are informative but we can summarize the characteristics of Next Generation Users in a more concise fashion using a multivariate analysis, based on the seven independent demographic variables

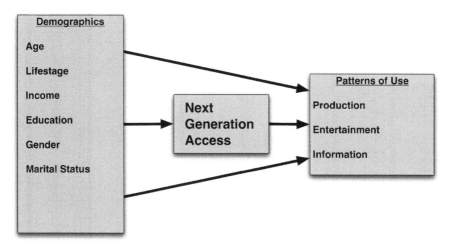

Figure 1.10   Next Generation Access shaping patterns of use.

we used to describe the characteristics of respondents.[8] They include age in years, household income, higher education degree, gender, employment status, use of the internet at work, and marital status.[9] This model includes all of the demographic variables that we have available in the OxIS 2011 dataset. The model we are testing is in Figure 1.10. The figures above show bivariate results denoted by the arrows between demographics and patterns of use, and the arrow between Next Generation Access and patterns of use. Essentially, the question we are testing is: Does the causal arrow connecting Next Generation Access with patterns of use remain statistically significant after we control for the demographic variables?

The results (see Table 1.2) are not surprising; they are largely similar to, and reinforce, the bivariate results shown in the figures. The multivariate analysis in the left-most column is a logistic regression predicting Next Generation Use. The coefficients are odds ratios. Six of the coefficients are significant. Comparing the odds ratios, it is clear that younger and higher income respondents are more likely to be NGUs. Students are more likely to be NGUs than employed, retired or unemployed people. Married people are less likely to be NGUs than singles, but no other marital status categories are significant. When life stage, income, and age are controlled, neither education nor gender has a significant effect.

The three right-most columns are ordinary least squares (OLS) regressions predicting three different kinds of activities: entertainment, information seeking, and content production. They enable us to determine whether the influence of being a Next Generation User for three major internet uses—entertainment, information seeking, and content production—disappears after controlling for other variables. The control variables are all the demographic variables we have available in OxIS. Even after introducing these

Table 1.2 Predicting Next Generation Users

Variable	Logistic regression Next Generation User	OLS regressions Entertainment activity	Information seeking	Content production
Next Generation User	—	1.630***	1.310***	1.790***
Age	0.953***	−0.066***	−0.025**	−0.059***
Female	0.955	−0.708***	−0.157	−0.194
Income	1.557***	0.005	0.054	0.238**
Non-white	0.845	−0.5	−0.057	−0.449
Lifestage				
Student	(base)	(base)	(base)	(base)
Employed	0.094*	−0.152	0.288	−0.82
Retired	0.064*	−0.392	0.3514	−0.124
Unemployed	0.067*	−0.473	0.166	−1.252
Marital Status				
Single	(base)	(base)	(base)	(base)
Married	0.506*	−0.048	0.403	−0.275
Living with someone	0.651	0.132	0.016	−0.22
Divorced/separated	0.894	0.403	0.389	−0.09
Widow/er	0.936	0.442	0.48	−0.039
Education				
No qualifications	(base)	(base)	(base)	(base)
Secondary school	1.601	0.326	0.773*	0.842**
Further education	1.358	0.071	1.401***	0.797*
Higher education	1.757	0.498	1.494***	1.122***
Constant	72.635***	6.465***	4.818***	4.310***
N	1181	1181	1181	1181
R^2	0.222	0.330	0.173	0.248

* $p < .05$; ** $p < .01$; *** $p < .001$.

Note: The logistic regression coefficients are odds ratios and the R^2 is McFadden's R^2.

controls, in all three regressions, the NGU variable remains statistically significant and strong. Being an NGU is highly predictive of these activities, even after taking into account age, income, education, lifestage, marital status, and gender (as summarized by the path model provided in Figure 1.10). The coefficient for gender is particularly interesting. It is significant only for entertainment activity, and it is negative indicating that being female reduces the use of the internet for entertainment. The centrality of the internet in the household has been associated with a narrowing of the digital divide. It might well be that the diffusion of more mobile devices that can be integrated into everyday life and work are reconfiguring gender divides to some degree.

BEYOND BRITAIN: THE WORLD INTERNET PROJECT

Finally, although these detailed analyses are limited to Britain, our participation in the WIP enables us to compare our findings with those of over two dozen other nations.[10] From our work in this context, we have no evidence to question the generality of these basic patterns being applicable in other nations. In less well-to-do nations, for example, there has been less focus on the household as the main site of access, and more importance placed on shared locations, such as a cyber café. Likewise, some countries, such as Poland (WIP Poland, 2011), have yet to see the rise in mobile and appliance-based access to the internet that Britain, the US, and many other nations have experienced. But those are some of the few differences and not findings that would raise doubts about the general conclusions of our analysis about the emergence of Next Generation Users over time, and the ways they have reconfigured their access to information, people, services, and technologies, such as appliances that complement other modes of access.

CONCLUSION: LOOKING TO THE FUTURE

Clearly, it is most likely that more mobile phone users will access the internet in the coming years, but this forecast misses the broader picture—the twin trends of mobility and the use of multiple devices, and the synergy of these two trends that creates Next Generation use. As Figures 1.1 and 1.2 suggest, these trends appear to be strong and likely to continue into the foreseeable future. Next Generation Users have become a major force in the internet. They have certain characteristics that may indicate how they are changing the internet. They are particularly important as consumers of entertainment and information, and they are disproportionately content producers. NGUs tend to be younger, wealthier, either students or employed, and they are not married.

It is therefore important for research to begin to differentiate among internet users in new ways. Speed remains one feature of new infrastructures that will shape patterns of access. But the days of narrow and broadband users are over, as nearly all users in Britain have some level of broadband access. Wireless access will also grow as more households have multiple and portable devices. It is because of wireless broadband access that portable devices are so capable of being used for accessing entertainment and information on the move. However, speed and wireless access are primarily enablers of new patterns of use and not the key factors discriminating among internet users.

The central, new distinction—from the perspective of this study—is between First and Next Generation use. It will be important to track the growth of Next Generation use in relation to non-users, former users, and First Generation Users. Research needs to look at the consequences of Next Generation use on patterns of use and their societal implications. If, as we find, this next generation is truly empowering users in new ways, then it will be equally important to address the new digital divides created by the multiple devices that enable Next Generation Users. The new divide in the use of the internet may influence inequality in several ways. Because Next Generation Users tend to be disproportionately young and wealthy, their mobile access may reinforce many existing inequalities. Their ability to access information may enhance their social capital. Their emphasis on content production could increase their influence in society. All these suggest that this divide would reward research attention over the coming years.

The key theoretical contribution of this study is to expose some problems of both technologically and socially deterministic perspectives. Innovations that define the Next Generation User are reconfiguring their access to information, people and services in ways that are likely to empower them in relation to other users. And those in school or work and with more schooling and higher incomes are more likely to have the skills and wherewithal to exploit this potential. However, this is in contradiction to the expectations of a technically dumb downed internet, as quite the opposite appears to be emerging. New devices are complementing and building on existing tools. In contradiction to the domestication perspective, some people are better able to domesticate these new technologies than others, and the technologies tend to have systematic implications for their users, such an enabling them to integrate them into their lives in ways that enhance their significance.

This study exposes a curious contradiction in domestication research. On the one hand it claims to have its origins in an attempt to construct theory that avoids technological determinism (Silverstone, 2006) and focuses on how people actually integrate technological objects into their lives. On the other hand most of the research focuses on individual objects, such as computers, mobile phones, and other ICTs. The complexity of the internet shows the difficulty of this approach: On the internet there is rarely a single 'object.'[11] Next Generation Users do not focus on objects. Their purposes include finding entertainment, finding information, finding a job, or publishing their creative work.

To accomplish these ends they combine and integrate an ensemble of objects: smartphones, tablets, readers, laptops, and desktops. For most people the objects are not the point. Their goal is most often not to 'use my tablet'; instead, they want to listen to music or watch a movie. A fascination with the technology per se might have typified early hobbyists, and still some users of the internet, but not most users. This understanding of how ICTs are used in service of people's goals is consistent with domestication research's emphasis on how people appropriate and domesticate an object, but it moves research away from a focus on the object to focus on the purposes that human beings wish to achieve through them. More concisely, research should shift from a device-centric analysis to a more practice-centered analysis.

One of the most remarkable aspects of the internet is its dynamic. It has never been the same object from year to year; for example, the dramatic rise in search, then the uses of social networking sites since 2007 have introduced a whole new way for people to communicate in large numbers. Another example: After more than a decade of languishing as 'Personal Digital Assistants' or PDAs, Apple introduced the iPad and newly renamed 'tablets' suddenly became the Next Big Thing. The internet is a site for multiple ICTs and multiple innovations. A weakness of domestication theory is that it assumes a certain level of stability, specifically that there is an identifiable and stable object that is slowly adapted to fit into the life of the household. But the internet is not stable, but constantly being reinvented. Each new development has brought with it new challenges for people to incorporate into their routines. Moreover, the technologies of the internet extend well beyond the household and enroll many actors in shaping their appropriation, objectification, incorporation, and conversion in ways that might diverge from the preexisting moral economy of households, continuing waves of innovation also challenge research. In the midst of continuing change the challenge is to identify patterns of incorporation that have stabilized and will persist for an extended period of time. Next Generation Users are the most recent of these patterns.

Other new research is also needed. Our survey data could well be complemented by more qualitative studies that would expand our understanding of Next Generation Users to describe the meaning of these patterns of use to Next Generation Users, how their identity is bound up in being a Next Generation User, how use is negotiated within households, and other topics that are difficult for survey research to address.

NOTES

This chapter is the latest in a series that explores the causes and consequences of the rise of Next Generation Users (Blank & Dutton 2014; Blank & Dutton 2013; Dutton & Blank 2011; Dutton & Blank 2013).

1. The case for viewing Lessig's argument as technologically determinist is developed by Mayer-Schönberger (2008).

2. These correspond to common stages in the adoption of an innovation, from adoption to implementation to routinization (Rogers, 1962).

3. Because users of new technologies adopt and integrate them into their existing lives it is possible for technologies to transform media-related practice. By privileging the role of the consumer in technology, however, domestication tends—more than any other perspective—to focus on what is stable during the adoption of new technologies and not on what is transformative.

4. For a more complete overview of the OxIS methodology, see: http://microsites.oii.ox.ac.uk/oxis/methodology.

5. Using response rate formula RR1 defined by the American Association of Public Opinion Researchers (AAPOR) (2011, p. 44).

6. For a more detailed description of the sample and methodology see Dutton and Blank (2013).

7. For example, Wei's (2001) study of mobile phones.

8. This model includes all of the demographic variables that we have available in the OxIS 2011 dataset. There is one exception: We also tried a variable measuring urban-rural residence but it was not statistically significant. For several variables in the model we tried numerous specifications. For marital status the full variable had five categories, but only the 'married' category was statistically significant. Similarly, for education only the higher education category was significant, and for 'life stage' only 'retired' was significant.

9. The variables are defined as age, a continuous variable ranging from 14–92 years; income, an eight category variable; higher education degree, a dummy variable indicating whether or not a respondent has a higher education degree; gender, a dummy variable using males as the comparison group; retired, a dummy variable indicating retired people; use the internet at work, a dummy variable indicating if the respondent uses the internet in their job; and married, a dummy variable indicating the respondent is married.

10. Information about the World Internet Project (WIP) and other national samples can be found online at: http://www.worldinternetproject.net/#news.

11. Quandt and von Pape (2010) also develop a critique of domestication research's practice of focusing on a single technology, rather than a 'mediatope' as a whole.

REFERENCES

American Association of Public Opinion Researchers. (2011). *Standard definitions: Final dispositions of case codes and outcome rates for surveys* (7th ed.). Retrieved from http://www.aapor.org/Standard_Definitions/3049.htm

BBC News. (2013). PC sales see 'longest decline' in history. Retrieved from http://www.bbc.co.uk/news/business-23251285

Blank, G., & Dutton, W.H. (2013). The emergence of Next Generation Internet users. In J.M. Hartley, J. Burgess, & A. Bruns (Eds.), *Blackwell companion to new media dynamics*, (pp. 122–141). London: Blackwell.

Blank, G., & Dutton, W. H. (2014). Next Generation Internet Users: Digital divides, choices, and inequalities. In M. Graham & W. H. Dutton (Eds.). *Society and the internet: How information and social networks are changing our lives*. Oxford: Oxford University Press.Danziger, J. N., Dutton, W. H., Kling, R., & Kraemer, K. L. (1982). *Computers and politics: High technology in American local governments*. New York: Columbia University Press.

DiMaggio, P., Hargittai, E., Celeste, C., & Shafer, S. (2004). Digital inequality: from unequal access to differentiated use. In K. Neckerman (Ed.), *Social inequality* (pp. 355–400). New York: Russell Sage Foundation.

Dutton, W. H. (1999). *Society on the line: Information politics in the digital age.* Oxford and New York: Oxford University Press.

Dutton, W. H. (2005). The internet and social transformation: Reconfiguring access. In W. H., Dutton, B. Kahin, R. O'Callaghan, & A. W. Wyckoff (Eds.), *Transforming enterprise*, (pp. 375–397). Cambridge, MA: MIT Press.

Dutton, W. H., & Blank, G. (2011). *Next generation users: The internet in Britain. Oxford Internet Survey 2011.* Oxford Internet Institute: University of Oxford.

Dutton, W. H., & Blank, G. (2013). The emergence of Next Generation Internet users. *International Economics and Economic Policy, 10.* DOI 10.1007/s10368-013-0245-8

Haddon, L. (2006). The contribution of domestication research to in-home computing and media consumption. *The Information Society, 22,* 195–205.

Haddon, L. (2007). Roger Silverstone's legacies: Domestication. *New Media & Society, 9,* 25–32.

Haddon, L. (2011). Domestication analysis, objects of study, and the centrality of technologies in everyday life. *Canadian Journal of Communication, 36,* 311–323.

King, R. (2012, October 29). Great PC exodus on the Internet. *ZDNet.* Retrieved from http://www.zdnet.com/idc-were-in-the-midst-of-the-great-pc-exodus-on-the-internet-7000006532/

Lessig, L. (1999). *Code and other laws of cyberspace.* New York: Basic Books.

Ling, R., & Campbell, S. W. (Eds.). (2009). *The reconstruction of space and time: Mobile communication practices.* New Brunswick, NJ: Transaction Publishers.

Livingstone, S. (1992). The meaning of domestic technologies: A personal construct analysis of familial gender relations. In R. Silverstone & E. Hirsch (Eds.), *Consuming technologies: Media and information in domestic spaces* (pp. 113–130). London: Routledge.

Mayer-Schönberger, V. (2008). Demystifying Lessig. *Wisconsin Law Review, 4,* 713–746.

Perlow, J. (2012, May 31). Post-PC means mass extinction for personal computer OEMs. *ZDNet.* Retrieved from http://www.zdnet.com/blog/perlow/post-pc-era-means-mass-extinction-for-personal-computer-oems/20514

Punie, Y. (1997). Rejections of ICT in Flemish households. The why-not question. In R. Silverstone & M. Hartmann (Eds), *EMTEL working paper no. 3. Media and information technology: Regulating markets & everyday life* (pp. 46–72). Brighton: University of Sussex.

Quandt, T., & von Pape, T. (2010). Living in the Mmediatope: A multimethod study on the evolution of media technologies in the domestic environment. *The Information Society, 26*(5), 330–345.

Rogers, E. M. (1962). *Diffusion of innovations.* New York: The Free Press.

Silverstone, R. (1996). Future imperfect: Information and communication technologies in everyday life. In W. H. Dutton (ed.), *Information and communication technologies—Visions and realities*, (pp. 217–231). Oxford: Oxford University Press.

Silverstone, R. (2005). Introduction. In Roger Silverstone (Ed.), *Media, technology and everyday life in Europe* (pp. 1–18). Aldershot: Ashgate Press.

Silverstone, R. (2006). Domesticating domestication: Reflections on the life of a concept. In T. Berker, M. Hartmann, Y. Punie, & K. J. Ward (Eds.), *Domestication of media and technology* (pp. 229–248). Berkshire: Open University Press.

Silverstone, R., Hirsch, E., & Morley, D. (1992). Information and communication technologies and the moral economy of the household. In R. Silverstone & E. Hirsch (Eds.), *Consuming technologies: Media and information in domestic spaces* (pp. 15–31). London: Routledge.

Van Deursen, A. J., & van Dijk, J. A. (2013). The digital divide shifts to differences in usage. *New Media & Society*. Online First: DOI: 10.1177/1461444813487959.

Wei, L. (2012). Number matters: The multimodality of Internet use as an indicator of the digital inequalities. *Journal of Computer-Mediated Communication, 17*(3), 303–318.

Wei, R. (2001). From luxury to utility: a longitudinal analysis of cell phone laggards. *Journalism and Mass Communication Quarterly*, 78, 702–719.

WIP Poland. (2011). *World Internet Project Poland 2011*. Warsaw, PL: Agora S.A. and TP Group.

Zittrain, J. (2010). *The future of the internet and how to stop it*. New Haven: Yale University Press.

2   The Internet in My Pocket

Stine Lomborg

The portable nature of smartphone and tablet computers is a crucial element in the ubiquitous internet. Yet, the ubiquity of the internet reaches beyond the existence of software-based mobile devices for going online and the associated abundance of communication and metadata. What is distinct about mobile internet is not only the character of the internet on mobile devices, but the fact that the internet becomes accessible anytime, anywhere (e.g., Campbell, 2013; Humphreys et al, 2013). Arguably, ubiquity itself has an experiential dimension concerned with the emergent layer of meanings of access to and communication on pocket-size, portable entry-points for going online in various situations in everyday life. The smartphone may be seen to represent the example par excellence of mobile internet. Echoing the work of Ito and Okabe (2005) on mobile phones (or keitai, as it is termed in Japanese), the smartphone is not just about 'a new technological capability or freedom of motion, but about a snug and intimate technosocial tethering, a personal device supporting communications that are a constant, lightweight, and mundane presence in everyday life' (Ito, 2005, p. 1) That is to say, the smartphone is a cultural object continuously infused with meaning as it is used and inextricably interwoven in the practice of everyday life.

As demonstrated in the previous chapter, indeed mobile devices for going online have in many contexts reached the mainstream of users. The case of Denmark appears to resemble that of Britain (Blank & Dutton, this volume). Hence, Denmark makes a good case for studying the user experience when ubiquitous internet has become mundane. In 2012, at least 50% of the Danish population owned a smartphone, according to Statistics Denmark (Wijas-Jensen, 2013, p. 29).[1] More than 40% of the Danish population had used mobile internet for various communicative as well as informational purposes in 2012, including podcasting, banking, reading news, using GPS, and social network sites (Statistikbanken, 2013). Hence, in terms of adoption and use, the smartphone and mobile internet appear to be not luxury or niche phenomena, but ordinary and used across broad segments of the Danish population.

This chapter explores the meanings of the ubiquitous internet for its users, based on a qualitative interview study with a set of adult Danes, aged twenty-five to forty—the group of adults with the highest adoption rate for smartphones in Denmark. The participants were interviewed about their mobile internet usage practices, values, and the experiential qualities that they ascribe to their smartphones in general, and social media applications in particular, as they go about their everyday business. The resulting analysis tells a story not so much about changes in mobile phone or internet usage practices brought about by the diffusion of the smartphone, but a story about how everyday situations and practices, including the mere awareness of the opportunities of the smartphone for going online, are part of the signification and ongoing negotiation of the smartphone as a ubiquitous internet device. Specifically, I would like to demonstrate how ubiquitous internet attains meaning for users in a negotiation between the affordances (Hutchby, 2000) of the smartphone for internet use and the everyday situations and practices in which the smartphone is part.

THEORIZING THE EXPERIENTIAL QUALITIES OF BEING ALWAYS ON

Several scholars have theorized and debated the social consequences of a media-saturated everyday life. In her book, *Always On*, Baron (2008) explores the cognitive implications of electronic communications, as studied through practices of multitasking and how individuals regulate their accessibility through digital technologies. She demonstrates how multitasking plays a crucial role as we engage in mundane activities and communications online, such as instant messaging or monitoring our profiles on social network sites. According to Baron, we manage these activities by *controlling the volume*, that is, regulating our accessibility, and through continuous *partial attention* to the service(s) that we are logged onto, while at the same time engaging in other everyday activities (doing homework, text messaging, etc.). Along similar lines, Turkle (2011) argues that the digital media we carry with us in the course of daily life have facilitated the tethering of the individual across contexts and social relationships. The consequences are at once the incessant socializing with others through digital media enabled when we are 'always on,' and a state of isolation—being 'alone together'— all immersed in our own, personal media bubbles, and always looking for and tapping into more interesting conversations and things to do elsewhere.

Related to the idea of partial attention in the engagement with digital media, Humphreys, Pape, and Karnowski (2013) compared the use of smartphones and laptops among college students and found patterns of engagement to differ with the device used for going online. Specifically, their study participants reported more extractive media use, such as briefly checking something, when on their smartphones, whereas their laptop uses were comparably more immersive. Mapping the ideas of extraction and immersion onto Turkle's (2011) analysis of us being alone together, one might suggest that the smartphone crystalizes the very idea of superficial tethering through personal devices even more so than the laptop, simply because of its affordances for extractive engagement.

In their analysis of mobile communication, Ling and Donner (2009) describe how the mobile phone enables the *interlacing of activities*: As we carry our devices everywhere, activities and contexts of interaction become more interlaced in everyday life. We may use the small breaks during the day to call our spouses to 'micro-coordinate' dinner plans and who will be picking up the kids after work (Ling & Ytri, 2002) or check our Facebook accounts while waiting for the bus. Studies suggest that the mobile phone plays a significant role even in situations of in-person interaction, thus supporting Turkle's observation that we constantly keep ourselves tethered and available for communications elsewhere (e.g., DiDomenico & Boase, 2013; Humphreys, 2005). Taken together, mobile communication enhances a sense of 'connected presence' (Licoppe, 2004) among and 'ambient accessibility' (Ito & Okabe, 2005) of individuals during almost every aspect of daily life, owing to the interlacing of activities.

As suggested by Helles (2010), the ability to communicate and make oneself present across contexts through mobile devices may be dubbed *transsituational agentivity*. With smartphone applications for social media, the repertoire of social situations readily available for the individual to act in through their devices is extended—it is not only possible to call or text a specific person, or send somebody an email while simultaneously engaged in activities at home, for instance; through social media applications, the smartphone user may easily tap into a wider network of communicating peers. In short: smartphones enhance the scope of transsituational agentivity.

The experience of interlacing activities and creating a sense of connected presence extends to other forms of digital communication. Lomborg (2014) suggests that social media may also be seen to nurture of a sense of *liveness* through the interwoven contributions and comments of many individual users in the personalized news feeds of Twitter and Facebook, for instance. The concept of *liveness* invoked here was originally used to designate an experiential quality of live broadcasting on television and its interplay with digital platforms in the transmission events, unifying the disparate components in a single flow (e.g., Ytreberg, 2009, p. 477). On social media, liveness is experienced in the flow of disparate users' communications, which intersect and accumulate in a manner that both reflects and *augments* everyday life, by means of textually representing and sharing it with others (Lomborg, 2014, p. 184). Taking this idea even further, Deuze's (2011) perspective on what he labels 'media life' echoes the notion of liveness in relation to media in general. Deuze argues that as media pervade contemporary life, individuals increasingly live *in* rather than with media, thereby making the media themselves invisible. Arguably, this idea overlooks an important reflexive dimension in media use: The fact that although media may be 'taken for granted' (Ling, 2012) as a natural part of the fabric of everyday life, users continue to question their media, draw boundaries around them, and thereby negotiate their character, function, and significance in concrete situations of use.

Together, the literature on digital media in general is rife with useful concepts for beginning to theorize the engagement with smartphones in particular, and the associated experiences of being always on. A common denominator in the literature is the emphasis on the affordances of digital media as enabling specific uses and types of engagement. I would like to suggest that, complementing an affordances-based perspective, the contexts in which we tend to use different devices for going online play a crucial role in negotiating certain types of usage practices and associated experiential qualities. In stressing the role of context in the meaning-making of media, my approach has affinity with domestication research on digital media (e.g., Hartmann, 2006; Horst, 2012), but whereas domestication research takes as its main context the home, my scope is broader, as I consider 'context' to comprise everyday life as such, that is, the range of social situations that individuals traverse as they go about their daily business. The approach taken here is thus one that analyzes the experiential qualities of ubiquitous internet for users in their daily lives as an ongoing negotiation between the affordances and the situational uses of the smartphone.

METHOD AND DATA

In order to gain empirical insight into the experiential qualities associated with ubiquitous internet and elaborate the relationship between affordances and usage practices in context, the present study relies on qualitative data gathered through interviews conducted over an extended period from 2010 to 2012 with twelve Danish smartphone users. Although the quality of an experience for an individual is difficult to measure, because it is intangible, qualitative, open-ended interviews provide a means for generating data that address smartphone user experiences indirectly, by way of making participants describe and reflect upon their smartphone practices and the embeddedness of these practices in the broader trajectories of everyday life.

Participants were purposively sampled to ensure richness in the material, in terms of tapping into broad range of meanings emerging around the smartphone in general, and social media use via smartphones in particular. The sampling followed established guidelines for sampling for qualitative research to balance homogeneity and variation with regard to central dimensions (Kuzel, 1999; Stake, 2003), and participants were recruited using snowball sampling. Thus, the present study concerns adults aged twenty-five to forty, who use social media on their smartphones.

First of all, participants were sampled to ensure that they use social media via the smartphone to some degree. All the participants included in the sample used Facebook, the by far most widely adopted social media service in Denmark, and some participants also used Twitter, Tumblr, and other services on their smartphones. The participants' social media use varied in intensity from constant to more casual and sporadic uses, assuming that intensity of use would likely be one important parameter for eliciting experiential differences among users. Furthermore, the participants differ in gender and age, factors widely documented to account for differences in media use (Jensen & Helles, 2011). To install a measure of homogeneity in the sample, the age span for the study was delimited to adult smartphone users between the age of twenty-five and forty. According to Statistics Denmark (Statistikbanken, 2013), the younger parts of the population (those under forty) account for the most diversified uses of mobile internet and are more likely that older age groups to use social media via their smartphones. At the same time there are likely profound differences between for instance teens, young adults and those aged thirty and above who are typically more settled in terms of family, employment, and so on. The systematic analysis of age-specific differences in relation to smartphones is beyond the scope of this empirical study (but for some detail on this matter, see Blank and Dutton, this volume).

The interviews were conducted using loosely structured interview guides with three key themes framing the conversation between the author and the interviewee: participants' histories of social media and smartphone use; common situations of using the smartphone in daily life; and communication on social media through the smartphone. Expecting that it would be difficult for interviewees to put into words the experiential qualities associated with the ubiquitous accessibility of the internet via their smartphones, the interviews sought to access the user experience by asking questions regarding the everyday situations and practices in which the smartphone played a role for the participants. As argued by Pink and Leder-Mackley (2013, p. 682), it may be particularly fruitful to look for the often-implicit meanings of media, by addressing them indirectly through people's recounting of their everyday routines and practices. Furthermore, the interviews used prompts such as 'Imagine that you have forgotten your smartphone, what do you do?' in an attempt to address the implicit meanings attached by participants to their smartphones (Merriam, 2009, p. 97). Hence, everyday usage practices were assumed to reveal the patterns of significance emerging from and meanings ascribed to the smartphone as an entry point for the ubiquitous internet.

The interviews were transcribed and coded inductively through a close reading of the transcripts, thereby generating an unstructured set of codes describing patterns of activity with the smartphone, and suggesting tentative experiential qualities across interviews. These were then systematized into overarching empirical categories and linked to theoretical concepts emerging from the theoretical review, thus giving guidance to the structure of the analysis presented in the subsequent sections of this chapter. All participants have been anonymized.

Although crucial for generating fine-grained data the qualitative approach taken here does not allow for generalizing conclusions about the prevalence of specific usage patterns or attitudes in specific target groups. However, the study is pattern-seeking and aims to document meanings that reach beyond the individual level, as a foundation for developing a theoretically informed, and more general, understanding of the relationship between affordances and context in the experience of ubiquitous internet. In this respect, the analysis presented subsequently focuses mainly on similarities in the participants' accounts (Stake, 2003, pp. 151–153), whereas the analysis cannot draw valid conclusions about the particularities of individuals' experiences and any systematic differences in the sample.

NEVER FORGOTTEN, NEVER OFF: THE CRISIS OF DISCONNECTION

The smartphone is integral to the participants' daily routines of leaving the home, an item to be collected and put in the pocket or purse, alongside keys and wallet. It is almost never forgotten at home but travels with the participants as they do their daily business of work, picking up children, grocery shopping, and seeing friends. Indeed, it is taken for granted—a natural part of in everyday life. The few times that participants report having forgotten their smartphones at home are recollected as prompting a state of crisis. As one respondent frames it,

> it is your life nerve in some way, without it sounding all wrong. And you do not want to be addicted to it, but I have to admit that I am . . . and it is stupid, really, because if somebody calls you and you don't pick up, then you just call them back, so it should not mean anything. But it IS the calendar, the phone book, the notes and all.
>
> (woman, age 28)

As suggested in this quote, the smartphone is considered a multifaceted device, essential for organizing and managing daily life. It embeds not only the user's personal schedule (calendar), but also the social relationships of the individual user (e.g., as displayed in contact information and on social media apps).

It appears not to be enough to keep the smartphone close at all times. The participants also report never turning the smartphone off. One of them notes,

> then it would not be alive . . . it is never turned off unless the battery is empty, but then I get a little fidgeted when I realize that it has been turned off. Then I want it on so I can see if there is something . . . it makes me feel safe to be able to turn it on and see that there is nothing there.
>
> (woman, age 27)

In a sense, what is expressed here goes beyond the idea of the smartphone as a *life* nerve—it is also a *live* line to the world. The smartphone is always on, and apparently *should be* always on so the users can connect beyond their immediate surroundings in an instance.

At the same time, most of the participants contend that it can be quite liberating to be without the smartphone—and thus out of reach except for those within physical proximity—every now and then. However, the participants voicing this relief all recount only 'leaving' the smartphone behind when they are at home—hence it is still within reach, if needed, but it may disappear from their conscience for a while. For instance, one participant consequently leaves her smartphone in the living room before going to bed at night, instead of keeping it right beside her at the bedside table (woman, age 34), which most of the participants do. The act of leaving the smartphone is to be seen as a deliberative move to cut off the smartphone during the night.

The analysis above seems to suggest what could be labeled an experiential crisis of disconnection when the smartphone is not at hand in at least two senses: one concerns the idea that without the smartphone at hand, valuable *information* becomes unavailable to the user; the other concerns a felt need or compulsion to be available for *communication*. Hence the smartphone has come to be seen as a tool for making things, other people, and oneself immediately available, across contexts of action. Common to the participants' statements in relation to availability is a sense that the smartphone does not necessarily cater to a *demand* to actually be 'always on,' but simply offers the *option* for users to 'control the volume' (Baron, 2008) and tap into other contexts at all times at their convenience. Although Ling and Donner (2009) and Licoppe (2004) stress the ongoing communication as a key element in creating a sense of connected presence and interlacing activities, my analysis perhaps aligns more with Deuze's (2011) idea of living in media. That is to say, by its mere availability in the hands of the user, the smartphone offers the user an experience of connectedness, only waiting to be actualized by engaging various functionalities of the device, including calling, text messaging, and going online (also, Chayko, 2008).

AN INFORMATIONAL DEPENDENCY

Mobile information access has been found to be a key motivation for owning a smartphone. For instance, Bertel (2013), in an analysis of informational uses of smartphones among Danish youth, suggests two principal components of the informational use of smartphones: flexibility and autonomy. The smartphone allows users to flexibly align their everyday activities by way of offering just-in-time access to relevant information such as navigation and schedules, and the smartphone offers increasing individual autonomy, because it affords looking up information online and thereby decreases the dependence on others (e.g., through calls and text messages) for retrieving relevant information.

In the present study, several participants similarly describe the smartphone as 'practical,' in part related to the ideas of flexible alignment of activities and autonomy. One participant describes how 'the smartphones changes the way I act in certain situations' (woman, age 28), referring specifically to dealing with practical household matters, such as using an app for checking the price of a commodity across stores, before going to the preferred physical store to buy it (a practice analyzed by Turow, this volume). Other participants report on the experienced utility of their smartphones for keeping work documents at hand on the fly (woman, age 27; man, age 40), finding information about tourist attractions and directions when abroad (man, age 30; man, age 34), checking the weather forecast as a means of dressing accordingly (woman, age 35), and providing a background of music or speech radio when biking through the city on their way to work (man, age 29). Indeed, these are examples of flexible alignment and individual autonomy in the practices of daily life.

The informational dependency on the smartphone, chiefly associated with apps for podcasting, entertainment, grocery shopping, planning, banking, and travel, suggests that the smartphone offers itself as a practical tool for doing all sorts of everyday stuff, and by extension, has come to be seen by the participants as something that integrates and in some instances effectuates their personal everyday routines and duties. This supports previous findings of a similar integration between life conduct and mobile phone habits, as documented by Helles (2010), in a study of mobile phones in Denmark before the smartphone had reached the Danish market. At the same time, specifically the app-based uses of the smartphone (e.g., checking grocery prices before going shopping [woman, age 28] or the weather forecast before going out [woman, age 35]) seem to enhance and broaden the scope of possibilities for integration of relevant information in practical everyday activities.

Yet, there appears to be something more to the informational experience, in the way the interviewees talk about their smartphone. One participant describes how his smartphone, because of its enabling access to the internet, makes him happy:

> I have been thinking about it, because I am actually quite fond of my phone. . . . I have been slow deciding to buy one as I thought, well, I sit by the computer almost all day, so that thing about also having the internet in my pocket. . . . Is it really necessary also to have it on the bus? But I have actually become very happy that I have it. I think it is quite handy in many situations.
>
> (man, age 34)

As we have also seen in the previous section, the considerations of, or tension between, necessity and possibility of having information at hand are highlighted in the account of the smartphone experience. It is not like users would be impeded in doing their daily stuff without the smartphone—they did well before. Still, it makes them 'happy,' but the quote above suggests that it may be difficult to pinpoint exactly why this is so. The fondness of the smartphone appears not directly linked to its instrumental functions in supporting daily practices, but perhaps more closely related to the intangible value of having it at hand. Similarly, another participant considers the smartphone so ingrained in habits that it has become a source of mental lifeblood:

> well, primarily because it has become a habit . . . the feeling that if I were to need to know what Wikipedia thought an orangutan is, then I have that information at hand. Being wired to this . . . cloud of information, yes, it is a sense of being cut off if there is no internet. It has become an extension of my everyday life to such a degree that it is almost like not having running water. It is not a physical need, but a GREAT mental need.
>
> (man, age 26)

One might suggest that the smartphone is more than just a practical tool for accessing information on the fly and supporting the routines of everyday life: It represents a means for being wired to the world, and receives part of its significance from exactly that fact. These quotes demonstrate how, in terms of accessibility, ubiquitous internet is an important element in the interlacing of everyday activities—practically by making relevant information available at hand, just in time (Bertel, 2013), and mentally, by simply being available all the time.

A PERSONAL BUBBLE

The constant availability of information through the smartphone does not only come in handy in situations where information is needed. Because the smartphone integrates all existing media on one platform, it affords a range of additional uses beyond seeking information and briefly looking things up and goof off online—it also provides an opportunity for entertaining and goofing off. For some of the participants, the smartphone looms them into incessant checking of everything, not the least newsfeeds and notifications on social media. These participants report finding themselves checking sports results, gossip, news, social network sites, and so on at a much higher frequency than they would otherwise do, had they only accessed the internet via their laptops. This leads one participant to bluntly conclude, 'I feel more updated on irrelevant information . . . it is not necessary serious stuff, I think it all has an entertainment aspect to it' (man, age 29). This respondent elaborates how the information he checks on the smartphone is superfluous, and that we would never check it, if it was not for the smartphone. He does it, because he can.

Mihailidis (2014), analyzing an international cohort of college students' uses of the mobile phone for information and communication, contrasts the goal-oriented looking for valuable information with tethering for the sake of keeping up to date, that is, constant checking so as not to miss out on anything (Mihailidis, 2014, pp. 66–67). Whereas in Mihailidis's analysis, constant checking is specifically tied to social media use on the smartphone and the social information about ones' network, this practice seems prevalent for participants in the present study in connection with other types of apps, including news and entertainment apps as well. The tapping into and out of the flow of information, whether for finding valuable information or entertainment or simply for the sake of checking, corresponds to the extractive use of smartphones found by Humphreys and colleagues (2013). Hence, arguably, the practice of 'just checking' is suggestive of a general experiential quality of the smartphone as such: the creation of a personal space for oneself.

In one of the interviews, a participant reflects on her smartphone as an egocentric device:

> the text messages are mine, the emails are mine, the Facebook profile is mine . . . and if I read something in the [online] newspaper, it is something I find interesting. . . . And this may be why I come to care so much about my smartphone, because it allows me to be just me. (Interviewer: so when you sit with it, it is like withdrawing into yourself?), yes, I withdraw into myself, but also extend myself, me suddenly spanning several platforms.
>
> (woman, age 27)

Here, being engaged with the smartphone entails extending oneself across contexts (or 'platforms' as the participant describes above); but the same engagement also creates a personal bubble. The quote suggests that using the smartphone means carving a space for oneself, where others in the immediate surroundings can be shut out. This observation is not entirely new—it has been richly documented in relation to 'old' media such as the Walkman (du Gay et al., 2013) and print media (Radway, 1987). In relation to digital media, Humphreys (2005) and Ito and Okabe (2005), for instance, have vividly demonstrated how the use of mobile phones in public spaces serves similar functions of creating a shield of protection from the social world. However, the present data tell a story of how the idea of using the mobile phone to enter a personal bubble has moved into the private sphere of the home as well. Additionally, in contrast to newspapers (which are large enough to create a physical 'wall' around the reader) and music players (which are used with earplugs), with the smartphone the personal bubble is not drawn by way of its materiality. The smartphone instead draws a mental boundary of attention around oneself, and ones individual business, in the presence of others. Interestingly, in some instances the smartphone also functions this way when the individual user is alone: One participant recounts sometimes locating himself in the seemingly most private place in the home, the bathroom, to go online with his smartphone, just to take a five minute break from the everyday. The extractive use of the smartphone for checking stuff fulfills exactly that function: to give the user a short moment where the immediate surroundings and tasks are relegated to the background, and the world can wait. It is a time for relaxation, and for letting the mind wander.

Although the smartphone offers a way to 'go elsewhere' mentally, a key element stressed by participants concerning the extractive use of the smartphone in small breaks is that the smartphone is always of secondary importance in relation to other activities: 'I am always ready to close it, right, put it back in my pocket and let it wait until there is time' (man, age 35). With that, it becomes clear that a crucial experiential quality of being in the personal bubble with one's smartphone is simply that of passing time while waiting for the bus, in the supermarket line, at breaks at work, or at home. The experience of entering and leaving the personal bubble created with the smartphone is thus not tied to specific locations, but instead very much tied to specific *situations* that offer 'time outs' before more important concerns of the everyday take over again.

This section has highlighted the smartphone experience as tightly interwoven with the conduct of everyday life, and at the same marking a break from everyday life. Used in brief moments during the day, the smartphone carves out a space for the individual to take a few minutes for him or herself. As the next section will elaborate, the space carved out may also be seen as a way for the user to embrace the sense of wiredness with world at large.

WIRING UP FOR COMMUNICATION

One of the key affordances of the smartphone is the capability of individuals to connect across space and time. The concept of transsituational agentivity (Helles, 2010) denotes the individual's ability to—while physically present in one situation—make him or herself present in another social situation through a phone call, text message, or by logging onto social media applications and tapping into conversations on Facebook, Twitter, and so on. Among others, Fortunati (2002), conceptualizing the capability for transsituational agentivity reversely in terms of *present absence*, argues that this form of mental engagement elsewhere signifies an experiential shift in the individual's sense of social belonging: it is detached from space and instead attached to a communicative network. In this section, I explore the experience of transsituational agentivity through entering flows of communication, focusing chiefly on participants' engagement with social media applications on the smartphones. These applications offer themselves specifically to the type of abstract social belonging to dispersed communicative networks described by Fortunati (2002).

Looking at the present data, part of the engagement with smartphones as a device for communication resonates with ideas of social connectivity at various levels of intensity. According to the interviewees, the communicative crisis of disconnection described in the first section of the analysis not only relates to everyday practical issues of micro-coordination through text messages and phone calls (Ling & Ytri, 2002), although this dimension is recognized as central in the interviews, but also to a great extent to the affordances of the smartphone in terms of socializing and relaxation with others. The experience of transsituational agentivity and connected presence, and the associated expression of social belonging (Chayko, 2008), becomes visible in the present data primarily in the participants' accounts of using social media applications on their smartphones: to keep themselves in the loop of communication, and to make themselves present and available for communication with important peers.

Staying in the Loop

In Mihailidis's (2014) study of mobile communication, the availability of social media applications such as Facebook and Twitter was seen by some participants as an invasive force in their daily lives, compelling them to constantly check for new activities by their friends to feel socially included.

For the participants in the present study, checking social media applications several times during the day was common even before they had smartphones, because most of them spend much of their day in front of a computer at work. One participant describes Twitter as a source of major entertainment and distraction always looming in the background during working hours. 'Well, it is terrible, it is always on. I can check almost incessantly if there is something new' (woman, age 33). The incessant checking appears almost compulsory in the participants' description: Since it is available, she cannot help but take short peaks into the stream of communication on Twitter—and occasionally tweet something herself. In a sense, then, social media engagement may run in parallel to other activities during her workday, but in a different 'window' demarcating another social situation. She handles this transsituational agentivity of work and play on her desktop computer by multitasking. That is to say, when in front of the computer, she constantly shifts between situations and their associated activities, with a partial awareness to each of them (Baron, 2008).

The smartphone does not fundamentally alter the experience of partial awareness and juggling of engagement in simultaneously evolving situations, but it may reinforce and enhance it, because the smartphone is always at hand. As was also found in relation to informational smartphone use, the participants report on their smartphones enabling them to check their social media profiles more frequently than they would otherwise do, simply because they are always at hand. Moreover, most of them say that even though they occasionally use their desktop computers to log onto Facebook and Twitter, their social media use now is primarily based on their smartphones. This is, again, because the smartphone lends itself particularly well to extractive engagement, sifting in and out in brief moments during the day. Whereas desktop-based use requires switching between windows on the screen (i.e., between the work place intranet and websites such as facebook.com), the smartphone presents an additional, albeit small, screen. This enables a different organization of the situations in which the user simultaneously acts, as the switch between devices marks a shift of situation. By relegating social media activities to the smartphone, this device becomes a vehicle for procrastination and leisure, and by extension is reinforced as a tool for creating small time-outs during the day, as was also seen in the previous section.

The incessant checking of communicative activities on social media applications attests to the distraction and 'pulling' in of users' attention. Yet, according to the participants' accounts, social media applications are opened not so much with the intention to post something, but simply to browse the feeds and check out what others have been up to. At face value, this practice confirms Mihailidis's (2014) observation that users feel they have to make an effort to stay socially included by checking their social media accounts all the time. Participants in the present study, however, tend not to see striving for social inclusion to be key here. For instance, one participant says she checks her Facebook account frequently, and typically while waiting for something or someone, simply 'because I have the opportunity to have a look at it' (woman, age 27). As we have seen with informational practices as well, the use of social media applications for monitoring the flow of communication from friends and acquaintances seems motivated by the option offered by the smartphone to quickly engage, rather than a strong need for social inclusion in a group. This observation is supported by the fact, that although most of the participants say that they frequently run through their newsfeeds, they rarely post anything themselves. The extractive, momentous checking of social media apps suggests a loose and spontaneous sense of commitment to engaging with the people in one's social circles through the smartphone.

Frequent checking enables an experience of being in the loop—of knowing if anything important has happened in one's social circles, without requiring a lot of effort at socializing. In addition to everyday chatter, the newsfeed exposes if an old friend or acquaintance is looking for an apartment, got a new phone number, had a baby, is traveling, and so on. Hence, although Mihailidis's (2014) finding that incessant checking is driven by the fear of social isolation might—in the case of the present study—overstate the importance of social media in participants' everyday lives, checking does produce an experience of being up to date with friends and acquaintances. It is sociality without the effort of actually being together, simultaneously, in a conversation—and with less commitment than a communicative exchange (say, a phone call or an email) would require.

Signs of (social) Life

Whereas the study participants' reflections on their use of smartphones for socializing tells a story mainly of effortless, non-committal and somewhat superficial sociality through being aware of what others are up to, there are occasions when participants actually communicate on social media via their smartphones: by entering a conversation or sharing content with others. These occasions bear witness to how the smartphone can support sociality in a stronger sense, through experiences of liveness and intimacy at a distance.

With the smartphone at hand, some of the participants report a greater inclination to post snapshot photos on their Facebook profiles than they had before they got a smartphone. Apart from being attributed to the high technical quality of the built-in camera application and various applications for photo manipulation, participants emphasize the easiness and aesthetic pleasure of using photos to document their whereabouts instead of written statements. Arguably, the posting of photos augments everyday life by creating an instantaneous connection between the physical context of the individual user and his or her broader social circles on Twitter, Facebook, and so on. 'I like posting photos of things I see. . . . I think it is more fun to post a photo because it means . . . it is more real' (man, age 29). What this quote suggests is that photos offer a better, more authentic, representation of everyday activities than simple written text such as status updates and tweets. It not only does so, because it is visual communication, but also because the photo has a specific live 'feel,' as it presents a snapshot of the here-and-now.

Although photos seem to have obtained a special status for communicating the live experience, the small blurbs of written text posted through the smartphone in tweets and status updates may serve similar functions of representing the live experience. As one participant explains it:

> If I'm with the kids in the wood, then I have my phone and then I log onto Twitter and I can write 'I'm playing with the kids in the wood' and then I have this mental connection to the world even though I'm in the wood. And that is extremely important to me, that experience of connectedness. If, at some place, there is no internet I become all irritable, it is like I have not gotten enough sleep, really. It is not obsessive, but it is a very important part of my life to constantly feel wired.
>
> (man, age 26)

This quote highlights how smartphone in itself, as a ubiquitous access point to the internet, offers the experience of connectedness in the here-and-now, of being able to make oneself present to 'the world' at large by sharing live experiences during the day. Arguably, reflecting and sharing one's activities at a broader scale with others involves an augmentation of these very activities (Lomborg, 2014). It designates the mundane, individually based living as part of something greater. At the same time, liveness functions as a reminder to others that the individual is 'alive' and reachable: It opens the line for communication.

In addition to reflections on instantaneous communication of everyday activities to one's social circles as an augmentation of the everyday experience, communicating through social media may serve as a basis for enhancing a sense of togetherness with close friends and family. For one participant in particular the smartphone serves as a basis for a constant sense of intimacy with important peers through social media. She indicates that it was the engagement with social media that made her buy a smartphone in the first place. As she was going on a weekend trip without her computer, she became acutely aware of her dependence on access to social media to stay in touch with her friends.

> I almost could not bear being away from it and that is when I felt that 'this has really caught me', because I was leaving home Sunday and knew I would not be back until Thursday. That is a long time being offline. I knew I could borrow a computer there, but it was more the sense that 'oh', one suddenly realizes how much one talks to these people every single day.
>
> (woman, age 39)

The way this interviewee talks about her commitment bears witness to the experienced importance of being always on: Being available for continued conversation all the time everyday enables her constant maintenance of social relationship with important peers online. Remarkably, text messages and phone calls are not enough. Although it is not the smartphone in itself that offers her the experience of intimacy, the smartphone provides the internet connection and the applications needed to stay accessible all the time—it facilitates a continuous awareness of others. It is thus a precondition for the 'always on' sociality—for being able to stay in tune with specific others. Through communication on social media this participant and her peers display signs of life throughout the day to support an experience of liveness—whether in front of the computer or on the smartphone while on the fly.

Returning to Mihailidis's (2014) point about constant checking as compulsory behavior to avoid the feeling of social isolation, this participant's account of her need for constant accessibility through social media stands out as reminder that although the simple *possibility of constant checking* 'just because I can' seems to be an important driver of participants' social media use via the smartphone, for some, the smartphone plays an important role in terms of experiencing a *deep sense of connected presence* and intimacy with important others in the moment.

AMBIVALENCE TOWARDS TETHERING

Throughout the interviews, it appears that the participants experience a tension between, on the one hand, the '*crisis of disconnection*'—a feeling of being amputated when they don't have their smartphones with them, and on the other hand, a normatively grounded inclination toward being a bit ashamed of this felt need to be (or at least have the opportunity to be) always on. In the interviews, it is expressed that the ambivalence principally has to do with a wish not to let the smartphone take up too much of the users' time, because is presents a distraction from other activities, and may disturb the individual's sense of presence in the here-and-now.

Most of the participants tell stories of how they try to regulate their accessibility through the smartphone. For instance, only two of the respondents have enabled social media notifications, thereby trying to control when they access the apps on their smartphones. Notifications 'push' communications to the users by making them aware (through sound and graphics) of every time someone has mentioned them in a tweet, commented in a thread to which the user has also contributed, written on their Facebook wall, and so on. Similarly, most participants keep their smartphones on silent mode unless they expect a call. This indicates that the study participants actively and deliberately choose to increase and decrease their accessibility, to control the volume (Baron, 2008), rather than let others determine when connections (calls, chat on social media, etc.) should be made through the smartphone. They may check their smartphones frequently, but at their own convenience, in an attempt to draw boundaries around the ubiquitous internet. As one participant frames it, 'the smartphone should not be the basis of social interaction. It should be picked up from the pocket when I want to use it' (man, age 30). Resonating with the use of the smartphone to create a personal bubble, this effort at controlling the volume points to the experience of ubiquity and tethering created with the smartphone at hand as orchestrated carefully by the user so as not to let the distractive and invasive potentials of the smartphone take charge.

Against this background, the critical story told by Turkle (2011) of the tethered and lonesome self might miss a key point. The smartphone is seen as indispensable, yet, although it facilitates transsituational agentivity and partial awareness, and carves out personal bubbles for small breaks during the day, it does so at the convenience of the user who seeks to navigate reflexively, practically, and purposefully in the opportunities for looking up information, relaxing, connecting and creating through the smartphone in everyday life.

CONCLUSION

In this chapter, I have explored the experiential dimension of the ubiquitous internet, as it lends itself to informational and communicative activities during the course of everyday life, through a qualitative interview study with twelve Danes on their everyday uses of smartphones. The analyses suggest that for the interviewees it is almost unthinkable to be without ubiquitous internet access: It is taken for granted and closely intertwined with various everyday activities. Extending the toolkit of regular mobile phones, the smartphone and its wealth of dedicated apps is a tool for accomplishing mundane practical stuff from coordination with family, friends, and colleagues, to accessing relevant information and performing various tasks (e.g., banking, navigation) on the fly. The smartphone also enables connectivity in various forms—access to social media applications presenting the most important add-on when compared to regular mobile communications. In contrast to this interlacing of everyday activities and the smartphone, and perhaps most importantly, the study has demonstrated how the smartphone may also be seen as a tool for taking a timeout from the everyday: five minutes alone here and there in a personal bubble, just to relax for a moment. The engagement documented in this study is extractive, the user is always partly focused and ready to put the smartphone back into the pocket and flow back into the everyday.

Although the empirical findings have limited generalizability in terms of establishing how users across the board, or specific target groups of users, experience the ubiquitous internet on their smartphone, the study has shown how the smartphone experience is negotiated at the intersection of the affordances of the smartphone and the concrete practices and situations in which the smartphone is embedded in everyday life, and how the situations of use signify the smartphone in various ways: as a practical tool, a source of happiness, mental life blood, personal space, and social connectivity. That is to say, for the individual users, the smartphone to some degree changes its character and meaning according to the situation at hand. Future studies on the experiential quality for the users of being 'always on' should probe the negotiation between media and contextual practices further through empirical study to establish and access the possible consequences of ubiquitous internet in everyday life.

NOTE

1. The estimate is based on reports on the use of applications. Statistics Denmark does not measure smartphones and mobile phones separately, but the use of applications is measured and may be considered a relatively reliable indicator of the minimal level of diffusion of smartphones.

REFERENCES

Baron, N. S. (2008). *Always on. Language in an online and mobile world*. Oxford, UK: Oxford University Press.

Bertel, T. F. (2013). "It's like I trust it so much that I don't really check where it is I'm going before I leave": Informational uses of smartphones among Danish youth. *Mobile Media and Communication, 1*(3), 299–313.

Campbell, S. W. (2013). Mobile media and communication: A new field, or just a new journal? *Mobile Media and Communication, 1*(1), 8–13.

Chayko, M. (2008). *Portable communities. The social dynamics of online and mobile connectedness*. New York: State University of New York Press.

Deuze, M. (2011). Media life. *Media, Culture & Society, 33*(1), 137–148.

DiDomenico, S., & Boase, J. (2013). Bringing mobiles into the conversation: Applying a conversation analytic approach to the study of mobiles in co-present interaction. In D. Tannen & A. M. Trester (Eds.), *Discourse 2.0: Language and new media*. Washington, DC: Georgetwon University Press.

du Gay, P., Hall, S., Janes, L., Koed Madsen, A., MacKey, H., & Negus, K. (Eds.). (2013). *Doing cultural studies: The story of the Sony Walkman* (2nd ed.). London: Sage.

Fortunati, L. (2002). The mobile phone: Towards new categories and social relations. *Information, Communication & Society, 5*(4), 513–528.

Hartmann, M. (2006). A mobile ethnographic view on (mobile) media usage? In J. Höflich, R. Joachim, & M. Hartmann (Eds.), *Mobile communication in everyday life: Ethnographic views, observations and reflections* (pp. 273–297). Berlin: Frank & Timme.

Helles, R. (2010). Hverdagslivets nye medier. *Dansk Sociologi, 21*(3), 49–63.

Horst, H. A. (2012). New media technologies in everyday life. In H. A. Horst & D. Miller (Eds.), *Digital anthropology* (pp. 61–79). London; New York: Berg.

Humphreys, L. (2005). Cell phones in public: Social interactions in a wireless era. *New Media & Society, 7*(6), 810–833.

Humphreys, L., Pape, T. v., & Karnowski, V. (2013). Evolving mobile media: Uses and conceptualizations of the mobile internet. *Journal of Computer-Mediated Communication, 18*(4), 491–507.

Hutchby, I. (2000). *Conversation and technology: The telephone, the computer, and the nature of human communication*. Cambridge, UK, Malden, MA.: Polity Press.

Ito, M. (2005). Introduction: Personal, portable, pedestrian. In M. Ito, D. Okabe, & M. Matsuda (Eds.), *Personal, portable, pedestrian: Mobile phones in Japanese life* (pp. 1–14). Cambridge, MA: MIT Press.

Ito, M., & Okabe, D. (2005). Technosocial situations: Emergent structuring of mobile e-mail use. In M. Ito, D. Okabe, & M. Matsuda (Eds.), *Personal, portable, pedestrian: Mobile phones in Japanese life* (pp. 257–273). Cambridge, MA: MIT Press.

Jensen, K. B., & Helles, R. (2011). The internet as a cultural forum—implications for research. *New Media & Society, 13*(4), 517–533.

Kuzel, A. J. (1999). Sampling in qualitative inquiry. In B. F. Crabtree & W. L. Miller (Eds.), *Doing qualitative research* (2nd ed., pp. 33–46). Thousand Oaks, CA: Sage Publications.

Licoppe, C. (2004). 'Connected' presence: The emergence of a new repertoire for managing social relationships in a changing communication technoscape. *Environment and Planning D: Society and Space, 22*(1), 135–156.

Ling, R. (2012). *Taken for grantedness. The embedding of mobile communication into society*. Cambridge, MA: MIT Press.

Ling, R. S., & Donner, J. (2009). *Mobile communication*. Cambridge, UK: Polity Press.

Ling, R. S., & Ytri, B. (2002). Hyper-coordination via mobile phones in Norway. In J. Katz & M. Aakhus (Eds.), *Perpetual contact: Mobile communication, private talk, public performance* (pp. 139–169). Cambridge, UK: Cambridge University Press.

Lomborg, S. (2014). *Social media—Social genres. Making sense of the ordinary*. London and New York: Routledge.

Merriam, S. B. (2009). *Qualitative research. A guide to design and implementation*. San Fransisco, CA: Jossey-Bass.

Mihailidis, P. (2014). A tethered generation: Exploring the role of mobile phones in the daily life of young people. *Mobile Media and Communication*, 2(1), 58–72.

Pink, S., & Leder Mackley, K. (2013). Saturated and situated: Expanding the meaning of media in the routines of everyday life. *Media, Culture & Society*, 35(6), 677–691.

Radway, J. (1987). Reading reading the romance. In A. Gray & J. McGuigan (Eds.), *Studies in culture: An introductory reader* (pp. 62–79). London: Arnold.

Stake, R. E. (2003). Case studies. In N. K. Denzin & Y. S. Lincoln (Eds.), *Strategies of qualitative inquiry* (2nd ed.). Thousand Oaks, CA Sage Publications.

Statistikbanken. (2013). Anvendelse af internet på mobiltelefonen (16–74 år) efter tid, formål og type. Retrieved from http://www.statistikbanken.dk/Statbank5a/SelectVarVal/Define.asp?MainTable=BEBRIT15&PLanguage=0&PXSId=0&wsid=cftree

Turkle, S. (2011). *Alone together. Why we expect more from technology and less from each other*. New York: Basic Books.

Ytreberg, E. (2009). Extended liveness and eventfulness in multi-platform reality formats. *New Media & Society*, 11(4), 467–485.

Wijas-Jensen, J. (2013). *It-anvendelse i befolkningen 2013*. Danmarks Statistik. Retrieved from http://www.dst.dk/pukora/epub/upload/18685/itanv.pdf

3 Managing the Interoperable Self

Anja Bechmann

The ubiquitous internet is characterized by services that offer users the chance to share their self-reported and behavioral data in one service with another service. Internet services promise visibility, performance optimization, customized solutions, and convenience if the user chooses to share data. From a commercial point of view, user data is a valuable commodity because it makes customer service and business risk management more effective, for instance by providing accurate information on the user's reported health situation or by providing information on the user's engagement in a game app. At the same time, trade data has become a new type of marketing with 'data brokers' at the center, with segmentation now taking place at the individual level (see also Bodle, this volume). The same is happening in crime investigation and prevention (Bechmann, 2013). The collection of as many different data points as possible tends to construct the individual human subject on the ubiquitous internet through algorithmic processing. This means that the internet is filled with tracking and data-capture technologies, collecting data across services and offering to share data between services. Under the term 'interoperability,' this chapter will look at how users navigate and manage the offer of data sharing and connectivity between different services.

The largest, most interoperable, and diversified social media data company on the internet is Facebook. Facebook collects personal and sensitive self-reported data (e.g., religion and politics) as well as behavioral data across platforms in various contexts, such as different mobile platforms and services including Spotify, Runkeeper, and Instagram. Facebook shares the digital footprints of the users in almost unlimited fashion with third-party companies and developers. Plugins such as Login with Facebook, also called Facebook Connect, are one of the most widespread 'trackers' that track user behavior and self-reported data on the internet along with Facebook Social Plugins (Gerlitz & Helmond, 2013). This schism between the user's self-portraying and Facebook's commodification of data sharing is the underlying premise for interoperability on Facebook.

This chapter focuses on the interoperable character of Facebook as a data hub on the ubiquitous internet. More specifically, the chapter seeks to investigate the interoperable self by posing the following questions: to what extent do users connect services and share data; to what extent do users choose to use more than one platform to access Facebook (thereby providing Facebook with more behavioral data and different kinds of content); and what kind of strategies do users apply in order to keep data private despite the promises of interoperability, including the characteristics of this sensitive content?

The research questions will be answered through a case study of Danish and US Facebook users aged 18–20 years using an ethno-mining inspired research design (Anderson, Nafus, & Rattenbury, 2009). The chapter will analyze Facebook data using a content analytical approach (Weber, 1990) combined with the thematic and narrative coding of interviews (Kvale, 1994, pp. 198–201). Before presenting the method in detail and the findings in the study, the following section will conceptualize interoperability and the interoperable self more closely in relation to social media and Facebook.

INTEROPERABILITY AND THE INTEROPERABLE SELF

Interoperability allows companies, public institutions, and users to connect (personal) data in diverse IT systems through open application interfaces in products and services, for instance. In a policy perspective, Tsilas (2011 pp. 103–104) distinguishes between technical and people interoperability. Technical interoperability connects to considerations regarding out-of-the-box product design, shared development communities, securing access through licensing, and securing open and non-proprietary standards. People interoperability, on the other hand, relates to considerations regarding compatible business goals and business models between organizations, and semantic clarity to secure the (same) precise meaning of data when exchanged between systems.

Inspired by Tsilas' distinction between technical and people interoperability, this chapter will use the notion of technical and social interoperability to analyze how end-users link different services together. Technical interoperability will refer to the potential for data interoperability between two or more services, for instance by accounting for the number of Facebook apps installed by the user enabling data exchange, and the amount of content posted from external services. Social interoperability, on the other hand, will refer to the social compatibility of services and identification of the social arena ('audiences') that Facebook users have in mind when they share data.

Following this understanding of interoperability, the interoperable self in this chapter is understood as an individual human subject that uses different platforms and services on the internet, as well as having the possibility of choosing to share his/her data across these platforms and services with the associated companies, networks of friends and third-party companies.

Numerous scholars have characterized the practice of sharing data deliberately as an act of impression management (e.g., boyd, 2007), with information playing a central role for the self-portrait of who we are, where we are, what we do, and how (well) we do it. On Facebook as a social arena this impression management takes place toward networks of friends as well as companies and state agencies (Bechmann, 2013). And when data is shared across services, the impression management in turn takes place across social arenas such as Facebook and Instagram. Socially we benefit from this because we are visible in our different networks of friends (Albrechtslund, 2008). Functionally, Facebook may provide a convenient and easy access to different networks of friends.

The promises of convenience may overshadow the perils of interoperable data sharing in terms of lack of overview and control for the user. Many studies of data disclosure relate to the dominating discourse of privacy as a paradox (Barnes, 2006). On the one hand, it is convenient to disclose information online and it is too complex to understand the consequences of this disclosure. On the other hand, when asked, users do care about privacy and want to protect and control their identity online (Nissenbaum, 2011).

Building on classical theories about privacy, among other things (Westin, 1967; Altman, 1975), scholars have analyzed how users disclose data in social media and especially on Facebook, and how users manage this data disclosure (e.g., Ellison et al., 2011; Acquisti & Gross, 2006; boyd, 2007, 2008; boyd & Hargittai, 2010; Raynes-Goldie, 2010; Young & Quan-Haase, 2013). Altman suggests that we understand privacy as the 'selective control of access to the self' (Altman, 1975 p. 24); and within the field of computer and information ethics Floridi (1999) proposes, 'we are our information' (Floridi, 1999 p. 53). When information objects connect to a human being, he speaks of a 'mee-hood' (Floridi, 1999) that deserves privacy because it contains personal information.

Altman (1975) and Margulis (2011) focus on characterizing privacy as a process that necessarily involves multiple parties. Focusing on this bi-directionality, Raynes-Goldie (2010) proposes a distinction between social and institutional privacy, emphasizing that users worry about how they are portrayed as 'selves' in their (close) network of friends but not about the data that they provide to institutions or companies. Young and Quan-Haase (2013) find similar results in their study of undergraduates in the US. They account for privacy strategies on Facebook that involve excluding contact information, using the limited profile option, untagging and removing photos, and limiting friendship requests from strangers to manage their self-presentation to friends. However, they find that the participants have few concerns when it comes to sharing data with companies.

According to Taddicken (2012), the schism between self-portraying and commerce is not well described in the literature. Furthermore, none of the studies listed above have a primary focus on how users manage interoperability across social media, or how they protect and share data across social media services and with third parties connecting to social media data. Due to the increasingly complex nature of data exchange in interoperable services, it is interesting to examine whether the focus on the interoperable character of Facebook may add to the need for control in the impression management process identified in existing studies.

The study presented in this chapter also contributes to the field both by studying actual data patterns through the use of Facebook API, and by contextualizing these patterns in interviews with participants. So far most of the existing studies in the field have used surveys and interviews as their methodological tools for examining data disclosure without studying the actual digital footprints. Due to the privacy paradox, the digital footprints in combination with the reflections of the participants may reveal other practices and strategies than question-based methods reveal. The next sections will report in greater detail on Facebook as a case study of the interoperable self, the dataset collected, and the methods used.

FACEBOOK AS A CASE STUDY

Facebook has been chosen as a case for the study of the interoperable self because it is the most widely distributed social networking site in the world. Approximately half of the Danish and US population participate as members in this social network (Statistics Denmark 2011; Duggan & Brenner, 2013). Furthermore, Facebook, like Google, has managed to effectively draw data into its business from external sites and services through plugins such as like, Facebook Connect, and Facebook applications. Since Facebook was founded in 2004, it has gradually increased the use of interoperable tools such as APIs (Application Programming Interface) that extend the user data and traffic available for sale (Bechmann, 2013). API is a back-end interface through which third-party developers can connect new add-ons to Facebook (Lomborg & Bechmann, 2014). Facebook thereby becomes a data hub or what Sutor (2011) characterizes as a case of *intra*operability in which a service provider 'sucks all important data and processing into the central software ecosystem' (Sutor, 2011, p. 214). In this way Facebook and Google own and control massive amounts of user data. Software developers agree to an asymmetrical power relationship in which they connect to Facebook and Google, enhancing the importance of their standards. This makes the services currently the most powerful hubs in the ubiquitous internet network, along with Apple and Amazon (Catells, 2011). By the end of 2010 Facebook's advertising revenue surpassed $1.2 billion (Bodle, 2011 p. 328), and the interoperability of user data stands at the center of this lucrative ad-based revenue model as a way to generate more aggregated data about users.

Users may indicate demographic data and optional interests. This data is combined with the information uploaded by the users, such as photos, likes, shares, status updates, comments, tagging of other users, and check-ins at various geographical locations. Furthermore, the information is connected to data from various devices and user behavior on external services through social and authentication buttons. The social and authentication buttons allow third-party developers to make use of the Facebook data, and in return Facebook can increase the social graph (the network of users) and obtain knowledge of user behavior from outside the Facebook universe. Even though interoperability takes many forms between Facebook and third-party services, the main focus in this chapter will be on the interoperability of the service between various devices (e.g., Facebook in the browser versus Facebook app for mobile phones and tablets), integration with third-party Facebook apps, and content uploaded from external services (e.g., links to YouTube videos).

Facebook has many communicative features, but this chapter focuses primarily on studying the newsfeed, the timeline (also called profile feed or wall in this chapter), and groups. The newsfeed enables users to keep updated on recent activities and posts in the network of friends. The wall or timeline is the user's personal page, which is visible to the network of friends, whereas groups may be visible for invited members only. The term 'Posts' used in this chapter refers to images (photos), links (to external content like YouTube videos), status updates (written text by the user), and 'other.' The category 'other' contains uploaded videos in particular. 'Content units' cover both posts and user comments. Furthermore, the chapter uses the concept of 'activity,' which covers user likes and shares on comments and posts.

DATASET AND METHODS

Denmark has been chosen as the main case study country, and Danish high-school students have been chosen as participants in the study, because the market penetration of Facebook in this user group in Denmark is among the highest in the world. In social network sites Danes are the most active sharers in the EU. Thirty seven percent have shared photos, videos, and music compared to the average of 22% in the EU (Statistics Denmark, 2011, p. 24). Sixty one percent of Danish internet users are members of at least one social network service, of which the majority use Facebook (57%), LinkedIn (10%), Myspace (5%), Twitter (4%), and other services such as Foursquare (9%).[1] Among 16–19 year olds, 93% (of all internet users) are members of at least one social network service. The social network service pattern among 16–19 year olds is different from the average. Ninety percent use Facebook but only 1% LinkedIn, and as many as 17% use other services (Statistics Denmark, 2011). Compared to the Danish Facebook penetration, 67% of the American internet population use Facebook and 86% in the age group 18–29 use Facebook. However, the American survey was conducted two years after the Danish one (Duggan & Brenner, 2013).

Fifteen Danish high-school students and two American college students all in the age group 18–20 (seven males and ten females) participated. By integrating American students in the study, I aim to provide an American perspective to the Danish-anchored study. This is not with the intention of presenting cross-national comparative studies of the interoperable self, but to acknowledge the international character of Facebook as a ubiquitous internet service. Since the data patterns are very similar the participants will be treated as a part of the same group (18–20 year olds).

The students were recruited in the classroom in order to ensure their proper consent as well as ensuring that they were in fact students in this particular age group. If recruitment had been done from inside Facebook, the researcher could not have been sure that the self-reported parameters corresponded with the actual demographics of the individuals concerned (Lomborg & Bechmann, 2014). The participants were informed both in speech and writing about the purpose of the study, the data we needed to retrieve, and how we would use it. The participants were also informed of previous cases of unintended data disclosure in research projects on social media, as well as being informed of their right to withdraw their participation at any time during the data retrieval period. Even though the research team knows the identity of the persons, the data from Facebook will be presented in the form of aggregated statistics to prevent identity disclosure. The research project has been authorized by the Danish Data Protection Agency.

Inspired by ethno-mining (Aippersbach et al., 2006; Anderson, Nafus & Rattenbury, 2009), data collection took place as an iterative process between collecting Facebook data and finding patterns (e.g., number of apps and types of posts) or outliers (e.g., facerape posts), and initially interpreting them. The participants were interviewed subsequently to contextualize and validate patterns and interpretations, and then to collect different Facebook data (in this case groups).

Empirically, the study presented in this chapter combines API data retrieval, screen dumps of Facebook apps, and semi-structured group interviews (Kvale, 1994). The data collection took place in the spring and fall of 2012. All the participants took screen dumps of their privacy settings and Facebook apps so we could see how many times they had made this interoperable connection. Moreover, we acted as third-party developers and retrieved all their data from Facebook from the time they first joined Facebook and onwards in order to analyze patterns in interoperable use and data sharing. In total, the API data in the dataset consisted of:

- Seventeen records of personal data such as name, age, civil status, and hometown
- Seventeen timelines/walls: 24,062 posts plus comments, likes, and check-ins
- Seventeen newsfeeds: 41,168 posts plus comments, likes, and check-ins on their newsfeed for fourteen days
- Nine participants' groups: 10,213 posts in 116 closed, secret, and open groups plus comments and likes

Nine participants were chosen for interviews, and I collected data from groups after interviews because I was not aware of the widespread use of groups among the participants. Although it would have informed the research question, the Facebook inboxes were not collected. Instead I told the participants of the possibility of retrieving inboxes as third-party developers using the API and included their attitudes toward this kind of interoperable access in the analysis. The Digital Footprints Research Group designed the software Digital Footprints (http://digitalfootprints.dk) to collect the data and visualize patterns.

As noted by Anderson, Nafus, and Rattenbury (2009), quantitative and qualitative methods go hand in hand in ethno-mining: 'ethno-mining does not separate out the quantitative and qualitative data from an ethnographic ethos' (p. 125). Instead, quantitative methods such as data mining or (in the case of this study) manual and software-supported content analysis supplement qualitative data such as interviews to describe qualities of a specific user practice, in this case the interoperable self. The method is not a mixed-method design in the sense that you can distinguish different items of data from each other. The methods are intertwined or hybrid (Anderson, Nafus, & Rattenbury, 2009), for instance when the interviewer refers to the data in the interviews and the interviewees react to the data patterns.

Even though ethno-mining inspires the data collection in this study, the data analysis and presentation of findings still draw on classical methods. The interviews were coded thematically and with a focus on narratives (Kvale, 1994). Manual and software-supported content analysis (Weber, 1990) were applied to the Facebook data. Basic descriptive statistics were built into our software to get an overview of the different patterns of data sharing and interoperability. To understand the content units shared by the students, we ran statistics on content types across walls and groups. Afterwards the groups were manually coded, looking at their content in order to decide on the general thematic patterns. Last but not least, we sorted all groups in these grounded themes and ran statistics on them correlating them with group status (Weber, 1990). The data retrieval through Facebook's API is not flawless (Lomborg & Bechmann, 2014), and therefore important methodological limitations will be presented and accounted for in the findings sections.

The study reported in this chapter takes a methodological route to examine interoperability that focuses on in-depth understanding of the interoperable self. By using this hybrid method of self-reported and behavioral data and reflections in interviews, the next sections will present the findings of the study.

PATTERNS IN POSTS, COMMENTS, AND LIKES ON FACEBOOK

This section will present, analyze, and discuss what kind of content units are circulated in the interoperable network of Facebook. To do this, the section draws on descriptive statistics of the content units and 'likes,' as well as trying to contextualize the patterns through the interview data.

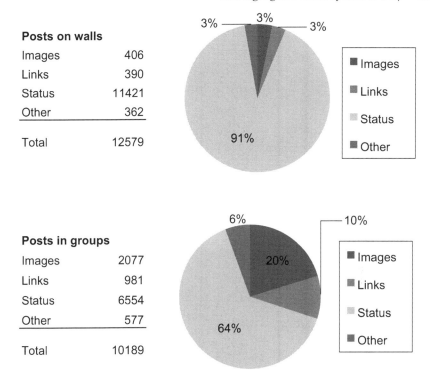

Posts on walls

Images	406
Links	390
Status	11421
Other	362
Total	12579

Posts in groups

Images	2077
Links	981
Status	6554
Other	577
Total	10189

Figure 3.1 Descriptive statistics on the types of posts on walls and in groups.

The participants had 409 Facebook friends on average. However, the user data (content units and activities) is potentially visible to friends of friends and other networks of friends in connected services as well. In the dataset the number of certain types of posts varies in the Facebook user walls and user groups.

In general the participants post more images in their groups than on their timeline (see Figure 3.1). Of the timeline posts, 90.8% are status updates. The interviewees generally see the timeline as a public 'face,' whereas groups allow the participants to communicate more selectively, not thinking of their general and public impression management. In other words, they see the groups as a safe place for selected friends and regard the social interoperability in these groups as limited. In comparison, status updates on the timeline are more carefully chosen according to the impression the participants want to give.

When it comes to engaging with other people's data, the dataset shows almost the same patterns of comments on the wall posts and group posts, with only a few more comments on status updates in groups than on walls (see Figure 3.2).

It is easier to 'like' something than to comment on something, and the behavioral patterns are different in the 'like' activity (see Figure 3.3).

The participants in the dataset tend to 'like' more images on the wall than in the groups, despite the fact that the analysis shows more photos in

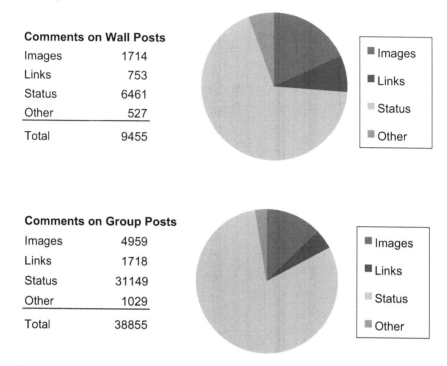

Comments on Wall Posts	
Images	1714
Links	753
Status	6461
Other	527
Total	9455

Comments on Group Posts	
Images	4959
Links	1718
Status	31149
Other	1029
Total	38855

Figure 3.2 Descriptive statistics on comments on wall and group posts.

the groups than on the wall. The interviewees all agreed that likes were a particularly good way of acknowledging their Facebook friends.

One interpretation of the smaller amount of likes on images in the groups could be that the acknowledgement of such private posts may be reduced in return for likes on status updates with micro-coordinating messages because groups in general have a specific audience.

Even though 'likes' in general is considered a way to acknowledge friends in the interviews, two of the interviewed students said that they found it annoying that the like activity of a Facebook friend appeared in their news-feed. They considered it to be useless information. If likes concerned their own content, they found the information valuable. The descriptive statistics of the API data show more likes (30,894) than posts (22,768). This may seem to contradict the expressed annoyance with likes. However, the pattern may occur because likes are easier to give than writing a status update. It may also suggest that even though the interviewees find it annoying to look at likes from Facebook friends in the newsfeed, they do not consider this social interoperability when clicking on the like button. The perceived social interoperability may be limited to the one Facebook friend receiving it.

This section has presented what kind of data potentially travels in the interoperable network of Facebook, and how users try to manage 'public'

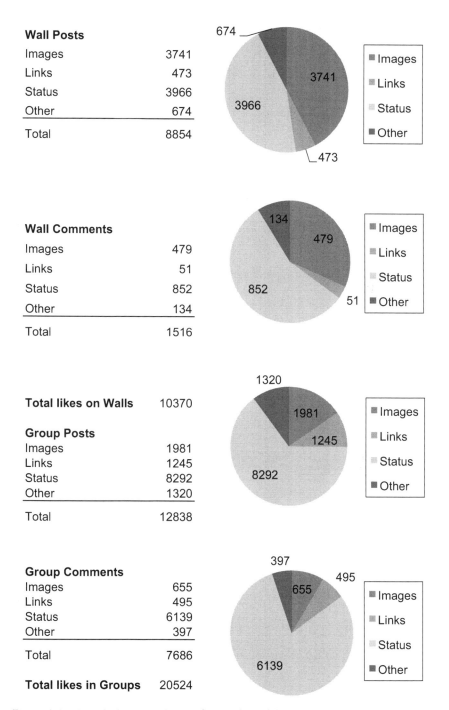

Wall Posts

Images	3741
Links	473
Status	3966
Other	674
Total	8854

Wall Comments

Images	479
Links	51
Status	852
Other	134
Total	1516

Total likes on Walls 10370

Group Posts

Images	1981
Links	1245
Status	8292
Other	1320
Total	12838

Group Comments

Images	655
Links	495
Status	6139
Other	397
Total	7686

Total likes in Groups 20524

Figure 3.3   Descriptive statistics on the number of 'likes' on different content units.

and specific targeted content on the different features of Facebook. The next section will analyze indicators in the dataset on how this data potentially 'travels' across devices and services, and how the participants try to manage this interoperability.

CONTROLLING INTEROPERABILITY: NAVIGATION IN THE SEAMLESS SERVICE OF FACEBOOK

This section will address three aspects of interoperability: platform interoperability, in terms of the use of different devices to access Facebook, technical interoperability, in terms of the use of different third-party apps, and social interoperability, understood in terms of attitudes toward data sharing with networks of friends and companies.

Interoperability not only happens across services, but also in cases in which the same features share the same user data (e.g., content units and activities are visible on both walls and newsfeeds), or when Facebook data is available on different devices. In the dataset only a few content units were uploaded using Facebook mobile smartphone or tablet apps. The participants used seven different mobile devices in total to access Facebook through designated apps.

The number of posts submitted from the official Facebook app is very low. As Table 3.1 shows, in total only 3.3% of all wall posts and 15.1% of all newsfeeds were sent from Facebook for a mobile device. However, these figures do not say anything about the total mobile use of Facebook, because

Table 3.1   Designated Facebook Apps on Mobile Devices

App name	Number of posts on walls	Percentage of total	Number of posts in newsfeed	Percentage of total
BlackBerry smartphone app	65	0.3	81	0.2
Facebook for iPhone	633	2.6	4668	11.3
Facebook for Android	61	0.3	1198	2.9
HTC Sense	2	–	39	0.1
Nokia	3	–	26	0.1
Facebook for Windows Phone	1	–	21	0.1
Facebook for iPad	27	0.1	195	0.5
Total	792 (24,062)	3.3 (100)	6228 (41,168)	15.1 (100)

they do not take into consideration when content is uploaded from other apps outside Facebook, for instance the photo snapshot social networking service Instagram. This points to the fact that the students in this small dataset prefer to use Facebook on their laptop when uploading status updates inside Facebook, something that they also confirmed in the qualitative interviews. They mainly used the mobile devices to check notifications and read the newsfeed on Facebook. This usage pattern corresponds with the pattern found in Lomborg's chapter in this volume, which deals with a different sample of participants. This may indicate that the pattern is not unique for high-school and college students.

The dataset shows a large amount of technical interoperability between Facebook and third-party companies. The average number of Facebook apps in the dataset is sixty. This means that the participants have agreed to share their data with an average of sixty companies (median forty five) that ask for permission to access their data in return for a particular service. Most of these services are quizzes such as 'How well do you know me'; games such as Farmville; or services such as MyBirthday Calendar, but the participants also often connect to Spotify and 'cities I've visited.'

Looking at content units and especially the status updates in the dataset more closely, the participants and their friends do talk about things on (for instance) Instagram or SnapChat, but very little content is uploaded from Instagram. Two participants had posted comments on Instagram pictures on the wall, and 148 content units appeared from Instagram in the newsfeed. There were no content units relating to SnapChat. The screendumps of apps showed that only one of the participants has connected the Facebook account with Twitter.

When we asked the participants about their strategies for data interoperability in third-party apps, they deliberately chose not to share data and activity on different services. The social networks are maintained as separate social arenas reserved for the networks of friends for that particular service. However, Spotify is an example of a service that forces them to use Facebook Connect in order to obtain an account. The standard setting in Spotify is that users reveal all their listening activities to their Facebook network of friends. Despite the settings, most of the participants chose NOT to disclose listening activity on Facebook. Corresponding with the privacy paradox (Barnes, 2006), participants in general see technical interoperability as a necessity in order to obtain the service they want in the most convenient way:

> I also have these games on my iphone that are connected to Facebook . . . such as SongPop, that kind of music quizzes . . . they are connected to Facebook . . . you had to . . . otherwise you aren't allowed to play the game . . .
>
> (Danish female high-school student, age 19)

However, the most frequently interlinked external service in the dataset is YouTube (0.7% of wall posts). YouTube is used for sharing video links and the interoperability is established on the content sharing level and not on the account level; hence distributed content is primarily not content created by the participant.

Even though the participants in general actively connect two services, the forced connections and the data disclosures that follow are not a problem for the participants as long as this data is only shared with companies, not people with whom they have a personal relationship:

> If some company sees what I have written on my wall . . . someone who wants to employ me . . . so what? Yes, and the fact that Spotify knows that someone has written on my wall, I really don't care . . . they don't know me personally.
>
> (Danish female high-school student, age 19)

As existing studies already point out (e.g., boyd & Marwick, 2011; Raynes-Goldie, 2010), the participants are focused on social interoperability in terms of people viewing the activity, not companies monitoring and storing personal data.

Boyd (2008) shows how young Americans use the network of Facebook friends as an address book to keep track of and information on people they barely know any more, because the information might come in handy in the future. In the dataset of this study the participants also have friends they barely know. However, three of the interviewees say that they find it difficult to keep them in the network if they are not really friends due to the 'closeness' they experience through Facebook. As one interviewee explains:

> I had many friends from when I was younger, people you barely knew and then you just sent them a friend request, but I have started to delete them, because there are so many, that, people that I wouldn't even say hi to if I met them and I find that weird. That you're friends on Facebook and then if you met them on the street you can't even say hi to them . . . you show them everything, everything you do on Facebook . . . pictures and stuff . . . and you get all this information about them every single day, you know exactly what they did yesterday morning . . . ate breakfast with someone.
>
> (Danish female high-school student, age 19)

It is awkward for the participant that such acquaintances know 'stuff' about them, and it is also awkward to follow the activity of a person that the participant hardly knows.

Based on the analysis of different forms of technical interoperability, the main findings in this section are that even though participants access data across devices, the number of status updates they make in the native apps is very small. However, the level of interoperability is high in the case of data exchange across services, with an average of sixty installed Facebook apps. Despite this high degree of technical interoperability across services, the participants did not want to connect the social media and other services, but wanted to keep them as separate social arenas.

The next section will further analyze the kinds of techniques and strategies that the students in this study apply to prevent content from being shared.

GROUPS AS A MAIN PRIVACY FILTER

One of the main findings of the study is that all the participants used groups as a privacy filter. They reported that they used groups to manage private content and only used the wall for non-personal and public information. On average the participants have seventeen groups each (median = 17). They did not use the privacy settings of Facebook because they were too complex and changed too often (see also Bechmann, 2014). It was easier for them to manage their circle of friends in the groups.

However, the participants were unaware of the possibility that third-party companies might gain access to the groups through Facebook apps (Bechmann, 2014). The participants regard groups as important tools to manage interoperability, in comparison with walls. Groups are considered 'safe ground,' like Facebook messages (inbox) that other applications and services cannot access. Groups are not a part of the public impression on the wall with the average of 409 friends. On the wall the participants were very aware of the exposure that these friends made on the participants' content units toward their friends. The interviewees had less considerations of data exposure in groups because they had already selected specific groups of friends to share content with.

The total number of groups in the dataset is 116. The privacy settings of the groups were either open, closed (default setting), or secret, and there were almost the same number of groups (1/3) in the different categories.

The percentages in Table 3.2 show that approximately one third of the groups are open to the public and therefore do not contain secret content per se. However, the groups may still function as a privacy filter because

Table 3.2   The Number of Groups Within the Three Categories Open, Closed, and Secret

Groups	116 groups	100%
Closed (Default setting: anyone can see the group and who is in it. Only members see posts)	42	36%
Open (Anyone can see the group, who is in it, and what members post)	36	31%
Secret (Only members see the group, who is in it, and what members post)	38	33%

even open groups have a specific targeted content for specific members of that group.

If we focus on the content units in the different groups, the result is that the participants tend to use groups for various purposes.

Table 3.3 shows that of the groups, 17.2% contain content that has to do with school or education, while 50.9% relate to sport, friends, or hobbies, and 17.2% of the groups have been made to support the communication for a single event such as a party or a holiday. Only 3.4% have the purpose of stating something that could be compared to a like or a dislike, and 10.3% of the groups were made for the promotion and sales of clothing for instance. The promotion sites were primarily open to the public.

Of the secret groups, 63.2% contained content related to sports, friends, and hobbies. This cluster of secret groups actually constituted 20.7% of the total number of groups. This type of content involved the micro-coordination of sport and hobbies that were only interesting to the people involved in the activity concerned. The groups also contained content that was shared among close friends or groups of friends, for instance confidential talk about boyfriends. As one nineteen-year-old female high-school student said about the group for past

Table 3.3   Thematic Coding of Groups

Code	Number of groups	School, education, class	Sport/ friends/ hobby	Event	Statement	Promotion and sale
Open	36	5 (official school sites) (13.9% of open)	15 (official sport sites) (41.7% of open)	1 ('are you in x town this summer') (2.7% of open)	4 (11.1% of open)	10 (27.8% of open)
Closed	42	11 (26.2% of closed)	20 (47.6% of closed)	9 (21.4% of closed)	0	2 (4.8% of closed)
Secret	38	4 (10.5% of secret)	24 (close talk btw. friends) (63.2% of secret) (20.7% of total number of groups)	10 (26.3% of secret)	0	0
Total	116	20	59	20	4	12
%	100%	17.2%	50.9%	17.2%	3.4%	10.3%

boarding school girlfriends: 'It's just easier to share this way, especially if you don't see them everyday because they are from your boarding school.'

Instead of focusing on the timeline as the central function of Facebook, most of the interviewees in their own words primarily used Facebook as an 'easy' and 'inexpensive' (compared to phone calls and texting) way to communicate with their friends through chat, inbox, and groups. Even though they focus on these features, the API data shows that the amount of posts is larger on the walls than in groups. This is also the case even if we take into account that the first wall post in the sample is from 2006 and the first group item is from 2007. This can either indicate that the participants are more engaged in the group communication, and/or that timeline communication happens more intuitively, effortlessly, and as an integrated part of the daily routine. They all describe precisely their own Facebook use as an integral part of everyday life.

The analysis in this section has shown that the students use groups as a privacy filter instead of using Facebook privacy settings to manage and control the circulation of data. The section also shows that these groups primarily contain content units related to sports, hobbies and friends, and that this content category amounted to 63.2% of all secret groups. In this content category, micro-coordination plays a major role. The last section will analyze the interview data according to the topic of private data, to show what the students consider private content that must be hidden in the interoperable network.

SENSITIVE DATA IN THE INTEROPERABLE NETWORK

The groups are used to control the circulation of content units and activities, and the analysis of API data shows what kind of data is placed in the groups. However, the data reported above does not describe in detail if the content is actually considered sensitive. When we asked in the group interviews what they consider sensitive, one of the nineteen-year-old female high-school students said: 'sensitive data is information you don't want to be confronted with.' She found it annoying that she was confronted with information about her partner's status if she had broken off with her boyfriend, and felt that it was impolite and awkward not to accept an invitation for a Facebook relationship if she was already in a real relationship. When we asked if secret groups contain sensitive information, all of the students agreed that some of the content was sensitive and should not be disclosed to the larger network of Facebook friends. For the participants this was primarily content on girlfriends/boyfriends, and hot girls/boys talk. During the interviews the participants also agreed that 'death' and serious 'illness' were sensitive matters that they would not post on Facebook because they would not want to be confronted with sympathy and questions if this kind of information was circulated across devices and services.

Supported by the API data laid out earlier, the interviewees agreed that images were more personal and sensitive than their names when we talked about how they felt about data disclosure in different unintended settings such as advertising on Facebook. They were also very protective about their private addresses and account numbers, but this was for security reasons rather than for impression management reasons.

The participants see data disclosure as a way to trade for free services and they are not concerned about data interoperability when directed toward third-party companies, advertisers, or people they do not know personally. However, they still have a code of conduct for securing their data. The study shows that sensitive data is shared in closed settings such as secret groups, chat, or inbox according to the interviews. All the participants also limit friendship requests from strangers and only see Facebook as an effective way to communicate with existing friends, albeit accumulated friends and family.

The students are much more concerned with social interoperability toward their close network of friends, and there are certain rules for data disclosure here as well. These rules are often connected to the management of 'the right to be forgotten' (Solove, 2013; Bechmann, 2014). One of the female participants said that she was in elementary school when she joined Facebook and had improved and developed her looks and interests since then. It is natural for them NOT to engage with content from earlier periods of their lives. For instance, they refrain from writing comments on each other's images to prevent them from resurfacing. However, they do not un-tag themselves from pictures because as one of the Danish eighteen-year old male high-school students says 'they will just tag you again.' He would rather adjust the disclosure settings. This finding stands in contrast to Young and Quan-Haase's (2013) survey study of undergraduates in the US in which they report on un-tagging practices and removing images. One possible explanation to this difference is that the methods used in this study allow for greater sensitivity and details in the practices of the participants than the survey study conducted by Young & Quan-Haase. On the other hand the study of seventy seven undergraduates deliver a broader picture of tendencies. However, the differences in the studies suggest interesting diversities in the strategies toward the 'right to be forgotten' on the ubiquitous internet.

DISCUSSION AND CONCLUSION

This chapter has investigated the patterns of data interoperability and sharing on Facebook among high-school and college students in order to analyze strategies of personal data sharing in the interoperable and ubiquitous environment of Facebook. The analysis among others shows that the participants do not use Facebook for mobile devices to upload content but rather to read and check activity on Facebook. The study also shows that the participants do not connect data across services deliberately unless they are forced to do so in order to optimize or obtain access to a certain service, for instance through Facebook apps.

This means that they do not share data across services with their network of friends (social interoperability), but only with the apps (technical interoperability). In this respect the study thereby confirms what we already know from existing studies (e.g., Raynes-Goldie, 2010; Young & Quan-Haase, 2013). The participants did not worry about institutional privacy or data retrieved by companies when they used Facebook apps, for instance. Returning to Floridi's (1999) notion of 'me-hood' and the idea that we are our information, this seems only partially to be the case for the participants when we compare their reflections on their behavior. They *want* their information to be themselves both when it comes to their network of friends and toward companies when they look good or when they obtain a better or more personalized service because the information matches the self. However, when data does not look good in front of their peers or when they are confronted with the massive amount of data that they send to third-party apps, they have a tendency to distance themselves from the idea of information as 'me-hood.'

This study differs from existing studies (e.g., Young & Quan-Haase, 2013) because it presents different strategies for data disclosure and managing the interoperable self. For instance, the participants tend not to un-tag themselves in pictures, they tend not to use privacy settings as their primary filter, but instead use groups as an informal privacy filter even though companies can gain access to this communication through the apps. The study also shows that the participants do have strategies to avoid the inappropriate use of data by third parties, mainly security aspects and less identity management (also, Bechmann, 2014).

The participants try to manage interoperability and the interoperable self by viewing the timeline as a public self-portrait and placing micro-coordination and non-public content in (for instance) secret groups that can only be accessed by invited members and apps. Non-sharing information is talk between close friends, micro-coordination of leisure activities, and information that they do not want to be confronted with such as break-ups, deaths, and illnesses. Furthermore, the American participants tend to view sexual orientation, alcohol, political views, and religion as sensitive as well. These are also kept in closed settings such as secret groups or inbox/chat, or safeguarded by participants by using social steganography (boyd & Marwick, 2011) deliberately indicating false information (e.g., false sexual orientation or civil status).

The existing literature on Facebook studies often focuses on timeline and newsfeed communication. However, in order to understand how users manage the interoperable self this study suggests the need to focus elsewhere on the more personal features of Facebook as equally (if not most) central hubs of communication. The participants in this case study need to use Facebook as an effective communicative tool to micro-coordinate and socialize with existing friends from different arenas without this communication being a part of their me-hood. In other words they do not use the full potential of openness, connectedness, and interoperability that the ubiquitous internet service of Facebook provides. Rather at times they deliberately circumvent this ubiquity.

NOTE

1. At the time of registration Google+ was not released yet. Release date June 28, 2011.

REFERENCES

Acquisti, A., & Gross, R. (2006). Imagined communities: Awareness, information sharing, and privacy on Facebook, *Privacy enhancing technologies: 6th international workshop*, *PET 2006* (pp. 36–58). Cambridge: Springer.

Aippersbach, R., Rattenbury, T. L., Woodruff, A., Anderson, K., Canny, J. F., & Aoki, P. (2006). Ethno-mining: Integrating numbers and words from the ground up (Technical Report No. UCB/EECS-2006–125). Berkeley, CA: Electrical Engineering and Computer Sciences, University of California at Berkeley.

Albrechtslund, A. (2008). Online social networking as participatory aurveillance. *First Monday*, *13*(3). Retrieved from http://www.uic.edu/htbin/cgiwrap/bin/ojs/index.php/fm/article/view/2142/1949

Altman, I. (1975). *The environment and social behavior: Privacy, personal space, territory, crowding.* Monterey: Brooks/Cole.

Anderson, K., Nafus, D., & Rattenbury, T. (2009). Numbers have qualities too: Experiences with Ethno-Mining, *Proceedings of EPIC2009*, 123–140.

Barnes, S. (2006). A privacy paradox: Social networking in the United States. *First Monday*, *11*(9). Retrieved from http://firstmonday.org/ojs/index.php/fm/article/viewArticle/1394/1312%2523

Bechmann, A. (2013). Internet profiling: The economy of data intraoperability on Facebook and Google. *Mediekultur. Jornal of Media and Communcation Research*, *29*(55), 72–92.

Bechmann, A. (2014). Non-informed consent cultures: Privacy policies and app contracts on Facebook. *Journal of Media Business Studies*, *11*(1), 21–38.

Bodle, R. (2011). Regimes of sharing. *Information, Communication & Society*, *14*(3), 320–337.

boyd, D. (2007). Why youth (heart) social network sites: The role of networked publics in teenage social life. In D. Buckingham (Ed.), *Youth, identity, and digital media* (pp. 199–142). Cambridge: MIT Press.

boyd, D. (2008). Facebook's privacy trainwreck: Exposure, invasion, and social convergence. *Convergence*, *14*, 13–20.

boyd, D., & Hagittai, E. (2010). Facebook privacy settings: Who cares? *First Monday*, *15*(8), Retrieved from http://firstmonday.org/article/view/3086/2589

boyd, d., & Marwick, A. (2011). Social privacy in networked publics: Teens' attitudes, practices, and strategies. In *Proceedings of A Decade in Internet Time*, 21–24 September 2011, University of Oxford.

Castells, M. (2011). A network theory of power. *International Journal of Communication, 5*, 773–787.

Duggan, M., & Brenner, J. (2013). *The demographics of social media users – 2012.* Washington, DC: Pew Internet Research. Retrieved from http://www.pewinternet.org/2013/02/14/the-demographics-of-social-media-users-2012/

Ellison, N. B., Vitak, J., Steinfield, C., Gray, R., & Lampe, C. (2011). Negotiating privacy concerns and social capital needs in a social media environment. In S. Trepte & L. Reinecke (Eds.), *Privacy online: Perspectives on privacy and self-disclosure in the social web* (pp. 19–32). Heidelberg: Springer.

Floridi, L. (1999). Information ethics: On the philosophical foundation of computer ethics. *Ethics and Information Technology, 1*, 37–56.

Gerlitz, C., & Helmond, A. (2013). The Like economy: Social buttons and the data-intensive web. *New Media & Society, 15*(8), 1348–1365.

Kvale, S. (1994). *Interviews.* Copenhagen: Hans Reitzels Forlag.

Lomborg, S., & Bechmann, A. (2014). Using APIs for data collection on social media. *The Information Society, 30*(4), 256–265.

Margulis, S. T. (2011). Three theories of privacy: An overview. In S. Trepte & L. Reinecke (Eds.), *Privacy online : Perspectives on privacy and self-disclosure in the social web* (pp. 9–17). Heidelberg: Springer.

Nissenbaum, H. (2011). A contextual approach to privacy online, *Dædalus, 4*, 32–48.

Raynes-Goldie, K. (2010). Aliases, creeping, and wall cleaning: Understanding privacy in the age of Facebook, *First Monday, 15*(1). Retrieved from http://firstmonday.org/article/view/2775/2432

Solove, D. J. (2013). Introduction: Privacy self-management and the consent dilemma. *Harvard Law Review, 126*, 1880–1903.

Statistics Denmark. (2011). *Befolkningens brug af internet – 2010.* Copenhagen: Statistics Denmark.

Sutor, R. S. (2011). Software standards, openness, and interoperability. In L. DeNardis (Ed.), *Opening Sstandards: The global politics of interoperability* (pp. 209–218), Cambridge, MA: MIT Press.

Taddicken, M. (2012). Privacy, surveillance, and self-disclosure in the social web. In C. Fuchs, K. Boersma, A. Albrechtslund, & M. Sandoval (Eds.), *Internet and surveillance: The challenges of web 2.0 and social media* (pp. 255–272). New York: Routledge.

Tsilas, N. L. (2011). Interoperability and open innovation. In L. DeNardis (Ed.), *Opening standards: The global politics of interoperability* (pp. 97–118), Cambridge, MA: MIT Press.

Weber, R. P. (1990). Basic content analysis. *Quantitative Applications in Social Sciences, 49*, 1–96.

Westin, A. F. (1967). *Privacy and freedom.* Atheneum: New York.

Young, A. L., & Quan-Haase, A. (2013). Privacy protection strategies on Facebook: The internet privacy paradox revisited. *Information Communication & Society, 16*(4), 479–500.

4 The Dynamics of Real-Time Contentious Politics

How Ubiquitous Internet Shapes and Transforms Popular Protest in China

Jun Liu

The growing ubiquity of mobile technology and internet-connected devices around the world has led to a burgeoning literature on the political role and implications of information and communication technologies (ICT) in contentious politics as an increasing number of people are appropriating and domesticating their digital applications for the initiation, mobilization, and coordination of contentious activities (e.g., van de Donk et al., 2004; Mercea, 2012; Rojas & Puig-i-Abril, 2009; Tufekci & Wilson, 2012; for a review, see Garrett, 2006). In the spring of 2011, for instance, the world watched as internet and mobile phone-facilitated revolutionary fervor swept the Middle East (e.g., Howard & Hussain, 2011). As one of the latest examples of eye-catching ICT-facilitated activism, the 'Arab Spring' not only mobilized widespread offline protests and toppled dictators but also stimulated further studies into the role of ICT in demonstrations and protests, in particular in authoritarian regimes, in the wake of increasing use of digital devices in political activism and contentious politics.

One hot topic in studies of ICT and contentious politics in authoritarian regimes is the question of how—and to what extent—ICT-enabled and facilitated contentions empower people to challenge and struggle against the authorities in China. Despite being the world's largest authoritarian state, China also has the world's largest internet and mobile phone populations. According to a report from the China Internet Network Information Center (CNNIC), the number of internet users in China reached 618 million by the end of 2013, equal to over 45% of the total population (CNNIC, 2014). The mobile phone population has surpassed 1.2 billion, or around 90% of the total population. As wireless networking becomes ever more prevalent, China has witnessed a surge in the use of mobile phones to access the internet. As CNNIC's latest report demonstrates, among all internet users, the proportion of the population using mobile phones surges to 78.5%. In other words, four out of five people today gain access to the internet through their mobile phones. The increasingly ubiquitous access to the internet enables people to maintain online chatting, carry out online shopping, surf social networking sites, and perform numerous other activities anytime, anywhere. With this in mind, we can enquire into the political influence of the increasing ubiquity of internet and mobile devices and their applications, as a large proportion of the population is now able to access to the internet whenever and wherever possible. More to the point, given that Chinese people have been adopting, appropriating, and maneuvering ICT against the authoritarian regime (e.g., Tai, 2006; Yang, 2009), how could current understandings of the political role of ICT (including the internet, mobile phones, and social media, such as the prevalent *Weibo*[1]) benefit from a discussion on ubiquitous internet's role in contentious activities?

This chapter explores this question through a preliminary study of the interrelationship between ubiquitous internet and contentious politics in China. More specifically, it investigates *how the use of ubiquitous internet, given its different ICT components, shapes and transforms the dynamics of contentious politics in contemporary China*. I first provide a critical review of current studies on ICT and contentious politics in China, addressing the relevance of approaching such a topic from a perspective of ubiquitous internet that combines *diverse* media uses via *multiple* digital platforms during and for contentious activities. I then elaborate on case selection, data collection, and analysis methods, followed by an overview of two protests in rural and urban areas: the anti-corruption protests in Wukan, southern China's Guangdong province, in 2011 and the anti-Paraxylene (anti-PX for short)[2] demonstrations in Kunming, western China's Yunnan province, in 2013. Both case studies show how Chinese people have taken advantage of ubiquitous internet in their struggles against the authorities. I further scrutinize how ubiquitous internet generates new dynamics of real-time contentious politics and empowers Chinese people by allowing quick and irrepressible dissemination of politically sensitive information despite censorship, facilitating a rapid and unprecedented scale of organization and mobilization within a short time frame, and consolidating large-scale solidarity beyond geographical boundaries. I conclude with thoughts on the political influence and implications of ubiquitous internet as an integrated part of contentious politics in contemporary China.

ICT AND CONTENTIOUS POLITICS IN CONTEMPORARY CHINA

The rapid development and proliferation of ICT has had a profound effect on political protests and contentious activities in contemporary China. The current struggle against the authorities is replete with examples of how ICT (including Bulletin Board Systems [BBS], online forums, blogs, mobile phones, and *Weibo*) has generated 'online activism' (Yang, 2009), mobilized offline contention (Liu, 2013a, 2013b), facilitated 'new media events' (Qiu & Chan, 2011), and nurtured an emergent cyber civil society (e.g., Lu & Qiu, 2013; Tai, 2006; Yang, 2003, 2007) to empower Chinese citizens and to change—and even undermine—the authoritarian regime (Esarey &

Xiao, 2011; Zheng, 2008, for a review on China ICT studies, see Qiu & Bu, 2013). Some studies suggest that ICT in general and the internet in particular have increasingly become vital access points into government bureaucracies and public policy-building processes, enlivening civil society, and constituting a virtual public sphere (e.g., Yang, 2003, 2007, 2009; Zheng, 2008). Others hold the opposite opinion, arguing that the party-state also modernizes itself with control strategies that rein in the internet to defend its autocratic rule effectively (e.g., MacKinnon, 2011; Morozov, 2011). Particularly in order to prevent internet contention from moving offline and into the streets, the Chinese government has established stringent information-filtering systems to eradicate online comments and discussions that could initiate or coordinate social mobilization (e.g., King, Pan, & Roberts, 2013). In short, there is no easy answer to the question of whether ICT, especially the internet, will automatically lead to empowerment and emancipation of political activism in authoritarian China.

Nevertheless, the impressive literature so far is vulnerable on two fronts as follows:

First, most literature is confined to the political use of *a single form* (e.g., online forums, blogs, mobile phones, or *Weibo*) *or genre* (e.g., SMS or the text modality of tweet) of ICT instead of taking into account the growing repertoires of digital channels and applications that engage in the practice and process of contentious activities as a whole. More specifically, for instance, studies on *Weibo* and political activism focus on either the textual content or the network structure of tweets on *Weibo* platforms (e.g., Huang & Sun, 2014; Tong & Zuo, 2014). As such, political communication on *Weibo* is lumped into a more or less single entity: the text tweet. However, in practice, '*Weibo*' embodies diverse forms of communication, including texts, pictures, photos, videos, and online links. As a result, focus on *Weibo*'s text modality alone fails to provide a comprehensive picture of *Weibo*'s political influence on contentious activities.

Similarly, studies exclusively addressing the use of the internet for political activism ignore that the internet itself is increasingly *only one element* of the ecology of (digital) media. In other words, 'the internet' ought to be understood as seamlessly linking and encompassing not just services/networks and users but also an array of digital devices, each with (potential) embedded internet connectivity. As people progressively gain access to the internet through digital devices besides laptops, it is necessary to consider the interrelationship between the uses of different digital media for and during contentious activities. For instance, taking pictures of protests on camera phones and disseminating these photos over the internet is a common practice in political activism today. Does such a practice refer to the political influence of the internet *only* or to a combination of the political uses of mobile phones (in this case, camera phones) and the internet simultaneously? In this sense, current discussions of ICT and contentious activities in China have failed to distinguish the political use of ICT (including 'the internet') into more discrete phenomena and to scrutinize the interplay between the political roles of different digital applications and platforms during contentious activities on the other. In order to address this, we must thus expand our discussion by interrogating diverse ICT uses during and for contentious activities or, as Chen (2014) suggests, 'to take into account individuals' media use via multiple platforms' (p. 5) in political protests.

Second, the existing literature largely treats the process of ICT-mediated contentious politics as linear, with normal Chinese people adopting available digital resources to struggle against the authorities. Nevertheless, as McAdam, Tarrow, and Tilly (2001) expound, the dynamics of contentious politics—whether through digital media or otherwise—involve a set of interactive mechanisms. Only by looking at 'the dynamic processes through which new political actors, identities, and forms of action emerge, interact, coalesce and evolve during complex episodes of contention' (McAdam et al., 2001), they believe, can we understand the dynamics of episodes of contentious politics. Following this suggestion, to advance our understanding of the political role and implication of ICT in contentious politics in China, we must nuance both how different types of ICT shape, transform, and have been integrated into the dynamics of contentious politics and how they interact with each other in the process of contentious activities.

Given the above discussion, this study approaches the question from the perspective of ubiquitous internet. Ubiquitous internet refers to the fact that people are able to access to the internet anywhere and at any time using a well-established telecommunication infrastructure and the proliferation of ICT devices and applications. As in other parts of the world, digital media and communication with embedded internet connectivity have become pervasive in people's everyday lives in China. An increasing number of Chinese people are therefore embracing the internet through various devices always and everywhere. How does this kind of ubiquitous internet shape political activism and further contribute to contentious politics in China?

The perspective of 'ubiquitous internet' holds several advantages in advancing our understandings of ICT and contentious politics in China. On the one hand, ubiquitous internet reminds us to segment the abstract concept of 'ICT' into more discrete phenomena. In other words, in order to specify the political role of ubiquitous internet, studies should explicate different (digital) media uses via multiple platforms in the process of contentious activities. On the other hand, the term 'ubiquitous internet' suggests that we consider its political influence as a combination of repertoires of various types of ICT instead of any individual one. The detailed research questions are thus:

How do Chinese people employ different digital media in concerted effort in contentious politics against the authorities?

How does ubiquitous internet, given its different digital media components, shape and transform the dynamics of contentious politics in contemporary China?

METHODS

This study employs a descriptive multiple case study design (Yin, 2009) to acquire a nuanced picture of the uses of ICT and their interrelationships with contentious activities. This design also allows the comparison of differences within and between cases and generalizing what is common across cases (Yin, 2009, p. 18). In other words, by looking into similar cases— ICT-mediated contentions—occurring independently in different situations, circumstances, or groups, we are better able to generalize our conclusions (Flyvbjerg, 2006; Yin, 2009, p. 54). The current study selects the following two protest cases: the anti-corruption protests in Wukan, one of the biggest 'mass incidents (*quntixing shijian*)' of 2011 (Jacobs, 2011) and the anti-PX demonstrations in Kunming in 2013 (Chang, 2013), one of a series of environmental protests in recent decades. The criteria for case selection required, first, the use of ICT as a key part of contentious activities. Second, the selected cases represent a variety of principles that have been echoed in other contentious cases, countering the common criticism that findings are unique to one particular case. As one of the landmark cases of civil disobedience in recent years, the Wukan incident demonstrates governance problems and injustices that beset many villages across China, thus generating far-reaching discussions on and implications for the political role of digital media in contentious politics (Mo, 2011; Wines, 2011). The anti-PX protests can be traced back to the demonstration in Xiamen as early as 2007 (Liu, 2013a). Learning from the Xiamen case, residents organized a series of protests against government decisions on PX projects in over five cities, such as Dalian, 2011 (BBC, 2011); Ningbo, 2012 (Liu & Yan, 2012); and Kunming, 2013, somewhat successfully forcing city governments to shut down PX refineries or move these factories far outside the city boundaries. The case of the anti-PX protest hereby becomes a 'prototypical' example of contentious politics in contemporary China. Third, the case's success (or otherwise) in, for instance, changing government policies through ICT-enabled contentious activities is not a necessary criterion for selection because there are too many other contingent factors influencing government decisions to act or adopt a certain plan. Thus, by focusing on the actual use of digital media in cases (instead of their results), this study can grasp the nuanced and detailed use of ubiquitous internet while avoiding exaggerating its role in contentious politics. The case description will be provided in the next section.

This study adopts qualitative approaches to collect and analyze data. Both case studies employ analysis of documents and materials, including public records, such as national and international news reports,[3] government reports and statements,[4] discussions from online forums and BBS,[5] and personal documents that are available online, such as blogs and Sina's *Weibo* tweets. The reason for choosing Sina *Weibo* rather than other social media platforms is that Sina *Weibo* is China's dominant and largest online social forum and most energetic micro-blogging platform, thereby exerting significant influence on social, economic, and political issues in contemporary China. Sina *Weibo* consequently becomes the preferred option for people to air their anger, pour out their grievances, reveal corruption, and so on. Meanwhile, Sina *Weibo* is also one of the largest online platforms that allow its users to access to and upload integrated text, image, and video content, among other things, via different digital terminals. It also employs a variety of interactive formats to create a rich, personalized experience of ubiquitous internet for its users. *Weibo* tweets have been retrieved from Sina *Weibo* by manually searching for keywords such as 'Wukan,' 'WK,'[6] 'Xue Jingbo,'[7] and '9.21'[8] between September 2011 and January 2012 in the Wukan case and 'Kunming,' 'PX,' and '*sanbu*'[9] during April and May 2013 in the Kunming case, respectively. The keywords are the most common euphemisms and alternative expressions of politically sensitive words in both cases.

In the Kunming case, I also carried out eleven interviews with protest participants for an investigation of their ICT uses in demonstrations.[10] To identify protest participants as interviewees, I more specifically first searched for keywords such as 'Kunming' and 'PX' on Sina *Weibo* and followed tweets covering the anti-PX demonstration in Kunming from May 3–13, 2013, before they have been eliminated by the service under the directive of the authorities. Among the tweets, those with real-time coverage or photos of demonstrations and local-based information enabled me to identify local residents who engaged in the anti-PX demonstration in Kunming. Second, I sent invitations to twenty-five *Weibo* accounts for confirmation of their participation and interviews. Third, due to the politically sensitive nature of protest participation in China, I requested that interviewees join this research on a voluntary basis. The sample has been reduced to eleven after removing those who withdrew from the research due to the sensitive subject matter. Among them, eight are male and three are female. Fourth, I employed a semi-structured interview guide (Kvale & Brinkmann, 2009) to probe the question of how participants utilize ICT and ubiquitous internet for contentious activities.

The interviews were structured as follows: (a) In an introductory section, I asked participants for basic personal data. (b) I established in detail the availability and forms of access to different types of media during protests (e.g., did interviewees have access to the internet for reading and distributing mobilizing messages?) (c) I collected data regarding information exchanged through ICT, such as type (tweet, photo, or mobile text), content, when this information was received, and how often it was received in protests. (d) I looked into the interpretation of both communication practices and information via ICT, including how interviewees perceived the messages from their digital devices or platforms, whether or not they followed these messages, and most importantly, why they did so. (e) I mapped out how interviewees dealt with these messages, such as whether they disseminated the messages or responded to it, to whom they forwarded the messages, via which channels, and why. Each interview was conducted in China and lasted around one hour.

The explanation-building approach and cross-case synthesis (Yin, 2009, p. 18) were employed following data collection to figure out questions as to *how* people used their ICT to facilitate protests against the authorities and *what* influence ubiquitous internet had on the dynamic of contentious activities in China. Importantly, as a piece of exploratory research aimed at shedding new light on the role of ubiquitous internet during and for contentious politics through investigating and generalizing cases of ICT-facilitated protests in China, this study used cross-case synthesis to identify the general features instead of to compare the differences between the two cases. It should be noted that these questions are not intended to apply to all contentious activities or all kinds of activism that involve ubiquitous internet. However, this study believes that these questions shed light on the contribution of ubiquitous internet to contentious politics in authoritarian regimes like China.

CASE DESCRIPTION

The Wukan Incident

As early as 2009, Wukan villagers started to organize and petition government authorities concerning illegal land grab issues while disseminating their appeal through BBS and online forums, but they failed to get any response from authorities. Villagers decided to take the law into their own hands and to demonstrate and express their anger by taking to the streets. The street demonstrations took place between September 21 and 23 when around 4,000 angry villagers protested using banners and placards with slogans like 'give us back our farmland' and 'let us continue farming' in front of a government building before attacking this building, clashing with police, and blocking roads. Mobile phone-captured videos and photos showing the clashes between the villagers and police proliferated across online forums and *Weibo* (Dafeng, 2011).

The situation worsened on December 9, 2011. When villagers again protested and carried out a demonstration parade on the way to a city government building, they had a confrontation with the police. The police detained five village representatives, and three days later, one of them, Xue Jinbo, died in local police custody. Local police asserted that Xue had died of a heart attack, but his family refused to accept the verdict and claimed instead that Xue had been beaten to death by the local public security bureau, given the signs of torture on his body. Xue's death intensified villagers' emotional reactions, and anger broke out in the village over the following days. The villagers forcefully evicted the entire local government, Communist Party leadership, and police from the village. The authorities responded by sending thousands of police and People's Armed Police to surround the village, preventing food and goods from entering. Government authorities also set up internet censorship against information related to Wukan. To protect against the authorities, Wukan villagers established a *de facto* militia to guard the perimeter and keep the police out. Throughout mid-December, local villagers protested daily against the local government and, at the same time, informed the outside world about the situation in Wukan using Sina *Weibo* (Goodman, 2011).

The situation started to change after 20 December under pressure from increasing protest reports by overseas media and new media, in particular *Weibo* and online forums. The provincial government had sent official representatives into the village to negotiate with the villagers, promising to acknowledge their demands, investigate the corruption issue, and redistribute land that had been confiscated by the local government. Villagers stopped their protest the next day, and on February 2012 carried out an independent election for a new village leadership to govern Wukan and guarantee the villagers' interests. Throughout the incident, Wukan villagers made use of diverse digital devices and platforms (including BBS, online forums, mobile phones, cameras, and *Weibo*) to keep themselves connected to the internet and contend with government authorities.

The Anti-PX Demonstration in Kunming

The anti-PX demonstration in Kunming is one in a long line of environmental protests, starting in 2007, against the government's decision to construct petrochemical factories that would endanger the environment. The earliest protest can be traced back to the one in Xiamen in 2007, in which mobile text messages played a vital role in proliferating government-censored, PX-related information and facilitating two days of demonstrations (Liu, 2013a). Unlike the Xiamen protest, the one in Kunming had been initiated and coordinated largely through the Chinese social media sites *Weixin* (WeChat)[11] and *Weibo*. On May 3, 2013, messages advocating a demonstration against the government's decision to build a PX factory went viral on *Weixin* and *Weibo*, stating 'Against PX project in Kunming: Join us at 1:30 pm on May 4 at Nanping Square for a peaceful demonstration. No disputes, no blocking streets, no garbage, civil expression!'[12] People discussed and circulated the potential environmental dangers of the PX project through *Weibo* and *Weixin* and further handed out masks and white T-shirts bearing slogan 'No PX in Kunming.' To prevent people taking to streets, students at schools and universities were confined to their dormitories. The local government even restricted mask and T-shirt sales and requested that photocopying at shops needed real name registration.[13] Still, the proliferation of messages calling for protests through *Weixin* and *Weibo* resulted in a demonstration of over 2,000 participants in front of government buildings. Participants disseminated real-time texts and images of the demonstration throughout the protest.[14] Some included locational information when they circulated the protest photos while calling for more participation to express people's concern and discontent. The demonstration eventually forced the local government to halt the construction of the PX project.

Although the two cases took place in different sets of circumstances (rural and urban areas), involved different groups (the rural residents of Wukan and the middle class of Kunming), and were motivated by different reasons (justice seeking and environmental concern), both embraced ICT as a crucial means for contentious activities. More specifically, both the Wukan incident and the Kunming anti-PX demonstration bore witness to not only the diverse uses of digital devices for political protest but, more importantly, the increasing relevance of the accessibility of ubiquitous internet in contentious politics in China. The next section will elaborate on the role of ubiquitous internet in both cases and how it shapes contentious activities in contemporary China.

FINDINGS AND DISCUSSION: HOW ICT AND UBIQUITOUS INTERNET SHAPE PROTESTS IN CHINA

By virtue of the popularization of digital devices and ubiquitous accessibility of the internet, people in Wukan and Kunming not only succeeded in ridding themselves of the government's harsh control over information and communication but also facilitated offline protests against local authority, influencing the power dynamics between the governor and the governed. Ubiquitous internet performs the following two functions in the two cases: First, it is a means of overcoming censorship, which enables information to be diffused in near-real time across a highly distributed network environment. Second, it is a means of mobilization, which encourages the real-time organization and coordination of political activism simultaneously with the diffusion of information. The intertwining of these two functions empowers ordinary Chinese people against the authorities while shaping and transforming the dynamics of contentious politics in China.

Ubiquitous Internet as a Means of Overcoming Censorship

The term 'overcoming censorship' addresses the fact that communication enabled by ubiquitous internet is poised to breach the authority-mandated information blockade, reshaping people's views and knowledge against the silence of local government and government-controlled media *before* and *during* political protests.

China's authoritarian government strives to maintain intense control over new media platforms to discover and extinguish internet-based political organization and mobilization (e.g., King et al., 2013). Nevertheless, ubiquitous internet allows people to disseminate politically sensitive information and circumvent censorship via various platforms. As soon as these messages had been distributed via diverse digital platforms, they were able to proliferate within a very short time and spread to services beyond the control of state censors. On the one hand, the messages diffused through decentralized network infrastructure before the government recognized it and initiated censorship. On the other hand, the rapid and widespread diffusion of these messages made it impossible for the Chinese government to eliminate them completely, as it is especially difficult to request overseas services such as YouTube, Facebook,[15] and Twitter to remove these messages.[16]

In the Wukan incident, for instance, ubiquitous internet enabled local villagers to employ the diverse digital media available to them (including BBS, online forums, camera phones, text messages, and *Weibo*) to disseminate not just their appeal, discontent, and anger towards the local government but also up-to-date information on the government siege and suppression, beyond the reach censorship. Such a role can be specified into three categories:

First, in the early period of the Wukan protest, BBS played a significant role in distributing across the internet the villagers' petition on the local government's illegal land grab. As early as September 2011, villagers sought to reveal the illegal local government land-grabbing issue by petitioning city and provincial authorities on the one hand and beginning to disseminate their petition on several BBSs on the other hand (Pang, 2012). Subsequent BBS posts made people outside of Wukan village aware of the villagers' petition and the illegal land-grabbing issue, even without mass media coverage due to propaganda directives.[17] Against this backdrop, according to a survey by the opinion monitoring office, *People's Daily* Online, online discussions and public opinion had expressed sympathy and support for this contentious issue already at the very beginning of Wukan protest (Pang, 2012).

Second, ubiquitous internet enabled Wukan villagers to spread up-to-date and real-time photos and video of their protests via different internet platforms, significantly influencing and shaping online public opinion during the protest, in particular after they had been besieged by the authorities. With the easy availability of mobile phones, in particular their camcorder functions, we have already witnessed that people in rural and urban areas need no longer depend on cumbersome and suspicious-looking video cameras and computers to capture their struggles and send them to their friends. Instead, 'a rapidly assembling and self-documenting public' (Shirky, 2010) has emerged as live reporting scooped by ordinary citizens with on-the-spot reports provides quick responses to the events. Citizens have become actively engaged in spreading information on politically sensitive topics, expressing different versions or opinions of events and even criticism of the government, and forcing authorities to tweak its propaganda war and hamfisted responses to challenges from below (Hung, 2010; Liu, 2013a).

Similar situations have been recognized in the Wukan case, in which the young generation of Wukan villagers played a crucial role as 'citizen journalists' (Allan, 2007) in documenting and broadcasting the protests throughout the entire process. Zhang Jianxing, a 17-year-old villager, worked together with his friends and used digital cameras, camcorders, and computers to take and later upload onto Sina *Weibo* up-to-date images and videos of, for instance, police charging into Wukan and beating villagers with sticks. Such images and videos proliferated within a short period before the government worked on censoring this information, sparking widespread online and offline criticism of the authorities' practices.

In addition to the photos and videos of protests, villagers' self-made videos that diffused across the internet also helped win sympathy and support around the country. Again, Zhang Jianxing working alongside his friend Wu Jijin recorded and edited a seventy-minute documentary entitled 'Wukan! Wukan!' to explain the reason for the protests (Reporter, 2012). This documentary was uploaded onto the internet following the protests. After being distributed to online forums and widely circulated around the internet, including on video-sharing websites such as YouTube, this documentary generated enormous effect outside of Wukan, attracting international and national media attention to the event.[18]

Most importantly, ubiquitous internet enabled Wukan villagers to maintain their connections with the outside world, speaking with their own voices beyond official reports, even after the government ordered the police force to besiege the village and control its connection to the outside. Wukan villagers used *Weibo* to update on the situation in the village, seeking to prevent the public from being misled by government accounts and its propaganda machine.[19] The villagers stated:

> We are only protesting against the illegal land-grabbing issue [instead of the leadership of the party]. Some of us are party members, others members of the communist youth league. To the government and mass media: Please do not distort or exaggerate our actions.
>
> (Zhang, 2013)[20]

Although the authorities tried to censor such information and even shut down several Wukan villagers' *Weibo* accounts to impede the information's distribution, this information still reached millions of *Weibo* users at a very fast rate—and these users were furious. A torrent of criticism followed, overwhelming the local government and police and forcing them to give up the siege.[21]

Third, the villagers depended on ubiquitous internet not just to disseminate information but also to keep themselves updated on the situation outside the village, to track the news reports by international and national media, and to keep an eye on the relevant messages from higher authorities.

Similarly, in the Kunming case, local residents established diverse communication channels to diffuse real-time information about the demonstration on the internet. They were even capable of setting up a Facebook group named 'Anti-PX Plant in Kunming' and a Twitter account to disseminate images and video of the demonstration.[22] The continuously uploaded, on-the-spot photos and videos not only breached the censorship blockade but also helped maintain sustained attention to this issue both online and offline. Meanwhile, once it spreads, this kind of real-time reporting also attracts attention from the media, including foreign media, which will send out journalists to cover these events. Accordingly, the real-time reporting succeeds in attracting more media coverage on demonstration and protests, making these events increasingly eye catching and preventing the government from concealing these unflattering activities from the general public.

Inasmuch as there had already been citizen journalism via mobile phones and that the overseas media had already taken note of the issue, any crackdown to prevent the protest would probably have made the situation worse and perhaps even sparked a violent conflict. The longer such protests continue, the more politicized they become. In this sense, the government was also forced to take a more nuanced approach to carrying out dialogue, leading to indirect empowerment of the people.

By utilizing different types of ICT to access ubiquitous internet throughout the process, people in both cases not only broke the censorship by authorities but also won moral support from the domestic public and international media.[23] More specifically, calls, photos, audio, and videos proliferating across ubiquitous internet enable ordinary people to broadcast to the world information (in multiple forms) concerning the demonstrations and protests, bringing inevitable and irresistible attention from the public at large, the central government, and even overseas media, which in turn empowers these citizens in way they had not even envisioned. In this process, the driving force is both the widespread availability of digital devices and the accessibility of ubiquitous internet, which allows participants as well as ordinary internet users to broadcast real-time protest activities to other people and to the wider world with remarkable speed. As a result, sources from the government and journalism are becoming a smaller part of people's information mix. The party-controlled media institution is thus no longer the sole gatekeeper of what the public knows. That power is in part moving away from those who cover the news to those who make the news. Even with a media blackout on news of the demonstration, the time, location, and target turnout of millions of people were spread almost exclusively by calls, SMS messages, BBS postings, tweets, and blog posts, making it a nationally and internationally observed act of political activism. Ubiquitous internet established real-time information on the protests as an inextricable part of contentious politics.

Ubiquitous Internet as a Mechanism of Mobilization

While ubiquitous internet enables and encourages people to broadcast the real-time situation they witness or engage in during contentious activities, the proliferation of smartphones and *Weibo* also allows people to diffuse real-time reporting on protests and demonstrations with locational information. As such real-time messages circulate through mobile communication or disseminate on the internet, they not only attract people's attention but also encourage residents in the same city to assemble as soon as possible at the site where the protest is to take place and join or cover these collective actions. In this sense, ubiquitous internet enables and encourages 'real-time' organization, coordination, and mobilization of contentious activities.

For instance, in the Kunming case, several interviewees recalled that they were unsure that a real-life demonstration against the local government would occur after they received the mobilizing message via *Weibo* or *Weixin*.[24] Then, on the morning of May 4, 2012, as soon as people updated the *Weibo* homepage or glanced at their *Weibo* feeds, they received photos that not only demonstrated the existence of the protest but also included detailed locational information. As one participant said:

> I read several tweets with photos of the demonstration and detailed locational information. The people who tweeted these messages called for people to join them. I thought I should join them [the demonstrators], be part of this event [the anti-PX protest], reinforce our power, and make our voice louder. I quickly forwarded this message through my *Weibo* account as well, set out, and went to join the demonstration.[25]

In this way, *real-time* messages with *real-time* locational information served as a 'call,' drawing residents to participate in protest activities, increasing the number of participants, and contributing to greater influence.

Ubiquitous internet moreover facilitates mobilization beyond the specific location where a protest takes place. In both cases, local participants used *Weibo* to upload images and videos and seek other internet users' attention and support. After Wukan villagers released on *Weibo* information about the government's siege, for instance, several big 'v's (verified and influential commentators on *Weibo*, with millions of followers) started encouraging and organizing people to deliver supplies to Wukan and to help them against the government's siege. Such practice greatly encouraged people to express their support towards the villagers and consolidate their solidarity against the authorities.

Reflection on the Role of Ubiquitous Internet in Contentious Politics in China

Existing research has already paid considerable attention to the role of ICT in political activism and contentious politics in contemporary China, covering the discussions from BBS to online forums, mobile phones to *Weibo*, and so on (e.g., Liu, 2013a, 2013b; Yang, 2009; Zheng, 2008). As the two cases in this study demonstrate, ubiquitous internet provides people—both rural and urban—with a convenient means of breaking censorship and disseminating real-time messages that are relevant to themselves via their internet-embedded digital devices, allowing people to more easily facilitate and coordinate collective action. The Wukan case involved a particular set of ICT-enacted political contentions in which the rural population, especially those without high-level technical skills (e.g., to evade the online censors), made their voices heard and their stories known in diverse media modalities (e.g., tweets, photos, and videos) to the public at large by virtue of the ubiquitous availability and accessibility of the internet and digital devices. Ubiquitous internet thus makes information (tweets, photos, audio, videos, locational messages) recording and dissemination available at any time, in any place, and in any situation. This feature encourages and turns more ordinary people into citizen journalists, in particular in circumstances in which the authorities do not allow the traditional media to cover certain events.

Equally important, the ubiquitous internet operates not only on the terminal (local) level but also on the service (international) level. International service providers such as YouTube or Facebook provided platforms that neither authoritarian regimes nor political parties could dominate for alternative sources of information production, its wide range of flows, extensive distribution, and differentiation of forms. Communication via ubiquitous internet thus has the potential to lead to a more open and free public communication domain, one that is less constrained by officially sanctioned agendas, editorial policies in traditional media, and censorship and subtle but effective controls over the internet. As this study demonstrates, ubiquitous internet enables and facilitates the emergence of 'real-time' contentious politics, in which *real-time* information—beyond simple texts—concerning protests and demonstrations have been distributed and proliferated over the internet, exerting great influence on public opinion in Chinese society. Meanwhile, ubiquitous internet initiates *real-time* organization, coordination, and mobilization of political activism, by which people assemble and consolidate their solidarity, online and offline, against the authorities.

It is nevertheless still necessary to remember that although ubiquitous internet provides people with more flexible ways of engaging in contentious activities, it is the government that still maintains general control over the operation of the internet. In several cases, the government has shown itself capable of shutting down the *entire* telecommunication service to ensure its control over society and 'maintain stability' (*weiwen*). Despite this, as the Wukan case illustrates, ubiquitous internet also enables and facilitates the articulation of public opinion, which in turn generates unprecedented pressure that keeps the government from employing censorship or even cutting off the telecommunication network so easily. In this sense, the integration of ubiquitous internet as a whole into contentious politics to some extent offers more opportunities for protests, enables diverse forms of contentions online and offline, and contributes to an increasingly relevant role for ICT in contentious politics in authoritarian regimes such as China.

CONCLUSION

As a preliminary study, this chapter aims to clarify the links between the proliferation of ICT and contentious activities and to lay the foundations for a comprehensive understanding of the role of ICT in protests and demonstrations in contemporary China. Analysts observe that ICT drives a number of profound changes in political activism and contentious politics: Information is free from centralized control, costs are plummeting, interconnected networks enable participants to access information stored on millions of computers beyond national boundaries, and real-time as well as asynchronous multicasting support entirely new modes of communication (e.g., Bennett, 2003, 2012; Bennett & Segerberg, 2012). Nevertheless, so far, little research about ICT and contentious politics in China has distinguished the political use of ICT into more discrete phenomena and scrutinized the interplay between the political roles of different digital applications and platforms during contentious moments. This chapter addresses this gap in the research by taking ubiquitous internet as a platform for integrating diverse digital devices into the process of contentious politics. As the chapter demonstrates, ubiquitous internet enables and facilitates the emergence of *real-time contentious politics*, in which it acts not only as means of overcoming censorship but also as means of organizing and mobilizing. Ubiquitous internet thus integrates the dynamics of real-time politics into the process of contentious activities and transforms contentious politics in contemporary China.

NOTES

1. *Weibo* is the Chinese word for 'microblog,' referring to microblogging services, including social chat sites and platform sharing. As a hybrid of Twitter and Facebook, *Weibo* has many functionalities similar to Twitter, such as allowing users to post with a 140-character limit, talk to other people using '@UserName,' and add hashtags with '#HashName#.' Among many *Weibo* service providers, Sina *Weibo* is one of the most popular sites in China, with over 500 million registered users as of December 2012 (Xinhua, 2013). For a general discussion on *Weibo*, see Sullivan, 2012.
2. Paraxylene is used in the production of plastics, polyester, and other synthetic materials.
3. For instance, reports from local media such as Guangdong-based *Southern Metropolis Daily*; national media such as Xinhua News Agency, *People's Daily*, *Global Times*, and *Beijing News*; and international media such as *The New York Times*, *South China Morning Post* (e.g., http://www.scmp.com/topics/wukan), Reuters, and Al-Jazeera.
4. For instance the report on public opinion in the Wukan incident by the Opinion Monitoring Office, *People's Daily* Online (Pang, 2012)
5. For instance, Tianya Club, one of the most popular internet forums for discussing issues including current events, politics, and culture (e.g., 'To

understand the role of new media in mass incident from the case of Wukan,'
retrieved September 1, 2014, from http://124.225.65.110/post-65-600512-1.
shtml).

6. A simple two-letter abbreviation of 'Wukan' after the word had been censored online.
7. A village leader who died in police custody in the Wukan incident.
8. Wukan protests are referred as 'the September 21 Wukan mass incident' by state media.
9. An alternative to 'demonstration' and 'protest,' both of which are politically sensitive words on the internet.
10. The original plan included recruitment of and interviews with participants in the Wukan case for exploring their use of ICT during contentious activities. However, the plan had to be dropped due to the difficulties and political sensitivity in identifying and locating participants after the Wukan protests.
11. *Weixin* is a mobile text and voice messaging communication service available on digital devices with Android, iPhone, BlackBerry, Windows Phone, and OS platforms. For more information, see http://www.wechat.com/en/.
12. Interviews with a graduate student in Kunming, January 2014.
13. Interviews with participants in the demonstration in Kunming, January 2014.
14. See, for instance, http://m.secretchina.com/node/496176; http://www.wenxuecity.com/news/2013/05/04/2375085.html.
15. For instance, the anti-PX group on Facebook, https://www.facebook.com/AntiPxPlantInKunming and the one for Wukan, https://www.facebook.com/groups/137610859683156/.
16. As several studies have pointed out, internet services in mainland China must abide by Chinese laws and regulations and cooperate with the government to impose censorship requirements on the internet (see, for instance, MacKinnon, 2009)
17. Interview with a journalist in Foshan, Guangdong Province, January 8, 2014.
18. For the video 'Wukan! Wukan!,' see http://www.youtube.com/watch?v=Lb_tto2GwoU.
19. For instance, the Chinese government utilizes the accusation of 'spreading rumors to mislead people' as an excuse for political suppression of contentious activities, see Liu, 2013b, chapter 7 for more detailed discussion of this issue.
20. It is necessary to address that the way of framing the protests could to an extent legitimate the contentions and influence government response (see, for instance, the discussion of 'rightful resistance' O'Brien & Li, 2006). Nevertheless, as the discussion in the methods section already noted, there are many contingent factors that can affect government response to conflicts. This issue is beyond the purpose of this study.
21. We have seen a situation in which the government cut off all internet connections to prevent the diffusion of protest information. But in the Wukan case, the government was forced to maintain internet access as the villagers had already demonstrated that they were only opposed to the illegal land grabbing and local corruption rather than to the party leadership.
22. The Facebook group 'Anti-PX plant in Kunming,' see https://www.facebook.com/AntiPxPlantInKunming; the tweets in Twitter, see https://twitter.com/search?q=%23AntiPX. The Chinese government blocked social media sites, including Facebook and Twitter, in mainland China following the 2009 Xinjiang Uyghur Autonomous Region riots, asserting that social networking sites abetted protesters.
23. Interviews with a journalist in Kunming, January 2014.

24. Interviews with participants in the demonstration in Kunming, January 2014.
25. Interview with a thirty-five-year-old engineer, who participated the demonstration in Kunming, January 2014.

REFERENCES

Allan, S. (2007). Citizen journalism and the rise of "mass self-communication". *Global Media Journal–Australian Edition*, 1(1), 1–20.
BBC. (2011). China protest closes toxic chemical plant in Dalian. Retrieved from http://www.bbc.co.uk/news/world-asia-pacific-14520438
Bennett, W. L. (2003). Communicating global activism. *Information, Communication & Society*, 6(2), 143–168.
Bennett, W. L. (2012). The personalization of politics. *The ANNALS of the American Academy of Political and Social Science*, 644(1), 20–39.
Bennett, W. L., & Segerberg, A. (2012). The logic of connective action. *Information, Communication & Society*, 15(5), 739–768.
Chang, M. (2013, May 17). Thousands protest Kunming PX plan. *Global Times*. Retrieved from http://www.globaltimes.cn/content/782252.shtml
Chen, W. (2014). Taking stock, moving forward: The internet, social networks and civic engagement in Chinese societies. *Information, Communication & Society*, 17(1), 1–6.
CNNIC. (2014). *The 33nd statistical report on internet development*. Retrieved from http://www.cnnic.net.cn/hlwfzyj/hlwxzbg/hlwtjbg/201401/P020140110639541 8429515.pdf
Dafeng. (2011). Wukan villagers took to the street this afternoon, the Communist Party of China kept censoring information. Retrieved from http://www.canyu.org/n36629c6.aspx
Esarey, A., & Xiao, Q. (2011). Digital communication and political change in China. *International Journal of Communication*, 5, 298–319.
Flyvbjerg, B. (2006). Five misunderstandings about case-study research. *Qualitative Inquiry*, 12(2), 219–245.
Garrett, R. K. (2006). Protest in an information society. *Information, Communication and Society*, 9(2), 202–224.
Goodman, J. D. (2011). *Video from inside rebellious Chinese village*. Retrieved from http://thelede.blogs.nytimes.com/2011/12/14/video-from-inside-rebellious-chinese-village/?_php=true&_type=blogs&_r=0
Howard, P. N., & Hussain, M. M. (2011). The role of digital media. *Journal of Democracy*, 22(3), 35–48.
Huang, R., & Sun, X. (2014). Weibo network, information diffusion and implications for collective action in China. *Information, Communication & Society*, 17(1), 86–104.
Hung, C.-f. (2010). The politics of China's wei-quan movement in the internet age. *International Journal of China Studies*, 1(2), 331–349.
Jacobs, A. (2011, 23 September). Farmers in China's south riot over seizure of land. *The New York Times*, p. A5.
King, G., Pan, J., & Roberts, M. E. (2013). How censorship in China allows government criticism but silences collective expression. *American Political Science Review*, 107(2), 1–18.
Kvale, S., & Brinkmann, S. (2009). *Interviews: Learning the craft of qualitative research interviewing* (2nd ed.). Los Angeles: Sage.Liu, D., & Yan, S. (2012,

October 29). Ningbo backs down from PX project. *Global Times*. Retrieved from http://www.globaltimes.cn/content/740943.shtml

Liu, J. (2013a). Mobile communication, popular protests and citizenship in China. *Modern Asian Studies*, 47(3), 995–1018.

Liu, J. (2013b). *Mobilized by mobile media-How Chinese people use mobile phones to change politics and democracy* (Unpublished doctoral dissertation), University of Copenhagen, Copenhagen.

Lu, J., & Qiu, Y. (2013). Microblogging and social change in China. *Asian Perspective*, 37(3), 305–331.

MacKinnon, R. (2009). China's censorship 2.0. *First Monday*. Retrieved from http://firstmonday.org/article/view/2378/2089

MacKinnon, R. (2011). China's 'networked authoritarianism'. *Journal of Democracy*, 22(2), 32–46.

McAdam, D., Tarrow, S.G., & Tilly, C. (2001). *Dynamics of contention*. Cambridge; New York: Cambridge University Press.

Mercea, D. (2012). Digital prefigurative participation. *New Media & Society*, 14(1), 153–169.

Mo, B. (2011). *Debriefing of Wukan incident*.Retrieved from http://www.shanwei.gov.cn/163747.html

Morozov, E. (2011). *The net delusion*. London: Allen Lane.

O'Brien, K.J., & Li, L. (2006). *Rightful resistance in rural China*. New York: Cambridge University Press.

Pang, H. (2012). *Research on the public opinion during Guangdong Wukan incident*. Retrieved from http://yuqing.people.com.cn/GB/16788483.html

Qiu, J.L., & Bu, W. (2013). China ICT studies: A review of the field, 1989–2012. *China Review*, 13(2), 123–152.

Qiu, J.L., & Chan, J.M. (Eds.). (2011). *New media events research*. Beijing: Renmin University Press.

Reporter. (2012). *Armed with cameras and the web, youth spurred Wukan protests*. Retrieved from http://www.wantchinatimes.com/news-subclass-cnt.aspx?id=201 20304000030&cid=1101

Rojas, H., & Puig-i-Abril, E. (2009). Mobilizers mobilized. *Journal of Computer-Mediated Communication*, 14, 902–927.

Shirky, C. (2010). *The Twitter revolution: More than just a slogan*. Retrieved from http://www.prospectmagazine.co.uk/magazine/the-twitter-revolution-more-than-just-a-slogan/

Sullivan, J. (2012). A tale of two microblogs in China. *Media, Culture & Society*, 34(6), 773–783.

Tai, Z. (2006). *The Internet in China*. London: Routledge.

Tong, J., & Zuo, L. (2014). Weibo communication and government legitimacy in China. *Information, Communication & Society*, 17(1), 66–85.

Tufekci, Z., & Wilson, C. (2012). Social media and the decision to participate in political protest. *Journal of Communication*, 62(2), 363–379.

van de Donk, W., Loader, B.D., Nixon, P.G., & Rucht, D. (Eds.). (2004). *Cyberprotest: New media, citizens, and social movements*. London: Routledge.

Wines, M. (2011, December 26). A village in revolt could be a harbinger, *The New York Times*, p. A4.

Xinhua. (2013). *Sina Weibo boasts 500m users*. Retrieved from http://www.chinadaily.com.cn/bizchina/2013–02/21/content_16243933.htm

Yang, G. (2003). The Internet and civil society in China. *Journal of Contemporary China*, 12(36), 453–475.

Yang, G. (2007). The co-evolution of the Internet and civil society in China. *Asian Survey*, 43(3), 405–422.

Yang, G. (2009). *The power of the Internet in China*. New York: Columbia University Press.

Yin, R. K. (2009). *Case study research: Design and methods* (4th ed.). London: Sage.

Zhang, C. (2013). *New media's influence on mass incident and possible response*. Retrieved from http://study.ccln.gov.cn/fenke/shehuixue/shglcx/24696–1.shtml

Zheng, Y. (2008). *Technological empowerment*. Stanford: Stanford University Press.

Part II

Commercialization, Standards, and Politics

As demonstrated in Part I, internet use is becoming increasingly multi-platform, portable, and interoperable from the users' point of view, but at the same time the four studies in Part I show limited use of some of the characteristics of the ubiquitous internet (e.g., Lomborg, this volume; Bechmann, this volume). The chapters in Part II discusses the same characteristics of the ubiquitous internet not as fixed entities but as fragile characteristics that are negotiated between different industry stakeholders. The chapters present studies on how technological standards and codes are created, negotiated, and developed over time, how policy and regulation influence the development of ubiquitous internet, how businesses handle and profit from the prospect of ubiquitous internet, and how users (by serving their data) are commodified in this process. Common for the four chapters is a reliance on cases and historical studies as traditionally seen in industry studies. Moreover, the questions of ubiquitous internet in the industry perspective is centered around classical perspectives of economics, standards, and regulation and questions of power, control, negotiations, and societal inequality (e.g., Havens, Lotz, & Tinic, 2009).

A common denominator of the four chapters in this section is that they challenge the idea of the ubiquitous internet as interoperable, seamless, and device-neutral, as experienced by users. Instead, the idea of seamlessly integrated platforms and services is counterbalanced with analytical insights stressing that the technological development underpinning the ubiquitous internet is characterized as a struggle of competing interests of various stakeholders. As a consequence, the interoperable character of both devices and data is debatable.

In the first chapter in this section, chapter five, Indrek Ibrus discusses the complex histories of the ubiquitous and multi-platform web with a special emphasis on the mobile web in terms of standardization practices. These practices took place at the interfaces of different industries (telecommunications, online services, content provision, handset manufacturing) that were on the course to converge and constitute the new industry of the ubiquitous web. The chapter focuses on the dialogues among these industries and demonstrates how their power struggles at different stages of the web evolution conditioned the design of the multi-platform web that currently appears as satisfactory for most industry players and sustains the value of the web as a global public good.

Complementing Ibrus' historical analysis of the mobile web, in chapter six of this volume Lela Mosemghvdlishvili analyzes mobile internet standards from a critical perspective, focusing on the politics of code and networks. In particular three cases are discussed: (1) the issue of net neutrality in relation to profit interests of mobile network owners, (2) the role of intellectual property regime (patents) in standardization of mobile technologies, and (3) the state of open source software production for mobiles. Through these issues, Mosemghvdlishvili reflects on the broader terrain of possibilities within which decisions regarding the pace and direction of mobile internet development are negotiated. The merits of current standardization procedures and the reification of intellectual property rights in relation to technology standards and code are discussed and questioned.

In chapter seven of this volume, by Robert Bodle, the critical lens of political economy is applied to a different dimension of the ubiquitous internet, namely the openness of data. Openness here takes the form of connecting and (algorithmically) interpreting user data to facilitate personalized services. Bodle looks at the implications of predictive algorithms used for personalization services on Facebook. Personalization is a characteristic of the ubiquitous, interoperable, and interactive web, where content conforms to the prior actions of the user (e.g., targeted advertising, personalized search, featured recommendations on Amazon.com, Promoted Tweets, Facebook's News Feed rankings). Personalization requires identification, tracking, and predictive analytics and should be considered a new and important modality of surveillance. Although personalization services can be useful and relevant, they can also have negative consequences for user privacy, autonomy, diversity, equality, and deliberative democracy. Predictive algorithms are neither neutral nor a-political and deserve special scrutiny when theorizing critical engagement within sociotechnical systems. Bodle's chapter examines the implications of Facebook's algorithms used to personalize content on the social network site and applies a political economy approach to identify the operational logics and underlying social relations between users, intermediaries, and advertisers. Although potentially valuable for the users, Bodle discusses how personalization services on social network sites can alter the balance of power for social network users to the detriment of human volition and personal autonomy. A focus on power offers suggestions for further study and examination of the potentially manipulative power of personalization algorithms.

Chapter eight of this volume, by Joseph Turow, rounds off the industry section. Continuing the focus on data exchange and user data commodification, Turow presents an analysis of how the collection of user data in the retail industry has developed over time into an aggressive and ubiquitous matter incorporating various self-reported and collected behavioral and sensory inputs. The digital/physical and offline/online distinctions that have become part of popular and some academic discourse are anachronistic when it comes to shopping. That is not just because physical stores have websites, but because those stores increasingly use the internet to connect to customers while they are moving through physical aisles. The dominant reason for this development is retailers' desire for data. Turow places these developments in historical context, sketches some of the data-gathering approaches retailers use and want to use, and considers their social consequences.

REFERENCE

Havens, T., Lotz, A. D., & Tinic, S. (2009). Critical media industry studies: A research approach. *Communication, Culture & Critique, 2*, 234–253.

5 Histories of Ubiquitous Web Standardization

Indrek Ibrus

The World Wide Web could be suggested to be the most important application that utilizes internet protocol and infrastructures. Hence, when discussing the 'ubiquitous internet' we should also inquire into the role of the Web within this 'anytime/anywhere' trajectory. For most of its history the Web has been a 'desktop' phenomenon. The visual layouts of websites have been designed and optimized for the 'big screens' of desktop and laptop computers. Yet, whereas the optimization of the Web layouts for other screenic devices such as game consoles, interactive TV, mobile devices, and even refrigerators has a long peripheral history, it has been the explosive popularity of advanced mobile devices such as smartphones and tablet computers that has in the last few years notably undermined the evolutionary trajectories of the Web's representational forms as taylored for desktops. The Web has become increasingly multiplatform and therefore fragmented in terms of its visual forms and customized services. Yet, it is exactly this fragmentation—that the Web is now accessed and displayed anywhere and on any device—that makes it 'ubiquitous.'

This chapter, therefore, is about such dynamics that have facilitated the ubiquity of the Web. It approaches these processes from the perspective of media production and industry studies. Since 'ubiquity' means in this context also 'multiplatform' its core focus is on the complex processes of convergence. The chapter asks what industry dynamics might be conditioning the convergence (i.e., homogenization of the forms, appearances, and contents of the multiplatform Web—so that while being 'ubiquitous' there would be conceivable continuities between the Web's appearances) and what dynamics might be conditioning the counter tendency—the divergence within the 'ubiquitous Web.' This discussion departs from the understanding that the internet is an indefinite compilation of technologies, institutions, and forms of media and communication that all continue to evolve. All its subparticles are undergoing a lengthy and highly social process of development, design, and redesign, hand-in-hand with the co-construction of associated markets and their institutions. In this context the chapter aims to interpret the dialogues among the relevant institutions and societal sub-systems and how such interactions have affected the evolutionary trajectories of the ubiquitous web. With 'sub-systems' I refer here to constellations of institutions, technologies, practices, and communications that are interconnected and coordinated and have therefore a tendency to co-evolve (i.e., 'mobile media' that is constituted by a specific set of relevant institutions, technologies, and practices such as mobile carriers, handset manufacturers, software vendors, value chains, and other exchange relationships, representational conventions, consumption practices, and so on).

A specific focus will be on the nature of dialogues, or negotiations, as part of different web standardization processes. That is, the focus is on how the complex processes of convergence and divergence have been shaped by a variety of standardization processes. These start with *de jure* standardizations at industry's meta-bodies, more specifically at the World Wide Web Consortium (W3C), and end with the emergence of various *de facto* standards at the grassroots level of 'web production.' I will ask what agents in what circumstances have been behind either convergence or divergence, respectively, and how have they then negotiated their objectives with a variety of others. The second question central to the analysis is the changes in the status of the Web as a 'public good'—how have these various convergence and divergence processes or industry dynamics in general undermined or further enabled this function. Altogether the objective of this chapter is to demonstrate some of the complexities of power relations, of historical contexts, and circumstantial motivations within media and telecommunications industries that have conditioned the emergence and the further evolution of the 'ubiquitous Web.' The chapter will investigate this evolutionary process since the late 1990 when the information technology and telecommunications industries started work on developing technical standards for the 'mobile Web' up until the ongoing era of advanced smartphones and high-speed wireless browsing. The chapter divides this period into three phases and discusses the constitutive industry dynamics and dialogues that have shaped the nature of the 'ubiquitous Web' in each of these. In the following section the conceptual framework for this analytic work will be laid out.

MULTISTAKEHOLDER GOVERNANCE, DIALOGUES, AND MEDIA EVOLUTION

In the case of internet governance it is the multistakeholder governance model that has been increasingly deployed at different levels and sites of internet standardization. Be it the internet Company for Assigned Names and Numbers (ICANN), International Telecommunication Union (ITU), World Wide Web Consortium (W3C), or mobile industry's Open Mobile Alliance (OMA)—all these industry meta-bodies accommodate rationales that are carried, to an extent, by multistakeholder governance ideologies. Despite the fuzziness of the multistakeholder governance concept and its very different applications across the board (Cammaerts, 2011) we can still suggest that part of the multistakeholder governance rationale is policy making that is in principle dialogic. But what does that mean?

Juri Lotman (2000, 2009) an Estonian-Russian literary scientist and a semiotician, elaborated Bakhtin's (1982) notion of dialogicality in a conceptualisation of cultural evolution. His conceptual framework serves as point of departure for this chapter's analyses of standardization as a dialogic proces. Lotman distinguished dialogic communication from auto-communication. The term auto-communication denotes communication from and to oneself, where the self-communicating entity can be both an individual and a larger social structure. As several authors have elaborated (Broms & Gahmberg, 1983; Christensen, 1997; Morsing, 2006) in a contemporary context all kinds of communications (such as strategic plans, codes of conduct, corporate reports, marketing communications) that organized bodies might produce could start working auto-communicatively. Even if the communicative act was originally not meant for internal use but for the outside audience, once the message feeds back to its authoring structure the auto-communicative effect could take place. Hence, the main function of auto-communication is the production of metatexts on the nature of the communicating structure. It could be suggested that such texts may often, especially if the communicating system is convergent (i.e., it is nascent, not yet established) contribute to 'confirming' the system and facilitate its self-creation by standardization and institutionalization. I have suggested elsewhere (Ibrus, 2010, 2013b) that in the technoculture the various 'dimensions' of convergence processes (of technologies, networks, institutions, markets, and policies, etc.) could be understood as contributing to the auto-communicative process that results in the emergence of a qualitatively new system—the one that is then converged. That is, in addition to various layers of metatexts that codify the distinctions of the new media system, also the 'system' itself—the harmonized communication protocols, the new universalized business models (as 'models'), shared exchange standards and codes of conduct for the industry—contribute to generating self-oriented aggregations of communicative acts and in this way in constituting and fixing the new system (see Ibrus, 2010, 2013a, 2013b).

It may be suggested that dialogues, in turn, are a side effect of auto-communicative processes. Following Lotman's (2000) theorization we can suggest that the cultural sphere is inherently infinitely heterogeneous, that 'well-defined and functionally unambiguous systems' never exist in isolation. Instead, they acquire their role and meaning when perceived as one segment of the continuum of variegated semiotic/social formations. That is to suggest that the cultural space consists of multitudes of sub-systems that are intertwined in complex ways and at different levels—i.e., some systems such as 'mobile media/communication' are larger than others and could include several smaller systems such as the telecommunications industry, handset production, app development, or mobile Web, etc. At the same time smaller systems could also be perceived as parts of several bigger ones—a 'mobile website' could be seen as an expression of the (ubiquitous) Web industry's technical standards for 'micro-sites,' or it could be part of an evolving genre of mobile web design as articulated by the 'Web design subsystem' of content industries, yet again it could be a component of a carefully orchestrated transmedia narrative, or perhaps be seen as an entity of a distinct national media system. Therefore, the evolution of mobile websites as distinct textual domains is conditioned by the semi-autonomous operations of all these super-systems. What is more, as such the 'websites,' as well as most individual media platforms, constitute dialogic spaces where the various super-systems meet, partly converge, and, therefore, are conditioned to co-evolve. That is, dialogues are conditioned by the attempts by various sub-systems to auto-communicatively reproduce themselves and for that to respond to changes in the environment constituted by other sub-systems—much in the spirit of Foucault's governance model and its idea of 'actions upon actions' (Foucault, 2002, pp. 201–222). That is, in terms of Foucault, to execute power is to foresee the actions of others and subsequently to guide and limit the choices of these others in ways that are preceived as beneficial for the 'order' of the own domain. We may therefore suggest that multistakeholder governance is dialogic in similar ways—it is about 'responses upon responses' whereas in such standardization processes all the participating actors are aiming at reproducing themselves and their environment according to their own specific preferences or path-dependencies. In such situations, as Pottage (1998, p. 22) has put it, each of the actors is dependent on the autonomy of the other, and it is in such situations of 'situated oppositions' that their power-relations are articulated. The eventual design of the Web (as in our case) therefore depends on such constant re-articulations of power—that is, whose principles of reproduction outperform the others.

Another aspect relating to the dialogic practices between institutional agents or sub-systems of various kinds is that these could facilitate the emergence of new systems. When different sub-systems are forced into dialogic contact it may lead to a new auto-communicatively functioning sub-system to emerge (read: converge). For instance, when telecommunications industries and web services/content industries end up in dialogic situation they may in the process articulate a certain shared identity or common interest, develop new frameworks for cooperation or interaction. But by doing this they may also be understood to be in the processs of convergence.

As suggested above, the various standardization or codification processes can take place at a variety of 'levels'—some 'higher' (at industry meta-levels—for instance by its standardization bodies) and some 'lower' (by individual companies or practitioners as they establish their codes of conduct, broker agreements, establish exchange relationships, etc.). Relating to this, another suggestion that can be made based on Lotman's semiotics of culture is that the evolutionary dynamics of culture is paradoxical for being bidirectional—it evidences both centrifugal and centripetal forces, which play themselves out on various, coexisting layers. That is, it is the auto-communicative functioning of larger systems, for instance the stan-dardization bodies of large industry fractions, that is having a centripetal effect—homogenizing the cultural space, creating unities between its smaller sub-systems, as for instance between different web access platforms. At the same time it is the autonomous evolution of these smaller systems and their acts of auto-communication that respond to changes in 'real semiotic/social milieu,' that are, in turn, conditioning the emergence of difference within the larger space of culture, facilitating plurality and constituting, in effect, the 'centrifugal' force of cultural change. It is important to understand that both of these forces are mutually conditioned, the need for creating unities is effected by growing entropy, whereas the act to create difference is moti-vated by the need for meaningful and socially relevant experiences in the too universalized culture.

The rest of this chapter discusses exactly how the industry dynamics con-ditioned such contradictory, but mutually conditioning tendencies—there were industry fractions that were more interested in homogeneity within the ubiquitous Web and others that saw themselves benefitting from more het-erogeneity and divergence within this space. That is, the following three sec-tions apply the above described conceptual framework in order to interpret the recent evolutionary dynamics of the ubiquitous Web. The sections divide this evolution accordingly into three phases—pre-smartphone phase (2000–2004); early smartphone phase (2004–2008), and the phase of advanced smartphones and tablet computers (since 2008).

PHASE 1: EARLY FIXED-TO-MOBILE
CONVERGENCE—WAP AND i-MODE

Web and mobile convergence has a long history. These communications plat-forms almost paralleled one another in terms of take-up by mass audiences in the 1990s and as a result, the plan of merging them was quick to emerge. This is evidenced, for instance, by a series of EU green papers[1] from the mid 1990s that were outlining and preparing the fixed-to-mobile convergence as a linear process in terms of (a) technology and network platforms, (b) industry alliances and mergers, (c) services and markets, and (d) policy and regulations. The first solution, however, to achieve the desired convergence of the internet and mobile phones was in the form of an artefact—the Nokia Communicator 9000 launched in 1996. Its innovative aspect that attracted worldwide attention (Sigurdson, 2001, p. 11) was the concept of a portable pocket-sized electronic office. The Communicator had a QWERTY key-board, enabled word processing, sending faxes or e-mails, and browsing the Web in a limited way—the many features that are now common on the so-called smartphones. However, when it came to its web browsing utility, as suggested by Hjelmeroos et al. (2000), consistency between the PC and the mobile browser was not always to be desired. It was realized at the time

(Roto, 2006) that mobile phones were not capable of displaying large web pages and that, therefore, specific mobile-optimized web pages would be needed.

Against this background, work was started to provide web-like services for mobile phones and for PCs. It started in two different camps and followed different strategies—one celebrated as a success, the other conceived as a failure. The first was the i-mode platform developed by Japanese operator NTT DoCoMo. The second was the Wireless Application Protocol (WAP) developed in cooperation between European and US handset and software vendors and deployed in many regions of the world.

The development of the WAP, a platform that was constituted at its early stage by the development of its own mark-up language, Wireless Markup Language (WML). This work started formally in 1996 and a year later WAP Forum, a dedicated standardization body, was established. After two years it had 500 members, including all the major telecommunications operators and information technology and software vendors from around the world. It could be argued to have been the first institutional catalyst for the auto-communication processes facilitating industry convergence. However, despite the first steps in industry formation, the platform itself failed to attract users. After being launched in 2000 in several European countries, the operators often marketed it in ways that suggested PC-level service quality, setting the expectations high. But the user experience of mobile browsing did not meet these expectations. The settings to be connected were hard to configure, circuit-switched networks required long connection times, once connected the speed was slow, WAP sites did not look like websites, the selection of content was very limited when compared to the full Web, and browsing costs were seen as high against the price of desktop browsing. As a result of this, by the end of the year the global number of WAP users was estimated to be only eight million, most of them in South Korea and Taiwan where there were better-designed services.

i-mode, the competing mobile internet standard that utilized a version of C-HTML as its mark-up language, was launched in Japan in 1999 and experienced rapid growth. More than 20 million users were attracted in only two years and 33 million in three years after the launch (Ishii, 2004, p. 44). Growth continued at a similar pace in the following years. What may have conditioned the differences in take-up between WAP and i-mode? Based on several commentators (Funk, 2001; Helyar, 2001, pp. 199–203; Lindmark, Bohlin, & Andersson, 2004, p. 353; Sharma & Nakamura, 2003, p. 162), these differences may be explained, first, by differences in the level of medium specificity and the 'emancipation' of the new platform—i.e., how independent the i-mode and WAP were in relation to the desktop internet and its services. Although both were designed as mobile-specific content platforms, the WAP was ambiguous in its relation to the desktop Web. Its initial promise as the internet on the phone established the expectation for continuity between the two. WAP also failed to introduce any new medium-specific forms that would be complementary, not supplementary, in relation to the regular Web and, as such, could have attracted users with new functionalities. The success of the i-mode at the same time was brought about by new communication and entertainment services that, despite being initially rather trivial, were attractive to young people (games and simple chat and communications applications at the time when the majority of adolescents did not have autonomous access to the Internet in Japan). After the critical mass of users was achieved with these services, new layers of sophistication were added. Hence, what the above commentators took away from this lesson for the future was that mobile and desktop Web should be developed, not as supplementary to each other, but as complementary platforms with differing functionalities and entirely new services, users, and emancipated, platform-specific forms of content (Funk, 2001, p. 17; Helyar, 2001; Lindmark et al., 2004, p. 353).

Another aspect that has been suggested to have led to the differences in user reception of the mobile Web in Japan and Europe was the nature of coordination in the development of the platform. In Japan NTT DoCoMo was able to fully control the introduction of the service and the related value chain. It dictated the terminal design; launch schedules, and the retail strategy together with the (subsidized) prices. It designed its micro-payment system and it established the guidelines for the content providers. The ability to coordinate all these components of the service was seen to enable DoCoMo to guarantee the quality of the service.

In Europe and North America such central coordination was not possible as there was no dominant party that could have controlled the whole value chain. WAP was, since its start, an evolving concept, a standard that was shaped in dialogues between parties of very different kinds (handset manufacturers, telecommunications companies, service and content developers, etc.). However, one of the fatal aspects in its development was that the initial specification for the WAP was devised one-sidedly by handset and software vendors and little was done to involve the operators and to optimize the platform for their networks in the light of their expertise in service provision or with respect to the preferences of their subscribers. As Kumar et al. (2003, p. 82) describe, WAP was a designer's nightmare. The problems designers faced—i.e., that applications were differently rendered by different phones and the incompatibilities between variations of WML (WAP's mark-up language)—suggest that the dialogic coordination within the nascent industries of the mobile web was still deficient. Hence, in 2001, the GSM Association, the telecommunications industry body, took the initiative by 'bringing together its operator community to provide clear guidance to handset manufacturers and software developers on the needs of consumers of mobile internet services going forward,' as stated in its press release (GSM Association, 2001). This step and the further inclusion of operators and content and service providers in the WAP Forum, later (tellingly) renamed the Open Mobile Alliance

(OMA), suggests steps towards improved multistakeholder dialogues and industry consolidation.

To conclude, this first phase of the evolution of the ubiquitous Web was on the one hand characterized by unsettledness (conditioned by rather limited technologies of handsets and networks at the time) of the convergent domain in terms of the autonomy of different access platforms—i-mode was found to be successful due its independence from the regular Web, whereas WAP was in trouble because of the false hopes created by its marketing as the 'mobile Web.' The poor usability of the WAP at this early stage was in turn conditioned by the limited dialogues between the relevant stakeholders, the limited possibilities of network operators and content providers to influence the service design of the 'mobile Web' of the time.

PHASE 2: 'ONE WEB' VERSUS ADAPTATION AND DIVERGENCE

Although the multistakeholder standardization efforts around WAP continued so that most of the above described problems were eventually resolved (which resulted in the steady growth of its take-up around the world), it may be suggested that the new phase of the evolution of the mobile Web arrived with the launch of 3G air interface standards together with more capable handsets. With the new 3G enabled services a new discussion emerged in the industry—whether access to the 'real Web' should be offered instead of WAP (with its still poor reputation) and whether, then, there is a need for special websites designed for mobile devices only—in order to avoid the risk of providing again the sub-optimal service for end-customers. At this point Nokia, together with several partners, launched a pro-active strategy to ensure that all mobile-optimized websites would be recognized by a new .mobi top-level domain (TLD). Approved by ICANN in 2005 as a sponsored TLD, it was governed by a multistakeholder consortium that included Google, Microsoft, Vodafone, T-Mobile, Samsung, Sony-Ericsson, and Nokia. The consortium (informally known as dotMobi) website stated in July 2006: '.mobi should stand as a trust mark for mobile sites and data services that says 'this works on my mobile."

DotMobi sparked criticism for breaking the principle of the 'device independence' of the internet. One of the opponents was Tim Berners-Lee, inventor of the World Wide Web. He expressed his concern about TLDs that promote the idea that the Web should be divided up into different device-dependent areas (see Berners-Lee, 2004). Berners-Lee, who heads the W3C, thought that .mobi could 'break' the Web. His main argument was that the Web was designed as a universal space and that its universality was its most important feature. He argued that the Web must operate independently of different hardware, software, or the network used to access it, of the perceived quality or appropriateness of the information on it and of the culture, language, and physical capabilities of those who access it. Berners-Lee pointed out that the Web is defined by the relationship between a URI (uniform resource identifier, a Web address) and what one finds by using that URI. The URI, he argued, should be universal as it is treated as being universal—people look up URIs in very different conditions and using various devices. It was therefore seen as crucial that the Web would stay compatible with all the different access devices including mobile phones. What Berners-Lee and other critics, in other words, were worried about was that the internet could be split into two because of potential device dependence.

In addition to the disputed and ambiguous line between the mobile and desktop Webs, the mobile content industry faced a mounting challenge from the fragmentation of the mobile platform itself. This fragmentation was conditioned by the generic dilemma confronted by the handset and software vendors at the time: Should their primary focus be on agreeing and meeting standards, or on creating devices and software that would be distinctive, differentiated, and desirable in a highly competitive marketplace? Then as now, most vendors were skewed towards favoring distinctiveness and, as a result, the notion of a 'common' handset specification was always changing. The situation was further complicated by manufacturers typically offering a broad portfolio of devices to accommodate to the sophistication and budget of any consumer. The problem that emerged for the content and service providers was that the devices tended to vary hugely in their input interfaces and screen specifications for resolution, aspect ratio, and the number of colors supported. Also, as described above, hasty non-consensual standardization in the early phases of the WAP mark-up languages (WML and XHTML-MP) had resulted in rather feeble output legitimacy of the already established standards and, hence, also in the emergence of their different interpretations by various browser and handset vendors. The outcome was an exceptional fragmentation in terms of the various sub-forms of the mark-up languages in use for the mobile Web.

The proliferation of technical standards was having a profound impact on the profitability of producing mobile content. Therefore, this technical challenge was addressed as a threshold. It was not long before the content and service industries called for standardization of the mobile Web, to enable content providers to 'create once and publish everywhere' with ease. The mobile industry (operators and manufacturers) took notice of this and started to look for a neutral institutional body for the standardization work. In the context of the regular Web, the best track record in this regard belonged to W3C and it thus gained mobile industry support. This marked a new step of the institutional convergence of mobile and web domains, that is telecoms and handset vendors with W3C and major online service providers (such as Google and Microsoft). In fact, the convergence agenda emerged as the common denominator of this constellation of institutions. It should be stressed that despite what is claimed the W3C has never been a neutral site for consensus-seeking standardization of grassroots innovation.

Instead, W3C's imperative has been the 'One Web' idea—that the Web should be indivisible, always the same on all possible access devices. This vision met a friendly response within the mobile and online industries. Companies and other institutions such as Vodafone, Deutsche Telekom, NTT DoCoMo, Google, Opera, dotMobi, and others agreed to sponsor or participate in W3C's new Mobile Web Initiative (MWI), which then became the core multistakeholder arena for the standardization of the ubiquitous, platform-independent 'One Web.'

The actions of this group were first focused on overcoming fragmentation in terms of mark-up languages, both within the WAP platform and between the WAP and Web platforms. The mobile industry facilitated dialogue between W3C and the mobile industry's own standardization body Open Mobile Alliance (OMA), that up until then had developed only mobile-specific standards that were not compatible with the 'big Web.' This cooperation gave rise to the formalization of XHTML Basic 1.1, a new standard for the mobile web, which was now also fully compatible with the 'full XHTML.' However, this development was only the beginning of an evolving effort to secure the convergence of mobile and desktop webs. Another step was undertaken with W3C's Mobile Web Best Practices guidelines (W3C, 2006). With these, a different attempt to achieve the aim of 'One Web' was made as compared to the earlier effort to make mark-up languages compatible. These were, in effect, design guidelines and were, in a rather accentuated way, independent of existing platforms. They offered guidelines on how to design a website in a way that did not presume the need for significant adaptation for being displayed on different access devices. The MWI hoped that it would be possible to achieve generic design—one that would be 'good enough' on devices with very different capabilities. All this was expected to help to overcome a division into two webs motivated by the existence of two different form factors: 'desktop' and 'mobile.'

All this happened in parallel with the institutional convergence of those industry players who were motivated to work towards merging the two platforms. I have identified the emergence of a new industry sub-system—which I have termed 'infrastructure enablers' (Ibrus, 2013a, 2013b). This new sub-system resulted from the described dialogues and associated auto-communicative processes that on the meta-level were facilitated by the joint standardization activities. This new sub-system came together, first, from the former major telecommunications industry players (operators, handset manufacturers, and specialized software vendors); and, second, from the major online players (in particular search engines) and Web-specific software vendors, including many of the major browser companies. The convergence was conditioned by the first of these groups being motivated to gain access to the Web as a functional market (as opposed to WAP as dysfunctional). For the second group, the motivation was to extend their business to yet another platform, to gain new customers and to cement their position in the context of the newly ubiquitous and cross-platform Web.

Once the new 3G networks were deployed in 2005 (in Western Europe), a variety of network operators launched business models that enabled unrestricted full Web browsing on mobile devices. To support this the above-described W3C standards of generic or platform-agnostic web design were popularized by a variety of means—dedicated seminars around the world, webinars, automated 'MobileOK2 checkers,' etc. But something still needed to be done with the 'legacy sites'—the majority of websites designed for desktop devices. This need motivated various software vendors—existing browser vendors and new 'transcoder' vendors to develop specific website re-rendering solutions. Such algorithmic *post factum* redesign of desktop designs for mobile screens seemed to emerge as an industry norm at the time. As revealed at the time by Opera (Ibrus, 2010, p. 153), their apparent agenda and that of similar software vendors was to turn their browsers and engines into the 'translating cores' of the multiplatform Web. This can be understood as a strategy to make themselves indispensable for the functioning of the emerging ubiquitous Web. Their positions as controllers of the transcoding technology were expected to give them the power to establish various norms for the ubiquitous Web. This holds especially for design norms, as it was to be their algorithms that were to determine how the designs were to be re-rendered and optimized for various devices. That meant seizing the initiative from the content providers—an aspect that makes this particular phase of media change historically distinctive. In other words, the aim was to extend the technological continuity that enabled the Web as a marketplace for goods and services. For this purpose a new and increasingly homogeneous mesh of technical and institutional systems was emerging consisting of the converging telecommunications and web enterprises (the 'infrastructure enablers') that were aiming to converge the technological systems in order to gain control over the new domain, over its media forms, and over the code of conduct for cross-platform publishing.

These hegemonic attempts, however, did not go uncontested. The historical consolidation of a competing social system, favoring a different evolutionary trajectory for the mobile Web, could also be traced. This second industry group was made up of various content and service providers. They were discursively cohesive in sharing similar interests and analogous perspectives on the further development of the mobile Web. Content and service providers resisted the proposed 'generic design' for all devices, because it would have meant leaving their content effectively 'un-designed,' ceding the power to determine the eventual design of their products to other parties such as browser and transcoder vendors. The content providers wanted to keep that power to themselves, to decide what content, in what form, to deliver in what circumstances to what platform. With this they were claiming the right to establish discontinuities between the various access platforms.

The technological solutions for how to create such discontinuities and to output content for different device classes or platforms differently—a technique now known as 'server-level content adaptation'—were developed by communities of independent mobile developers and by small content companies on the margins of the industry. The idea behind this was simple—to make servers to recognize the accessing device and then to deliver an appropriated service for this device. But as there was a penumbra of different devices out there a repository of their technical qualities needed to be created. Because handset vendors were not keen to disclose all the features of their products, it was the 'WML programming' web community (a forum) of independent developers that in 2002 created the new schema titled Wireless Universal Resource File (WURFL) and started filing device information in this repository. Finding wide take-up among independent developers, the content adaptation for different devices evolved as a code of conduct and a structuring principle for the Web-media—the one that—in contrast to the infrastructure-enablers—favored divergence within the Web in terms of its representational forms or service specifics across access platforms.

The two conflicting views and strategies collided at the negotiation desks (and the Web forum) of W3C MWI. Resulting from these dialogues the W3C chartered the Device Description Working Group (DDWG), which was assigned to develop and standardize a database of device descriptions that could be used by content authors to adapt their content to a particular device—i.e., following, in effect, in the footsteps of WURFL. The fact that all the related activities were re-chartered in spring 2007 to be integrated into a new Ubiquitous Web Applications Activity points to two issues. Firstly, by that time, the content re-versioning or service differentiation for different 'delivery contexts' had been 'legitimized' to become an acknowledged W3C priority. Secondly, resulting from the dialogues between the two sub-systems, the W3C began to give up on the idea of continuity in design (either content or service) when it came to web content. The 'One Web' was from then onwards to be defined so as to foster continuity in the technologies that would enable the 'thematically same' (W3C, 2005) content to be delivered to all access platforms, but not in the way the content (and exactly what content) was to be presented to users. In other words, the dialogical process between the different industry sub-systems yielded standards that were to condition the divergence in the media forms.

If to characterize this second phase of the development of device-agnostic and the ubiquitous Web we should first notice the mesh of power struggles taking place at different 'sites' of the industry and among different players. Alliances were changing, scenarios for the further development of the domain were manifold—the domain was unsettled. However, despite the ambiguity, there was evidence of two major constituent industry sub-systems when it came to creating continuities or discontinuities between the two main access platforms to the Web—the 'infrastructure enablers' and the content industries. The pursuits of these sub-systems resulted in the developments toward both of their respective aims—we recognized a paralleled creation of continuities and discontinuities within the disputed domain. This observation can be associated with Lotman's conceptualization that there are concurrent centrifugal and centripetal movements in culture, that unity and plurality presume each other. First, we have the systemic convergence of industries and homogenizing normative modelling conducted by the infrastructure enablers from a distance, on the industry meta-level. But we also have the divergence within the ubiquitous Web—content producers were ready to fragment the Web in order to retain the power to determine the forms of the media content. It was perceived that responsive design and context (device) specific forms of the Web would not only serve the interests of these particular industry players, but would also provide more accessible, usable, as well as meaningful experiences to users. The content adaptation technique and similar principles emerged from more immediate contacts with the governed objects, from their modelling in their contextual and circumstantial particularities.

PHASE 3: MOBILE WEB VERSUS APPS

A new phase to the development of the ubiquitous Web arrived with the development of 'smartphones' (and later also tablet computers) with touch screen interfaces and 'app stores' associated with these devices. The format of 'native' apps that were designed for specific mobile devices (using device-specific software specifications) was a new cultural form that enabled content and service providers to fully utilize the innovative affordances of advanced smartphones such as Apple's iPhone. What is more, the app-store platform enabled easy ways of monetization of the services and content provided. The app-format was well received by the content providers because it also enabled them to overcome the many uncertainties of the mobile web described above and to regain full control over what content was presented and how was it displayed on mobile devices. The Apple App Store was opened in the summer of 2008 and in only three and a half years, 1 billion third-party apps were created for the platform, indicating tremendous success of the new format and its associated mechanics of transactions (payment, subscription and promotion systems, etc.).

However, at the same time some control was again lost to Apple, Google, and other platform owners as the new hegemons of the mobile media domain. Similarly to i-mode ten years earlier the App Store is a strictly controlled platform. To publish an app for Apple iOS it needed to get officially accepted by Apple and therefore to follow its undisputed set of rules. Because most financial transactions needed to go through the App Store it not only controlled the distribution of wealth (and took 30% share of all sales), but what is perhaps even more important it controlled and refused to share most of its user statistics and contacts, denying the content and service providers a direct contact with their audiences. This became a source of tensions between Apple and content providers and created grounds for a search of an alternative.

The alternative had started to emerge as a set of new standards by W3C – HTML5 and its 'device API' (application programming interface) that allows developers to create web applications that interact with device hardware. Work on HTML5 enabled to turn the Web more interactive and visually attractive across access platforms. The work on device API (led by W3C Device API Working Group) enabled to turn Web-based applications as effective in exploiting the various new affordances of mobile devices (motion sensors, geolocation recognition, camera control, and other sensor-based features) as did the 'native apps.' The W3C was actively pursuing the work on both directions because it saw that mobile devices had came to dominate web access and therefore the emergence and dominance of the (native) app format were to undermine the Web as again the only platform holding the promise of a universally accessible information resource and a ubiquitous communications platform—a global public good.

As the W3C work and standards matured, these started to earn recognition and utilization by content providers due to the limiting conditions of 'native' applications markets. The instances of some of the biggest content brands experimenting with web apps became showcases for the rest of the industry. The most high profile standoff took place between Apple and the Financial Times (FT) in 2011. After Apple had announced its new Newsstand service (that reorganized its journalistic apps) the FT refused to comply to its terms and instead put out a new 'mobile web app'—effectively a HTML5-enabled website, promoted by the FT on its own, that could be downloaded to one's phone as a 'widget' and, based on the above described server-based adaptation technology, would be adapted for a series of devices in an automated way. This also indicated that the new strategy and reliance on W3C standards was not only driven by a need to dialogically respond to Apple's restrictive terms, but was part of the FT's larger 'ubiquity-strategy.' As explicated by an FT executive at the time, this move was motivated by their increasing difficulties in making apps for all devices and platforms available. 'It was months of work and as apps get more complicated was going to become a bigger and bigger problem and cost' (Sweney, 2011).

What was referred to here was one of the emergent arguments in support of Web apps in relation to native apps. As was demonstrated by leading industry analysts of the time (Visionmobile, 2011) app store, fragmentation had become a mounting challenge for content and service providers. The numbers of such stores were growing and each of these had its own developer sign-up, app submission process, artwork and paperwork requirements, app certification and approval criteria, revenue model options, payment terms, and taxation and settlement terms. Eventually the marginal cost of distributing an application through one more app store became significant.

To overcome the 'app store fragmentation' increasingly more companies turned to web apps because these offered architectural advantage and substantial savings when targeting a cross-device launch—develop once, run everywhere (Visionmobile, 2011). Other advantages that started to appeal to content developers were, first, the ease of updating their app, more flexibility in billing and much better user analytics, which in turn enabled more effective means for cross-media strategizing and for building customer loyalty. Altogether it had emerged by 2013 that HTML had become the main technology 'co-opetitor' to the Android-iOS duopoly—it had become the third most popular choice among mobile developers (Visionmobile, 2013). Fifty percent of them used the HTML-based set of technologies as a deployment platform (to create mobile web apps) or as a development platform (to create hybrid apps or HTML code translated into native apps). HTML had therefore become a platform that reduced externalities by lowering barriers to entry and exit from native platforms. Relatedly there was evidence that the mobile Web was proving to become a preferred tool for the related industries as they geared up for a multi-screen future—compared to other platforms, the mobile Web was the most versatile one, with web developers currently targeting on average the highest number of different screen types (Visionmobile, 2011). Therefore, at the time of writing this chapter it was still the web platform that had the potential to become the central facilitator of the ubiquitous internet as a universal resource of knowledge and a globally shared platform of communications.

To characterize this third and ongoing phase of the ubiquitous and cross-platform Web we should recognize that differently from the previous phase, it was this time the content and service providers that were looking for more of homogeneity and compatibility between media platforms. The centrifugal force of app-store fragmentation needed again a centripetal response in Lotman's terms. For this reason the content and service providers were supportive of all the standardization work at W3C that was aimed at overcoming the app-centric balkanization of internet services. And it was the large technology vendors (Apple) and online service providers (Google, Facebook, etc.)—the 'infrastructure enablers'—that were behind some actions contributing towards fragmenting the Web space. However, again we saw that the dialogic processes of responses upon responses were to affect the evolutionary trajectory of the Web towards a specific balance between these forces, the one that although favoring plurality in terms of representational forms or service design within the cross-platform web space, was still about technological continuities between the different access devices and as such, continued to support the idea of the global and ubiquitous Web as a universal public good.

CONCLUSION

This chapter has contributed a slightly unconventional view to the evolution of the ubiquitous Internet and to its governance processes. The approach here builds on specific evolutionary approaches in culture studies in order to studying the issues of media change and internet/innovation governance. Differently from political economy based approaches to Internet governance this humanities-informed approach put a special emphasis on how the various communicative (either auto-communicative or dialogic) actions and discursive dynamics may contribute to codifying media systems or to condition change in them.

In relation to the latter the specific focus was on the historical process of web-media convergence—how the uniplatform web became a mobile and multiplatform medium and how this was enabled by complex dialogic processes between the converging industries. The chapter demonstrated how media convergence tends to be nonlinear, complex and may involve innovative discontinuities as well as continuities with the structures of the past. We saw how different degrees of autonomy that the various converging industry subsystems may have at different stages may be both enabling as well as limiting for such processes of convergence. Relatedly, these processes may in fact be facilitating processes of divergence within the media space. In the particular instance of the ubiquitous Web the convergence was conditioned by the dialogues between partners that were in effect, new to each other, namely telecommunications industries, online service providers, and content providers. We saw how these dialogues, that were somewhat ineffective at first (the era of WAP and i-mode), have gradually, through the two following phases, produced an appropriated and balanced design for the ubiquitous Web that may be satisfactory for most of the interested parties for the time being. That is, the dialogues have resulted in the evolution of a relatively cohesive and auto-communicatively effectively functioning ubiquitous Web. Yet, we should also recognize that this process is not over, and the future evolutionary trajectory of the ubiquitous and cross-platform web will presumably depend on the similar mesh of power-struggles and complex dialogic processes.

To pin down the current situation we should first recognize how the evolution of the ubiquitous Web manifests what, according to Lotman, tends to be the general feature of cultural evolution—the parallel and mutually conditioned centripetal and centrifugal dynamics. That is, there have been industry sub-systems or institutional agents that at times have worked towards homogenising the web-media space and there have been others that at different instances have contributed towards creating distinctions within it. As a result, the status quo of the ubiquitous Web can be characterized both in terms of heterogeneity of its appearances on different access platforms, but also by technological continuities that condition the reasonable similarities between these appearances. The mutual effect of the textual forms and network technologies condition eventually what could be termed as 'ubiquity' in case of the Web. That is, the 'ubiquity' is defined by access and the expectation that the Web appears as relatively the 'same' anytime and anywhere (on all access platforms) and therefore warrants the universality of the associated experiences and functionalities. As such, the

Web continues to hold the potential ascribed to it by Tim Berners-Lee, to function as the universally accessible platform for shared knowledge and communications.

Yet, similarly and relatedly to the effect of the ongoing power struggles to the further evolution of the ubiquitous Web we can suggest that the balance between fragmentation and homogeneity within this web might still be fragile. For instance, the geolocation API that was recently standardized by W3C is also expected to condition more of the service design and content adaptation that is motivated by space, proximities, and localities. But that may also mean the increasing fragmentation of the Web based on the location of the access point. As the ongoing evolution of location-based web advertising evidences, there may indeed be economic rationales for such fragmentation and hence, for the evolving tension between the global universality and location specificity of the Web. The location-based services may well evolve to be a form of geographical walled gardens that as such threaten in a new way the universality of the Web. In other words, the further dynamics of parallel centripetal and centrifugal evolution of the Web may bring a new generation of ethical tensions and puzzles to its designers and standardizers.

NOTE

1. Green paper on the convergence of the telecommunications, media, and information technology sectors and the implications for regulation towards an information society approach, Com (97) 623. Green paper on a common approach in the field of mobile and personal communications in the European Union, COM (94)145.

REFERENCES

Bakhtin, M. (1982). *The dialogic imagination: Four essays*. Austin: Texas University Press.

Berners-Lee, T. (2004). New top level domains .mobi and .xxx considered harmful. W3C. Retrieved from http://www.w3.org/DesignIssues/TLD

Broms, H., & Gahmberg, H. (1983). Communication to self in organizations and cultures. *Administrative Science Quarterly, 28*(3), 482–495.

Cammaerts, B. (2011). Power dynamics in multi–stakeholder policy processes and intra–civil society networking. In R. Mansell & M. Raboy (Eds.), *The handbook of global media and communication policy. General communication & media studies* (pp. 131–147). Oxford: Wiley-Blackwell.

Christensen, L. T. (1997). Marketing as auto-communication. *Consumption, Markets and Culture, 1*(3), 197–302.

Foucault, M. (2002). *Power. The essential works of Foucault 1954–1984*. London: Penguin.

Funk, J. L. (2001). *The mobile internet: How Japan dialed up and the West disconnected*. New York: ISI Publications.

GSM Association. (2001). *GSM Association acts to support mobile internet services.* Retrieved from http://www.mobiletechnews.com/info/2001/06/13/230155.html

Helyar, V. (2001). Usability of portable devices: The case of WAP. In B. Brown, N. Green, & R. Harper (Eds.), *Wireless world: social and interactional aspects of the mobile age.* London: Springer.

Hjelmeroos, H., Ketola, P., & Räihä, K.-J. (2000). Coping with consistency under multiple design constraints: The case of the Nokia 9000 WWW browser. *Personal Technologies*, 4(2–3), 86–95.

Ibrus, I. (2010). *Evolutionary dynamics of new media forms: The case of the open mobile web* (Unpublished PhD thesis), London School of Economics and Political Science. Retrieved from http://etheses.lse.ac.uk/53/

Ibrus, I. (2013a). Evolutionary dynamics of media convergence: Early mobile web and its standardisation at W3C. *Telematics and Informatics*, 30(2), 66–73.

Ibrus, I. (2013b). Evolutionary dynamics of the mobile web. In J. Hartley, J. Burgess, & A. Bruns (Eds.), *A companion to new media dynamics* (pp. 277–289). Malden, MA & Oxford: Wiley-Blackwell.

Ishii, K. (2004). Internet use via mobile phone in Japan. *Telecommunications Policy*, 28, 43–58.

Kumar, V., Parimi, S., & Agrawal, D.P. (2003). WAP: Present and future. *IEEE Pervasive Computing*, 2(1), 79–83.

Lindmark, S., Bohlin, E., & Andersson, E. (2004). Japan's mobile internet success story—facts, myths, lessons and implications. *info*, 6(6), 348–358.

Lotman, Y. (2000) *Universe of the mind: A semiotic theory of culture,* Bloomington and Indianapolis: Indiana University Press.

Lotman, J. (2009) *Culture and explosion.* Berlin and New York: Mouton de Gruyter.

Morsing, M. (2006). Corporate social responsibility as strategic auto-communication: On the role of external stakeholders for member identification. *Business Ethics: A European Review*, 15(2), 171–182.

Pottage, A. (1998). Power as an art of contingency: Luhmann, Deleuze, Foucault. *Economy and Society*, 27(1), 1–27.

Roto, V. (2006). *Web browsing on mobile phones: Characteristics of user experience* (Doctoral dissertation), Helsinki University of Technology.

Sharma, C., & Nakamura, Y. (2003). *Wireless data services.* Cambridge: Cambridge University Press.

Sigurdson, J. (2001). *WAP OFF – Origin, Failure and Future, 135.* Stockholm: Stockholm School of Economics.

Sweney, M. (2011). FT admits 'Mexican standoff' with Apple. *The Guardian.* Retrieved from http://www.theguardian.com/media/2011/jun/07/financial-times-apple-website

Visionmobile. (2011). *Developer economics 2011* (p. 60). London: Visionmobile.

Visionmobile. (2013). *Developer economics 2013* (p. 60). London: Visionmobile.

W3C. (2005). *Scope of mobile web best practices.* Retrieved from http://www.w3.org/TR/2005/NOTE-mobile-bp-scope-20051220/

W3C. (2006). *Mobile web best practices 1.0, proposed recommendation.* Retrieved from http://www.w3.org/TR/2006/PR-mobile-bp-20061102/

6 Mobile Internet
The Politics of Code and Networks

Lela Mosemghvdlishvili

The term *mobile internet* refers to accessing the internet through (cellular) mobile devices and represents the convergence of mobile telephony, internet services, and personal computing. Whereas iMode (mobile internet and data services) was introduced in Japan as long ago as 1999 and became widely used (Barnes & Huff, 2003; Daliot-Bul, 2007), the release of the iPhone is commonly regarded as the decisive moment in popularizing mobile internet and smartphones in the West (Goggin, 2009; West & Mace, 2010; Campbell & La Pastina, 2010).

The convergence of mobile phones into programmable hand-held computers has reshaped the ICT industry and created a lucrative mobile internet business that spans the telecommunications, handset manufacturer, and software sectors. Goggin (2012, p.742) rightly points out that mobile media nowadays represents 'a new, exciting, but troubling set of developments.' Mobile technologies are indeed exciting, as they symbolize a new cultural platform and one of the most personal technologies available today. However, their development is also troubling, because critical issues such as net neutrality, access to the internet, and control over and the commodification of user data are extended to the mobile domain and require timely evaluation. Exploring the development of the mobile internet is crucial for understanding the ubiquitous internet. Indeed, it is not only that increasingly more users access the web through mobile devices, but industry standards, structures, and practices are also changing, with implications for society at large.

In this chapter, I aim to pinpoint the most discernible patterns of how the mobile internet is shaped. My focus is on the initial phase of design and development, rather than the end-users' appropriation of mobile devices. By drawing on the 'Critical Theory of Technology' (Feenberg, 1999, 2002, 2010; for a critique, see Vaek, 2006), I attempt to transcend the instrumental account of market analysis and evaluate the development of the mobile internet in the light of democratic rationalization (Feenberg, 2010). Democratic rationalization refers to the need to expand democratic procedures to the process of technological design and development by subjecting technological decision-making to social control, public participation, and conscious orientations towards politically legitimated human values, rather than profit-driven interests.

The remainder of the chapter unfolds in the following order: I first introduce the theoretical perspective and analytical tools (technical code, democratic rationality) that inform my analysis of the development process of the mobile internet. I then discuss three instances of how the interests of the decisive groups, namely mobile network carriers, handset manufacturers, and operating system owners, shape mobile networks.

TECHNICAL CODES OF CAPITALISM AND DEMOCRATIC RATIONALIZATION

Let me start with problematizing the 'standard image on technology' (Bijker, 2001, p. 26) in society and stressing that, regardless of academic work (especially in the tradition of social studies of technology), technological determinism is still the common view in political, corporate, and media discourses about the relationship between technology and society (Feenberg, 2010, pp. 8–9). As Feenberg highlights, technologically determinist stances share two basic premises. First, technological progress is believed to follow a unilinear course, namely a fixed, irreversible path, which means that even though political, cultural, and other factors may influence the pace of technological change, they cannot alter the general path. This premise does not bear close scrutiny, as there are a number of possible development paths available for the same technological artifact, and which of them will become standardized is the outcome of social processes (see, for example, the development of the bicycle in Pinch & Bijker, 1984). Second, determinism affirms that society must adapt to the imperatives of technological change (Feenberg, 1999, pp. 77–78; 2002, pp. 137–144; 2010, pp. 8–9). Conceiving technology in such terms depoliticizes its development and withdraws it from public deliberation.

Despite tremendous dependency on technology in almost every aspect of our social lives, mere women and men, as Feenberg writes (2002), are removed from the decision-making process of technological development and in principle have no say in deciding what type of technology will structure their lives at home, on the street, at airport check points, in their pockets, or in the workplace. In fact, citizens are left with the so-called consumer 'veto power' with respect to whether to adopt an artifact or not (Cockburn, as cited in Williams & Edge, 1996, p. 878). The situation is not very different when it comes to information and communication technologies, which, as Williams (1997) maintains, are predominantly shaped by the commercial strategies of the supply side-actors in order to create and maximize their market share.

In a capitalist society, what dictated the development path of technologies over the generations was the pursuit of efficiency and deeply ideological practices on restricting opportunities to participate in decision-making (Feenberg, 2010). To illustrate this, the operational rationality of capitalism presupposes the separation of workers from the means of production. This highly subjective, material, and historical aspect of a private-capitalist's enterprise became a *formal* structural element and the basis of what is considered to be rational in economic activities themselves. Likewise, the concept of efficiency became an unquestioned ideological justification for certain types of strategic decision. However, the problem lies in how efficiency is conceived. From an environmentalist perspective, efficiency would entail quite different measures than under capitalism, where profit is the most important element. It is through such justifications that an assembly line is a progressive form of technology that has increased the profits of company owners. The fact that this happened at the expense of de-skilling workers is of less importance, because the primary measure of efficiency does not account for the participation of workers. As a consequence, a subjective interest becomes the very structure under which choices about which technologies to develop are legitimated.

One of the most important contributions of the Critical Theory of Technology (CTT) is its critique of the very structure and processes within which technological decision-making takes place. Moreover, its framework, which classifies activities as permitted or forbidden, is a type of 'regime of truth' that brings the construction and interpretation of technologies into line with the requirements of the capitalist system. An analytical tool that I will draw on is *technical code*, which aims to capture such formal biases of technologies. As Feenberg defines it (2010, p. 68–69), a technical code is a rule under which technologies are realized in the social context, and serves as a criterion to select between alternative feasible technological designs. Crucially so, technical codes are always biased to some extent with respect to the values of dominant actors, and reflect the unequal distribution of social power (an understanding of a particular profit-measured efficiency is a good illustration of formally biased values in a capitalist society). However, subordinated groups may yet challenge the technical code and thereby influence the development of technologies.[1]

Accordingly, CTT rejects the neutrality of technology and enables commentators to uncover formal (ideological) biases. It is committed to subjecting the development of technology to democratic rationalization, which suggests a different rationalization based on responsibility for human and natural contexts and the democratic values of equality and participation, and not merely economic efficiency (with a narrow understanding of maximizing profits).

The agenda of democratizing technologies in the context of new information and communication technologies is primarily the struggle over the structure of communicative networks and practices. In what follows, I discuss three contested areas: the ownership of networks, power over setting technology standards, and gate-keeping power in permitting code production for mobiles. The three selected areas illustrate the operational rationality under which decisions regarding the architecture of mobile internet are negotiated; and at large define a 'terrain of possibilities' of how this complex technological assemblage will be developed. By highlighting the technical codes that over-determine the process, I aim to reveal broader ideological biases that, to a large extent, channel the development of the mobile internet.

MOBILE NETWORK CARRIERS AND NET NEUTRALITY

In this section, I illustrate the growing role of mobile network owners in altering the operational principle of the internet, namely net neutrality, on the example of recent changes in the US and EU.

The transformation of a mobile phone into an access device for the internet has brought about the long predicted convergence of the media and computing and telecommunications services, albeit with major implications for the future of the internet. These industries were hitherto considered to be distinct (Zuckerman, 2010; Goggin, 2011) in terms of their architecture, concentration of power, and organization of labour. Formerly, the government-owned telecommunication sector was traditionally centralized and monopolistic, but a massive deregulation process resulted in the establishment of regional and global network carriers. Ironically, deregulation, which was justified on the grounds of creating more competition and allowing new entrants to join the telecommunication sector, did not lead to a fundamentally different market structure (Wilson, 1992); historically dominant carriers still enjoy the privilege of providing mobile services as part of their integrated businesses (Goggin, 2011) under rebranded corporate identities. To illustrate this, in the US, the offspring of the American Telephone and Telegraph Company, Verizon Wireless and AT&T Mobility, together captured 70% of the market share (90% of mobile subscribers are tied to only four corporations; Statista, n.d.).

Mobile network carriers have access to cell phone subscribers' huge base, and retain strategic power with matters like investment, control, commissioning, and the closure of network infrastructure. Respectively, their role in channeling the development of the mobile internet has become decisive. The conflict of interest is critically seen in relation to net neutrality, which is an essential principle of the internet as a decentralized (and non-discriminatory) network (Cooper, 2004; Wu, 2003; Lessig, 2001), where no one single authority has the power to discriminate in terms of content and information flows (see also: Meinrath & Pickard, 2006; Barratt & Shade, 2007). The following two examples illustrate the conflict between the profit interests of large telecom companies and the democratic potential of having a non-discriminatory internet.

In the US on January 14, 2014, the Court of Appeals for the D.C. Circuit ruled in favor of Verizon (the largest mobile network in the US) and struck down the Federal Communication Commission's (FCC) Open Internet Order, which prohibited Internet Service Providers (ISPs) from blocking and discriminating against content. This means that network providers are able to engage in business deals with content providers, charge consumers differently for accessing various content (e.g., blogs and YouTube), and discriminate in terms of content by artificially slowing down traffic (Levy, 2014). Granting the power of gate-keeper to network owners is being actively contested and represents one of the crucial ongoing struggles. Indeed, two weeks after the court's decision, more than a million users signed a petition urging the FCC to intervene (Tropper, 2014) and safeguard freedom of expression on the internet.

The situation in the US is not exceptional; the same struggle is also evident in the eastern hemisphere, where the EU Commission has been promoting a new proposal to reform the EU telecom market since September 2013. The interests of leading European telecom companies are strongly represented in the proposed reforms. Indeed, activist groups were struck by the similarities between the reform proposal and the recommendations issued by the Economics and Technologies for Inter-Carrier Services consortium. This consortium was led by Alcatel-Lucent and was comprised of the dominant telecom operators such as BT, Orange, and Deutsche Telekom. During the negotiation stage, to which the so-called 'CEO-roundtable' representatives of the interested large private enterprises were invited, small ISPs as well as advocacy groups were excluded (La Quadrature du Net, 2013, July 9; Mangalousi & Mosemghvdlishvili, 2014).

These struggles over net neutrality are currently taking place on the regulatory level, and its outcome is critical to the future design of the internet. However, in the following section, my focus is on how technology standards are set by industry players, removed from public or political deliberation, and how intellectual property rights are used as tools to enable companies to profit from enclosed technological paths.

SMARTPHONE PATENT WARS AND STANDARDIZATION

In this section, I review the state of patents in relation to mobile technologies and networks, and demonstrate the process of how patents are used to secure the market share of well-known companies by establishing standards. I also explain the surge in patent litigation in relation to smartphones.

It is possible to connect a mobile device to the internet by way of various access technologies, the two predominant ones of which are so-called mobile broadband (3G, 4G) and wireless broadband (Wi-Fi). Although both Wi-Fi and 3G enable internet access, they differ in terms of their service, industry, architectural origins, and even philosophies. In an insightful comparison of Wi-Fi and 3G technologies as two (albeit different in their possibilities) development paths for accessing the mobile web, Lehr and

McKnight (2003, p. 353) point out that '3G offers a vertically integrated, top–down, service-provider approach to delivering wireless Internet access; while Wi-Fi offers (at least potentially) an end-user-centric, decentralized approach to service provisioning.' Moreover, the deployment costs of 3G (and 4G) are considerably higher than for Wi-Fi (or WiMAX, a successor technology of Wi-Fi). Nevertheless, 3G is still the favored option for mobile network providers due to its top-down and centralized architecture.

However, to use 3G, both mobile network providers as well as mobile device manufacturers need to comply with a set of essential standards, including the Third Generation Partnership Projects (3GPP and 3GPP2). These standards are set[2] within the industry by private companies that together hold a substantial share of the market (Lemley, 2002). In the case of 3G, the corporate members of these partnerships have identified up to 8,000 patents that they declared to be essential for 3G standards, 90% of which are owned by 13 companies. The following four entities account for 30% of these patents: Qualcomm, Ericsson, Nokia, and Motorola. Despite being declared as essential, a study revealed that only 21% were actually vital for 3G technologies (Goodman & Mayers, 2005).

As a consequence, a salient outcome is that companies that manufacture equipment or offer services for third generation cellular systems pay royalties for 80% of the patented technologies, which are too narrowly defined as being essential by patent owners (Goodman & Mayers, 2005). Even though the companies that own patents for standards are required to license them on fair, reasonable, and non-discriminatory terms, in reality royalties 'tend to be higher than the benchmark level' defined by law, and in the case of 3G phones amount to an increase of 30% of the total price of each phone (Lemley & Shapiro, 2007, p. 23).

The relationship between standards and patents has received considerable attention in policy and innovation studies (Bekkers et al., 2002; Bekkers & West, 2009; Gallini & Scotchmer, 2002; see also Ibrus, this volume), and has raised critical issues regarding the implications of increasingly patented standards. For instance, Shapiro (2001, p. 114) in a review of the literature regarding the patent system, argues that: 'our [US] current patent system is causing a potentially dangerous situation in several fields, including biotechnology, semiconductors, computer software, and e-commerce.' The interests of patent holders, in contrast to the public interest, are problematized in research that explored the GSM standard-setting procedure (Bekkers et al., 2002). Using the example of Motorola, the study's authors illustrate how patent ownership enabled the company to define the terms of the standardization process and argue that: at the level of the public interest in standard setting, the increasingly sharp negotiations about essential IPRs are not necessarily a positive development.' Lemley (2002, p. 1900), who focuses specifically on the process of standard-setting in the ICT sector, also argues that when standards are owned by a few of the largest companies, instead of promoting competition, patent owners act: 'as a cartel with the power to reduce output by excluding certain kinds of products.'

Another area of the mobile internet where patents are used as powerful tools to secure market share rather than promote innovation is the issue of design. Since 2011, several expensive legal disputes over patent infringements between giants like Apple and Samsung (Parish, 2011, Edwards, 2013), Google and Oracle, and Microsoft and Motorola became the subject of media interest, and terms like 'patent wars' and 'smartphone wars' appeared not only in the blogosphere and Wikipedia, but in academic work as well (Paik & Zhu, 2013). The number of court cases has risen so rapidly that even the most modest visualizations of patent litigation between corporations appear to be bewildering. The following estimations capture the magnitude of patent turmoil when it comes to phone design; since 2010, some $20 billion has been spent on patent litigation in the mobile phone industry (Cohan, as quoted in Paik & Zoe, 2013). With respect to smartphones alone, there are 250,000 active patents, which means that in the US every sixth active patent is used in these devices (O'Connor, 2012).

The reason for such a dramatic increase in patent litigation is that mobile devices are cumulative innovations, meaning that they are built on previous discoveries. As Shapiro (2001) explains in the case of complex information and communication technologies, new products will inevitably infringe patents, creating the so-called danger of 'hold-ups' (when companies avoid manufacturing new products in order to avoid patent litigation). Secondly, patents in the smartphone sector (as illustrated with litigation between tech giants) are not used to promote innovation, but as a strategic business tool. For instance, companies that are often publicly perceived to be rivals engage in cross-licensing (Shapiro, 2001). This explains a rather counterintuitive situation whereby when an HTC smartphone, which runs Android (Google's OS), is sold, its competitor Apple collects between $6 and $8 for each device. Similarly, Microsoft benefits from each LG, Acer, and Samsung phone sold by as much as $5 per device (Koetsier, 2012).

What the two examples discussed above point to is the alarming situation when patents, unlike their original conception to incentivize innovation (Gallini & Scotchmer, 2002), are used as a business tool for market competition and as a source of profit outweighing social benefits (Bessen & Meurer, 2008; Bessen et al., 2011; Coriat and Orsi, 2002, Cockburn & MacGarvie, 2009).

DEFINING FUNCTIONALITIES: HOW CODE
IS WRITTEN FOR MOBILE PLATFORMS

In this section, I review how code can be written for various mobile platforms, and how OS providers started to serve as gate-keepers. I also focus on the dominant platform, Google's Android,[3] and its particular business model that, by providing Android for 'free,' gives access to its source of capital—user data.

The importance of reviewing code/software in the mobile domain is determined by its critical function in modern technologies. As code serves as both a structuring and mediating framework, it not only *runs* on hardware and executes certain operations, but also defines the range of possibilities in terms of how a technological artifact can be used. Moreover, the importance of who is allowed to write code and under what conditions is a political question (Mosemghvdlishvili & Jansz, 2013, 2014).

Similar to the case of personal computing, in mobile devices there are likewise a number of locked-in platforms that are grouped around operating systems for which handset manufacturers build devices and programmers write apps. Currently, the most widely used platforms are Google's Android, Apple's iOS, RIM's Blackberry, and Microsoft's Windows Phone. Platforms differ in terms of being open or closed (i.e., the type of software licensing that is used), control over content (through a review process), programming language (platforms are tied to specific programming languages), and distribution (through which channels and under what conditions apps are allowed to be distributed, Mosemghvdlishvili & Jansz, 2013).

The distinction between proprietary (closed) and open platforms refers to the access to source code. When source code is not publicly shared, the platform is considered to be proprietary (e.g., Windows Mobile, iOS). In such cases, only prescriptive software is sold. However, when a source code is publicly shared to enable its use, repair, and modification, its platforms are regarded as open.

Currently, there is a crucial difference within open source software when it comes to copyright versus copyleft (aka free/libre software), as these are two ideologically distinct views on the mode of the production and distribution of software. When a license requires users who have used, modified or repaired a code to redistribute it under the same terms and conditions (hence enabling what was publicly shared to return to the public), we speak of copyleft. Whereas open source and copyleft initially represented one struggle against the enclosure of software production through copyright, since the late 1980s an important (ideologically motivated) split has occurred between open source and free/libre software (Berry, 2004, 2008; Elliott & Scacchi, 2008; de Laat, 2005; Sullivan, 2011). Correspondingly, a number or so-called *permissive* licenses were created, which even though they permit almost any use of the code, do not require it to be shared under the same terms, meaning that what was gained for free from the public domain can be enclosed and excluded from the public at large. This salient distinction is crucial in understanding how Google was able to capture more than 70% of the market share in five years, which will be revisited after a review of closed platforms (the example of Apple's iOS and Microsoft's Windows Mobile).

Because the success of an operating system is largely dependent on the number and quality of the application software, in the mobile sector proprietary platforms allow and even encourage third party developers to write software for their devices by releasing the software development kit (SDK). However, they retain control over the content through a mandatory app review process and exclusive distribution channels. To illustrate this, Apple allows apps to be distributed only via its exclusive channel, the App Store, whereas OS providers (including Google) charge fees to access their distribution channel, and also collect up to 30% from app sales (Mosemghvdlishvili & Jansz, 2013).

What emerged is the situation whereby mobile OS providers became important *gate-keepers*, retaining the power to review software not only for its technical compatibility with their platform, but also for content. This is a very sensitive issue if one takes into account the fact that apps define the functionalities of smartphones, meaning that OS providers have the power to channel what social uses are allowed through these devices.

In contrast to the positions of iOS and Microsoft Windows discussed above, Google appears to be the most lenient when it comes to control over the content of apps. Indeed, even though it favors its own Google Play (formerly known as Android Marketplace), it still allows other distribution channels. There is no official (content related) review process, and developers have to themselves ensure that their app is compatible with Android. However, ironically, in May 2013, Google removed advertising blocking apps from the Google Play store, one of which was Adblock Plus. This is not surprising because, even though Google appears to be geek-friendly and brands its Android as the developer-friendly OS, it is an advertising company at heart and evokes its power over the platform as soon as it interferes with its profit interests.

What is interesting in the case of Google is its unique model and approach to open source. The company is not interested in the commodification of code (unlike Microsoft or Apple), but in capturing Android user data and selling it to advertisers. It should be noted that Google's operations are predominantly driven by advertising services; in 2011, for instance, from total revenues that were estimated in its annual report to be US$37,905 million, $36,531 came from advertising. Accordingly, by giving away its OS for free and making it selectively open source, Google is able to achieve a critical level of dominance in having access to vast user data (Spreeuwenberg & Poell, 2012; Goggin, 2012; Mager, 2012; Mosemghvdlishvili & Jansz, 2014) and control of a large mobile ecosystem.

To respond to Google's selective adoption of open source strategies, a 'Free Your Android' campaign was initiated by the Free Software Foundation's European branch in 2009 (for more information about FSF, see: Berry, 2008; Elliot & Scacchi, 2008). The foundation maintains that access to software determines who can participate in a digital society. The freedoms to use, study, share, and improve software enable there to be equal participation, and are therefore extremely important. Indeed, the libre software community has developed the Replicant OS (a completely libre Android distribution) and the F-Droid (an alternative to Google Play that enables browsing and the installation of free/libre apps on mobile devices; whether an app is proprietary or libre software is not visible in Google Play).

Whereas user participation in code production has been celebrated as an example of user-led innovation (Von Hippel, 2004) and an alternative to capitalist modes of production and distribution (Benkler, 2006 Söderberg, 2008), in the case of Android, it resembles what Sawhney (2009, p. 113) calls the corporate effort to 'harness open-source energy for their own benefit.' The problem is further exacerbated by the concentration of large sets of heterogeneous user data within a single company (Mager, 2012), which in the wake of recent revelations about the NSA poses serious concerns.

If we apply the notion of democratic rationalization, as discussed in the theoretical perspective of this chapter, Google's selective open source strategies do not have an emancipatory or democratizing effect in terms of subjecting technological decision-making to social control and values (Mosemghvdlishvili & Jansz, 2014). Even though Google releases its source code, it does not involve developers directly in writing the code, and retains the right to integrate the contributions of others. The company certainly opened itself up to the range of groups that are involved in shaping the mobile internet (by writing apps for mobile devices), albeit while maintaining strict control, thus resembling what Goggin (2012) described as 'guided democracy.' I challenge the use of democracy in the metaphor, because Google's practices of mass surveillance and data commodification (Fuchs, 2010, 2011; Mager, 2012) are not in accordance with the principles of democratic rationalization.

CONCLUSION

The internet as we know it is changing. Mobile devices and networks are becoming pervasively ever more important in accessing online space, largely redefining established practices. As I illustrated with the example of the struggle over net neutrality, the owners of mobile network carriers are emerging as a decisive group in shaping the internet. The implications of the increased gate-keeping powers of internet service providers (who will differentiate among content that flows through their wires) is worrying for the democratic promise of the internet. Will it lead to a situation whereby content creators (for instance, bloggers, artists, small communities) who are unable to engage in financial deals with carriers will be trapped in slow traffic? The outcome of the struggle between the profit interests of large carriers and the millions of users who have benefited from having equal access to online content is yet to be seen.

Whereas the debate over net neutrality is evidently political, the second scenario that I discussed appears to be more subtle. Uncovering the subjective interests of the powerful group (in the light of patent owners) is possible through the analytical tool of technical code. As seen in the example of patents in 3G technologies, the private interests of patent holders are neutralized in standards. Technical codes, as defined in the theoretical framework of the chapter, represent such an abstraction, when the interests and/or values of powerful groups become embedded in technological design. The technical codes of capitalism draw on the reification of *intellectual property*, and so discussing the current terrain of possibilities in which technologies developed is not possible without considering the peculiarities of treating the forms of knowledge and information as property. What is currently legally safeguarded as intellectual property (particularly in the forms of patents) was considered to be a range of privileges, more in the category of welfare and the common good, than property. Concrete legal and institutional changes led to the establishment of the 'new IP regime' (see, e.g., Bessen & Meurer, 2008; Coriat & Orsi, 2002), when patentability was expanded to include new forms of information and knowledge (research on the human genome, software, and the so-called business models). However, unlike material property (which is naturally scarce), forms of information and knowledge are not scarce, but are *made scarce* to enable their commodification (May, 2006; Kleiner, 2010; Bessen & Mayer, 2008). A salient outcome of this in relation to the development of technology is that patents are not only used to extract rent (Vercellone, 2008), but also grant power to private patent holders to channel the development of technology in accordance with maximizing profits and securing market share.

In relation to the patterns of how code is developed for mobile devices, I addressed the differences between open and closed platforms. As seen from the selective adoption of open source strategies, code development for iOS and Android does not differ much. Google is more *permissive* and its platform is contingently open. The company, through the selective adoption of open source strategies (change of license, exclusion of developers from directly contributing to the development of Android, as well as use of its Android Compatibility Program), has redefined open source development in the mobile space. What has been argued as representing a challenge to the capitalist mode of labor organization is co-opted to fit Google's business model. Here, it is hard not to agree with Terranova's (2004) famous thesis that free labor has become structural to informational capitalism and its cultural economy. Yet, despite the widely practiced integration of open source development with business models of for-profit corporations, moments of rupture do occur, as seen in the efforts of free/libre software activists to re-politicize the development of code for mobiles.

My aim in this chapter was to consider the design and development phase of mobile technologies. I also wanted to reflect on the broader terrain of the possibilities within which decisions regarding the pace and direction of technological developments are negotiated. Moreover, I have both illustrated the prevalence of technical codes of capitalism that over-determine the process, and questioned the reification of intellectual property rights in relation to technological standards and code production.

NOTES

1. As an example, Feenberg (2010, pp. 100–104) discusses the case of French Minitel, which was hacked by users and transformed from a strictly informational utility into a communication medium.
2. There is also the possibility of *de facto* standardization, which is when certain products (e.g., Microsoft's operating system Windows) become widely accepted on the market, or standardization through government intervention, which sets the appropriate standard and compels all participants in the market to comply (e.g., the Federal Communications Commission; Lemley, 2002). (For a close analysis of internet standardization processes, see Ibrus, this volume).
3. Google's executives claimed that in 2012 some 1.3 million Android devices were activated and the total number of handsets that operated on this OS had surpassed 500 million (Shankland, 2012).

REFERENCES

Barnes, S. J., & Huff, S. L. (2003). Rising sun: iMode and the wireless Internet. *Communications of the ACM, 46*(11), 79–84.

Barratt, N., & Shade, L. (2007). Net neutrality: Telecom policy and the public interest. Canadian Journal of Communication, *32*(2), 295–305.

Bekkers, R., & West, J. (2009). The limits to IPR standardization policies as evidenced by strategic patenting in UMTS. *Telecommunications Policy, 33*(1–2), 80–97.

Bekkers, R., Verspagen, B., & Smits, J. (2002). Intellectual property rights and standardization: the case of GSM. *Telecommunications Policy, 26*(3–4), 171–188.

Benkler, Y. (2006). *The wealth of networks: How social production transforms markets and freedom.* New Haven, CT: Yale University Press.

Berry, D. M. (2004). The contestation of code—A preliminary investigation into the discourse of the free/libre and open source movements. Critical Discourse Studies, 1(1), 65–89.

Berry, D. M. (2008). *Copy, rip, burn: The politics of copyleft and open source.* London: Pluto Press.

Bessen, J., Ford, J., & Meurer, M. J. (2011). The private and social costs of patent trolls. *Regulation, 34*(4), 26–35.

Bessen, J., & Meurer, M. J. (2008). *Patent failure: How judges, bureaucrats, and lawyers put innovators at risk.* Princeton: Princeton University Press.

Bijker, W. E. (2001). Understanding technological culture through a constructivist view of science, technology, and society. In S. H. Cutcliffe & C. Mitcham (Eds.), *Visions of STS: Counterpoints in science, technology, and society studies.* New York: SUNY Press.

Campbell, H. A., & La Pastina, A. C. (2010). How the iPhone became divine: New media, religion and the intertextual circulation of meaning. *New Media & Society, 12*(7), 1191–1207.

Cockburn, I., & MacGarvie, M. (2009). Patents, thickets and the financing of early-stage firms: Evidence from the software industry. *Journal of Economics and Management Strategy, 18*(3), 729–773.

Cooper, M.N. (2004). *Open architecture as communications policy: preserving Internet freedom in the broadband era*. Stanford: Stanford Law School.

Coriat, B., & Orsi, F. (2002). Establishing a new intellectual property rights regime in the United States. *Research Policy, 31*(8–9), 1491–1507

Daliot-Bul, M. (2007). Japan's mobile technoculture: The production of a cellular playscape and its cultural implications. *Media, Culture & Society, 29*(6), 954–971.

De Laat, P. (2005). Copyright or copyleft? An analysis of property regimes for software development, *Research Policy, 34*(10), 1511–1532.

Edwards, G. (2013, September 25). Smartphone patent wars: Timeline of the Apple v. Samsung legal battle. *Quandary Peak Research*. Retrieved from http://quandarypeak.com/2013/09/smartphone-patent-wars-the-apple-vs-samsung-legal-battle/

Elliott, M.S., & Scacchi, W. (2008). Mobilization of software developers: The free software movement. *Information Technology & People, 21*(1), 4–33.

Feenberg, A. (1999). *Questioning technology*. London: Routledge.

Feenberg, A. (2002). Transforming technology. Oxford: Oxford University Press.

Feenberg, A. (2010). *Between reason and experience: Essays in technology and modernity*. Cambridge: MIT Press.

Fuchs, C. (2010). Labor in informational capitalism and on the internet. *The Information Society, 26*, 179–196.

Fuchs, C. (2011). A contribution to the critique of the political economy of Google. *Fast Capitalism, 8*(1). Retrieved from http://www.uta.edu/huma/agger/fastcapitalism/8_1/fuchs8_1

Gallini, N., & Scotchmer, S. (2002). Intellectual property: When is it the best incentive system? In A.B. Jaffe, J. Lerner, & S. Stern (Eds.), *Innovation policy and the economy* (pp. 51–78). Cambridge: MIT Press.

Goggin, G. (2009). Adapting the mobile phone: The iPhone and its consumption. *Continuum, 23*(2), 231–244.

Goggin, G. (2011). *Global mobile media*. Abingdon, Oxon: Routledge.

Goggin, G. (2012). Google phone rising: The Android and the politics of open source. *Continuum: Journal of Media & Cultural Studies, 26*(5), 741–752.

Goodman, D., & Myers, R.A. (2005). *3G cellular standards and patents*. Retrieved from http://ieeexplore.ieee.org/stamp/stamp.jsp?tp=&arnumber=1549445&isnumber=33022

Kleiner, D. (2010). *The telecommunist manifesto*. Amsterdam: Institute of Networked Culture.

Koetsier, J. (2012, November 13). Apple and Microsoft could make 600% more from Android than Google in 2013. *VentureBeat*. Retrieved from http://venturebeat.com/2012/11/13/in-2013-apple-and-microsoft-could-make-600-more-from-android-than-google/

Lehr, W., & McKnight, L.W. (2003). Wireless internet access: 3G vs. WiFi. *Telecommunications Policy, 27*, 351–370.

Lemley, M. (2002). Intellectual property rights and standard-setting organizations. *California Law Review, 90*(6), 1889–1980.Lemley, M., & Shapiro, C. (2007). Patent holdup and royalty stacking. *Texas Law Review, 85*. Retrieved from http://ssrn.com/abstract=923468

Lessig, L., (2001). *The future of ideas: The fate of the commons in a connected world*. New York: Random House.

Mager, A., (2012). Algorithmic ideology. *Information, Communication, & Society, 15*(5), 769–787.

Mangalousi, D., & Mosemghvdlishvili, L. (2014). The debate on establishing the digital single market in Europe and its implications for net neutrality. Paper presented at the International Association for Media and Communication Research (IAMCR) Annual Conference, Hyderabad, India.

May, C. (2006). The denial of history: Reification, intellectual property rights and the lessons of the past. *Capital & Class*, 30(1), 33–56.

Meinrath, S., & Pickard, V. (2006). The new network neutrality: Criteria for internet freedom. *The research conference on communication, information and internet policy TPRC 2006*. Retrieved from http://papers.ssrn.com/sol3/papers.cfm?abstract_id=2119750

Mosemghvdlishvili, L., & Jansz, J. (2013). Negotiating technology and its limitations: Politics of app development. *Information, Communication and Society*, 16(10), 1596–1618.

Mosemghvdlishvili, L., & Jansz, J. (2014). How free and open is Google's Android? An analysis into differences in open source code development for mobiles. Paper presented at the International Association for Media and Communication Research (IAMCR) Annual Conference, Hyderabad, India.

O'Connor, D. (2012, November 17). Breaking news on breaking stuff. *Disruptive Competition Project*. Retrieved from http://www.project-disco.org/intellectual-property/one-in-six-active-u-s-patents-pertain-to-the-smartphone/

Paik, Y., & Zhu, F. (2013, June 17–19). The impact of patent wars on firm strategy: Evidence from the global smartphone market. Paper presented at the 35th DRUID Celebration Conference, Barcelona.

Parish, J. (2011, November 2). Apple vs. Samsung: The complete lawsuit timeline. *The Verge*. Retrieved from http://www.theverge.com/apple/2011/11/2/2533472/apple-vs-samsung

Pinch, T. J., & Bijker, W. E. (1984). The social construction of facts and artefacts: Or how the sociology of science and the sociology of technology might benefit each other. *Social Studies of Science*, 14, 388–441.

Sawhney, H. (2009). Innovations at the edge: The impact of mobile technologies on the character of the Internet. In G. Goggin & L. Hjorth (Eds.), *Mobile technologies: From telecommunications to media* (pp. 105–117). New York: Routledge.

Shankland, S. (2012, September 12). Google: 500 million Android devices activated. CNET. Retrieved from http://news.cnet.com/8301–1035_3–57510994–94/google-500-million-android-devices-activated/

Shapiro, C. (2001). Navigating the patent thicket: Cross-licenses, patent pools, and standard setting. In A. B. Jaffe, J. Lerner, & S. Stern (Eds.), *Innovation policy and the economy*, (pp. 119–150). Cambridge: MIT Press

Söderberg, J. (2008). *Hacking capitalism: The free and open source software movement*. London: Routledge.

Spreeuwenberg, K., & Poell, T. (2012). Android and the political economy of the mobile Internet: A renewal of open source critique. First Monday, 17(7). Retrieved from http://firstmonday.org/ojs/index.php/fm/article/view/4050/3271

Statista. (n.d.). Market share: Wireless telecommunication carriers in the U.S. 2011. *Statista* website. Retrieved from http://www.statista.com/statistics/219720/market-share-of-wireless-carriers-in-the-us-by-subscriptions

Sullivan, J. L. (2011). Free, open source software advocacy as a social justice movement: The expansion of F/OSS movement discourse in the 21st century. *Journal of Information Technology & Politics*, 8(3), 223–239.

Terranova, T. (2004). Network culture: Politics for the information age. London: Pluto Press.

Topper, J. (2014, January 30). More than 1 million people call on FCC to save net neutrality. *Free Press*. Retrieved from http://www.freepress.net/press-release/105672/more-1-million-people-call-fcc-save-net-neutrality

Veak, T. J. (2006). *Democratizing technology: Andrew Feenberg's critical theory of technology*. Albany, NY: State University of New York Press.

Vercellone, C. (2008). The new articulation of wages, rent and profit in cognitive capitalism. Université Paris Panthéon-Sorbonne (Post-Print and Working

Papers), *HAL*. Retrieved from http://EconPapers.repec.org/RePEc:hal:cesptp:ha lshs-00645055

Von Hippel, E. (2004). *Democratizing innovation*. Cambridge: MIT Press.

West, J., & Mace, M. (2010). Browsing as the killer app: Explaining the rapid success of Apple's iPhone. *Telecommunication Policy*, *34*(5–6), 270–286.

Williams, R. (1997). The social shaping of information and communications technologies. In H. Kubicek, W.H. Dutton, & R. Williams (Eds.), *The social shaping of information superhighways: European and American roads to the information society* (pp. 299–338). Frankfurt: Campus Verlag.

Williams, R., & Edge, D. (1996). The social shaping of technology. *Research Policy*, *25*(6), 865–899.

Wilson, K.G. (1992). Deregulating telecommunications and the problem of natural monopoly: A critique of economics in telecommunications policy. *Media, Culture & Society*, *14*(3), 343–368.

Wu, T. (2003). Network neutrality, broadband discrimination. *Journal of Telecommunications and High Technology Law*, *2*, 141–179.

Zuckerman, E. (2010). Decentralizing the mobile phone: A second ICT4D revolution? *Information Technologies and International Development*, *6*(SE), 99–103.

7 Predictive Algorithms and Personalization Services on Social Network Sites
Implications for Users and Society

Robert Bodle

As we face an online environment of ubiquitous surveillance, it is worth noting the commercial forces that have provided the rational for tracking users, combining databases, and personalizing the web. Personalization is when online content conforms to the prior actions of the user in an algorithmically generated feedback loop. Examples of personalization include Google's personalized search, behavioral advertising, featured recommendations on Amazon.com, taste preferences on Netflix, headlines on Yahoo! News, Twitter Trends, and Facebook's News Feed rankings. The personalized web can provide convenience, efficiency, interestingness and relevance to users who are served with content that they themselves help to generate. However, there may be unintended consequences, biases, and costs including social discrimination, political polarization, coercion, and the erosion of personal autonomy and human volition. The chapter uses a political economy approach to identify operational logics and unintended consequences for users.

Social network sites (SNS) are ideal sites of inquiry for assessing the developing dynamics of personalization services, which include opaqueness (the black boxing of technological processes), algorithmic-human interfacing and enactment, the reliance on big data including data trails and user-generated content, and the role of advertising as a driving factor. Facebook is particularly important as the dominant SNS and a strong indicator of industry trends that can migrate to other sites. A critical examination of the ubiquity of personalization services provides an important and valuable contribution to the understanding of the underlying logic of interconnectivity, the economic processes of value-creation, and the human rights and democratic implications of personalization. Looking at personalization services on Facebook as a case study, this chapter will analyze advertising trends on the network, examine the role of predictive algorithms and their implications for users, and arrive at conclusions to help formulate user empowerment and agency.

THE PERSONALIZED WEB

The personalized web uses extensive customer data and predictive algorithms to conform content to the prior actions of the user; one's digital past is used to personalize new online experiences in real time. The personalized web includes Google's Personalized Search, behavioral targeting (e.g., when a specific ad appears on a variety of websites by tracking the user with cookies placed on their computer), locative mobile ads (Delo, 2013), Sponsored Ads and Suggested Posts on Facebook, and Promoted Tweets on Twitter. Technological, social, and cultural factors contribute to an online ecosystem that tracks and collects user data to serve personalized search results, ads, and entertainment. Cloud applications, web cookies, and Open APIs (application programming interfaces) such as social plug-ins (e.g., the 'Like' button) enable third parties to track people's activities from site to site, and from desktop to mobile device (Bodle, 2011). Social media sites encourage social behavior by rewarding participation with increased visibility and attention (Bucher, 2012; Bosker, 2013), that, in turn, produces a trail of data harvested as secondary information products shared, traded, and sold for personalization services.

The collection of valuable user data has given rise to a rapidly growing surveillance industry that includes digital advertising networks and marketing firms, data-brokers, as well as data-mining, tracking, and optimization companies (e.g., Acxiom, RapLeaf). These companies help amass and sort through big data in order to identify people's browsing, viewing, and purchasing habits used to predict behavior and personalize content in real time. They also help comprise 'digital dossiers' (Solove, 2002) that are used to make inferences, correlations, and predictions about future behavior. Although personalized services curate content that is deemed relevant to one's prior interests and activities, the algorithms also decide what is irrelevant for the user, and filters out content.

Google's personal web search demonstrates the filter in-filter out dynamic of personalization services. In December of 2009, Google introduced personal search results based on a user's semantic history (search terms run and results selected), location, time of year, language, and linked social networks (Notess, 2012, p. 43). Personal web search can provide timely and relevant results, but it can also limit one's exposure to information outside of one's range of knowledge and experience. In a recent Pew Internet & American Life Project survey (2012a), approximately 65% of respondents thought that it was 'a BAD thing if a search engine collected information about your searches and then used it to rank your future search results, because it may limit the information you get online and what search results you see' (Pew Internet & American Life Project, 2012a, 2).

Personalized search has proven to be successful for Google's ad business that sells 'personalized audiences' (Feuz, Fuller, & Stadler, 2011, p. 7) to advertisers (AdSense for search, AdWords for syndicated texts, and DoubleClick for graphics) generating $30 per user, towering well above Yahoo at $7 and Facebook at $4.39 (Manjoo, 2012). Research suggests that personalization services benefit advertisers more than users, actively furthering a commercial agenda by pushing users toward 'criteria predefined' by the company (Feuz, Fuller, & Stadler, 2011, p. 7).

APPROACH

This chapter looks at the development of Facebook's advertising practices—from simple visual display ads in 2009, to the algorithmic personalization of the News Feed—to identify potential implications and unintended consequences for the user. This work draws on industry press reports as well as empirical observation of how advertising is integrated and personalized on the site. Algorithms used for personalization are proprietary and prevent access and a perfect understanding of their underlying technological processes (Beer, 2009; Feuz, Fuller, & Stadler, 2011; Bucher, 2012). Thus, this study examines general processes and their implications. Although it is impossible to break open the black box of Facebook's algorithms, this limitation is a clear indication of asymmetrical power relations between Facebook, its advertisers, and its users; selective insights about users are shared with advertisers and brands, but not with the users themselves. Realistically, advertisers and third party data brokers also do not have total access to Facebook's analytics and databases (Peterson, 2012). Maintaining a power differential is not uncommon in ad-dependent industries when 'Marketing is a war of knowledge, insight, and asymmetric advantage' (Nichols, 2013, p. 8).

Applying a political economy of communications (PEC) approach helps to identify unequal power relationships and critique them (Greenstein & Esterhuysen, 2006). PEC examines the 'underlying social relations' and potential conflicts of interest between market logic and user needs. Analysis of asymmetrical relationships between online services, advertisers, and users suggests a process of commodification of social labor where personal information is turned into product, reconfiguring social relations as a result (Erickson & Wasco, 2009; Mosco, 2009; Terranova, 2000). 'With its focus on institutional structures and practices,' offers Bettig (1996), 'the political economy of communications is poised to help explain the forces driving these processes and to offer up predictions about their implications' (p. 1).

Information advertising on Facebook is the primary means of revenue for Facebook and drives the company's privacy policies: 'we may use all of the information we receive about you to serve ads that are more relevant to you' (https://www.facebook.com/legal/proposeddup). If information is the new currency, the underlying market logic of personalization is to learn as much about people, in order to monetize them. This is accomplished by providing user data that enables advertisers to place finely tailored ads on one's Facebook page and to pay a premium for it. General knowledge of how algorithms work will also provide context for a critical discussion of the power of personalization.

THE POLITICS OF ALGORITHMIC POWER

Recent interdisciplinary work in software and information studies helps explain the sociotechnical dynamics of algorithmic decision-making processes (Beer, 2009; Kitchen and Dodge, 2011; MacKenzie, 2005; Mayer-Schönberger & Cukier, 2013). Algorithms are used to make sense of (infer, filter, and correlate) big data for a wide range of purposes: to personalize cultural production (music, literature, film scripts; Steiner, 2012), regulate incivility on blogs (Morozov, 2013), shape social behavior (Bucher, 2012), target advertisements (Turow, 2011), guide public opinion (Sunstein, 2009; Pariser, 2010), predict future crimes (Mayer-Schönberger & Cukier, 2013), and screen terrorist threats (EFF, 2013). Although Web 2.0 rhetoric celebrates an era of disintermediation, predictive algorithms have been interposed as society's new gatekeepers, information filters, social shapers, and causal agents (Mayer-Schönberger & Cukier, 2013). New empirical and theoretical work from social science and communication studies proposes how seemingly neutral and inscrutable machine processes have political effects that reveal corporate agendas (Bucher, 2012; Gillespie, 2013). Algorithms are not neutral or 'a-political' prediction engines, suggests McStay (2012, p. 138). They are 'codified politics' (McStay, 2012, p. 138); ideological formulations about social relations embodied in code, insulated from political debate, about which most people are unaware' (Bucher, 2012, p. 1171) and 'an important terrain upon which political battles are being fought' (Gillespie, 2013). A better understanding of the politics of algorithmic power can help inform user participation and agency.

Research in behavioral advertising also provides insight into the data-sharing relationships between third parties (i.e., data brokers and tracking companies) and digital intermediaries (SNSs, search companies, user generated content sites, e-tailer sites, etc.) (McStay, 2011; Turow, 2011). Empirical research into other forms of personalization, especially personal web search, helps point to new methodologies for assessing the value, benefits, and ambiguities of personalization for users (Feuz, Fuller, & Stalder, 2011). Political critiques based in liberal democratic theory are used to examine the gatekeeping, censoring, and ideologically polarizing function of personalization (Bollinger, 2010; McChesney, 2013; Morozov, 2013; Pariser, 2010). Other studies cited indicate the harm of racial discrimination as a result of social sorting and personalization services (Gandy, 2003; Lyon, 2003; Nakamura, 2002; Sweeney, 2013). And theories of digital labor exploitation, human rights, and ethics lay out a framework to speculate on user empowerment (Ess, 2009; Fuchs, 2012; La Rue, 2013; Tavani, 2010; Terranova, 2000).

THE RISE OF PERSONALIZED ADVERTISING ON FACEBOOK

Advertising on Facebook gradually proved more effective after the SNS learned how to use user data to personalize ad content and better integrate ads within the user experience. Facebook collects information about its users from its social network (clicks, likes, shares, posts, comments, check-ins, RSVPs, apps used, friend activity) and from data-brokers (offline information), creating aggregate profiles that enable advertisers to more accurately serve ads to members on the site. In keeping with broadcast-era advertising strategy based on return on investment (ROI), ads are considered more cost-effective if they can reach the right viewer; corresponding to existing tastes, preferences, and habits of viewers. Personalized ads help provide more ROI for advertisers, support an ad-funded social media industry, and benefit users as well. Finely targeted ads help people find what's relevant to them and reduce clutter.

Facebook initially abstained from advertising (unlike its failed competitor MySpace), instead growing its service's functionality with open application programming interfaces (APIs), and building its user base. The company then leveraged this audience commodity to help commercialize the site. Today, the publicly traded company is heavily dependent on advertising with 85% ($1.24 billion) of its Q1's total ($1.46 billion) earned from advertising revenue (Delo, 2013) and is under intense pressure to grow its ad revenue, while mitigating the over-commercialization of its site and services (Manjoo, 2012). As a result, advertising on Facebook has grown increasingly sophisticated, nimble, and nuanced by visually integrating advertisements into the page layout and by serving real time personalized ads based on user data and inferences made by predictive algorithms. With over one billion members, Facebook harvests 2.7 billion likes, shares, and comments posted daily on the SNS (Manjoo, 2012). These interactions feed an adaptive News Feed algorithm that learns how to encourage more interaction and has, in fact, 'increased people's likes, clicks, and comments by 50%' (Bosker, 2013).

Facebook's growing ad business benefits from blurring the lines between paid advertisements and social status updates, which can minimize awareness of the distinctions and provide a persuasive social context to view ads. Facebook's first social advertising services began in 2009 with 'Marketplace ads' featured on the right hand margin of its homepage. These direct-response ads that were based on click-through rates (CRTs) performed 'about half as well as traditional banner ads' (Wasserman, 2011). In 2010 the average click-through rate for Facebook ads was 0.051%—'half as much as the industry standard of .1%' (Wasserman, 2011). Facebook responded to criticism of poor CRTs by partnering with Nielsen Co. to create a new rating system based on 'gross rating points' that uses 'mixed-media modeling' methods to measure the combined metrics of sales, awareness, and reach

(Wasserman, 2011). The underperforming 'Market-placed ads' were gradually replaced by 'Sponsored Stories,' 'Page Post ads,' and 'Premium ads' (May, 2011), which provided greater targeting options and more closely resembled friend's posts in both design and functionality, enabling interactions (the ability to comment, share, and like) and deeper engagement with the ad. The next development is brand pages that encourage people to share ads with their social graph (in exchange for coupons, discounts, and prizes), and allows brand access and reach to 'fans' and 'friends of fans.' The 'Reach Generator' feature enables advertisers to use Facebook's analytics to place ads, which the company claims can reach 75% of a page's fans (as opposed to the 16% without ads; Cohen, 2012). 'Page Post ads,' 'Premium ads,' and 'Sponsored Posts' occupy the right hand margin of the page. It is important to note that 'Sponsored Stories' (now called 'Suggested Posts;' Sept. 2013) are placed upon users' News Feed, appearing in the center column alongside friend's photos and status updates. Althoughe ads in the right hand column average 0.04%–0.05% (McDermott, 2012), ads placed within the News Feed earn 1.0%–7.0% CTR, with mobile CTRs earning higher than desktop only (McDermott, 2012). Thus, the enhanced integration of advertisements within social production spaces appears to be successful.

Facebook reports that the increase in advertising is not alienating users (measured by sentiment and satisfaction), however, anecdotal evidence on Twitter typifies a concern: '#Facebook, there are too many freakin ads on my news feed! fix that . . . ' (Bosker, 2013). And discontent with how the company shares member's 'likes' on ads in 'Sponsored Stories' resulted in a class action lawsuit (Facebook settled for $20 million; Fraley, 2012).

Personalization tools and analytics are used to help the company further enhance its advertising efforts while preventing the alienation from over-commercialization. An advertisement is far more likely to make a favorable impression when it is targeted because it conforms to the relevant needs and interests of the user and therefore predicts what the user will want. Facebook provides brands with filtering tools—'selected targeting parameters that are as relevant to your product or service as possible' (Facebook, 2012a), which includes: location targeting (country, city, IP address, and zip code—within the US), age and birthday, interests (likes, interests, and topics), education (college, university, major, graduation year), and connections and/or friends of connections. A brand or ad placement company can use these criteria to broaden or narrow the level of personalization, and reach existing and/or potential buyers. Facebook also provides third party access to members' aggregate user data obtained outside the SNS. The drive to gain perfect knowledge of the user suggests the more information known about a person the more likely to predict that a personalized ad will result in a future purchase. With the development of analytical services based on predictive algorithms Facebook pushes personalization beyond predicting to shaping 'what people want or don't want even before they realize it' (Simonite, 2012, p. 7).

FACEBOOK'S PERSONALIZATION SERVICES AND PREDICTIVE ALGORITHMS

Algorithms are a digital mode of statistical analysis (McStay, 2011) and are programmed with an adaptable set of procedural inputs, instructions, and rules used to draw meaning from large data sets. Algorithms are not 'cameras' but 'engines,' in that they 'performatively enact' (MacKenzie, 2005) results based on the 'intentions of the programmers' (Introna & Nissenbaum, 2000). Facebook's predictive algorithms are used to select and tailor posts on one's News Feed and thus determine visibility on the social network—who/what is seen and who/what is made invisible. News Feed algorithms rank users' interaction and engagement according to three criteria or three procedural inputs (among others): affinity (popularity), weight (relevance), and time decay (recency). However, these three factors have grown quite sophisticated; there are now multiple weight levels, categories and subcategories of affinity, and Facebook now bends 'decay' rules by keeping older posts alive if they continue to generate interactions (McGee, 2013). Although 'the exact workings and logics . . . include more factors than is publicly known' (Bucher, 2012, p. 1172), the company provides a glimpse to advertisers with the 'Insights API' to conduct real time tracking of 'News Feed Post Performance' (clicks, likes, comments, and shares), 'Virality' (organic propagation), and 'Negative Feedback' (unlikes and hides; Constine, 2012).

Facebook's News Feed algorithm processes are perhaps the most comprehensive collection of offline and online data 'assembled on human social behavior' (Simonite, 2012, p. 3); 'a previously unimaginable trove of information about what consumers see and do' (Nichols, 2013, p. 1). This 'trove' includes all information shared with Facebook, data garnered from user activity external to the SNS through social plug-ins (e.g., the ubiquitous 'Like' button) and cookies (e.g., Facebook Exchange), combined with offline data provided by data mining (e.g., Datalogix) and tracking companies (e.g., BlueKai). The algorithm analyzes personal and public information such as 'names, addresses, phone numbers, and details of shopping habits' (EFF, 2013). Facebook's predictive algorithms discern relevancy, importance, and 'interestingness,' but is also modeled on 'anticipated or future-oriented assumptions about valuable and profitable interactions' (Bucher, 2012, p. 1169). The underlying purpose of personalization is to identify and exploit the cause and effect relationships between advertising and purchasing, referred to by marketers as 'war gaming' (Nichols, 2013, p. 1). In this way predictive algorithms can increase the value of the social audience commodity (Smythe, 1981). 'Contrary to the laws of economics, information increases in value with greater supply; 'The more information you provide to companies, the more value they can extract from it' (Cochran, 2013).

Personalized advertising that includes both the social integration of ad messages and the analytic targeting of users drives the company's privacy practices as well as the company's control over how information is disseminated on the social network, with unintended consequences for user privacy, autonomy, and freedom.

IMPLICATIONS OF PREDICTIVE ALGORITHMS AND PERSONALIZATION SERVICES

Insights into the operational logics of Facebook's algorithm reinforce an understanding of the company's underlying business model that is predicated on tracking users and amassing data tied to fixed identities. Close examination of Facebook's data-driven personalization practices reveals the fundamental inequality between members, advertisers, and the company. Recognizing Facebook's asymmetrical algorithmic power can provide insights into the implications of personalization for privacy, civic engagement, diversity, and freedom from discrimination.

Informational Privacy and Personal Safety

Although Facebook provides real time insights to advertisers and brands to stimulate engagement, the company does not provide the same to members, revealing an important power differential. Access and control of one's own data is an integral component of autonomy and without it self-determination is relinquished (Tavani, 2010). Withholding what information is known about users and how it is used prevents people from anticipating potential consequences and making informed decisions. For example, recent revelations by NSA contractor Edward Snowden reveals an alliance of internet companies and the US government (e.g., PRISM), where tracking of user data for advertising purposes can also be used to identify enemies of the state. Predictive analytics can undermine user privacy; the unintended consequences are difficult to predict. However, they can include threats to one's personal safety.

Facebook enforces a 'real-name only' policy in order to fulfill a business model, predicated on tracking users and amassing data to fixed identities. The SNS also prevents pseudonyms in order to identify users, but also to provide safety and security for the social network: 'We take the safety of our community very seriously. That's why we remove fake accounts from the site as we find them' (Facebook, 2012b). Facebook's strategic adherence to real-name only norms, however, also prevents anonymity, which is a universally acknowledged extrinsic good of privacy and a fundamental prerequisite to achieving safety and protection from reprisal for expressing one's political beliefs and for freedom of association (UDHR, 1948).

Facebook, along with Twitter, YouTube, and other major platforms, have become critically important means to reach a global audience and to access information. For example, information about Gezi Park protests in Istanbul was not televised by Turkish media but disseminated via social media (Tufekci, 2014). Yet, Facebook's real-name only policy puts the internet's most vulnerable people at risk, including political dissidents, whistleblowers, people holding minority views, people oppressed for their religious beliefs and sexual orientation, and victims of abuse. The Facebook fan page 'We are all Khaled Said,' instrumental for organizing the protests that led to the ousting of Egyptian President Mubarak (January 25, 2011), was suspended due to the page administrator's violation of its real-name attribution policy. The Pew Research Center's Internet and American Life survey, 'Social Networks and Politics,' found that people are discouraged from expressing political views when their real names are attached (2012a). Indeed, the attributes of anonymity, including minimal accountability, disinhibition, and deindividuation, can permit the freedom to speak freely and provide safety from reprisal (Bodle, 2013).

Facebook claims that it does not share the names of people whose data is used to target them. Turow (2011) suggests, however, that 'when companies simply strip the name and address off of data that is sorted and labeled and combined with a telephone number—its claim that you are anonymous is meaningless' (p. 190). If advertisers can use predictive algorithms and social network data to identify and track its users, so can state security forces. Not knowing what personal data is available and how it is used can have a chilling effect on freedom of expression due to an internalized threat of discipline and punishment. Freedom of expression is also undermined through predictive algorithms that filter opposing views.

Algorithmic Gate-Keeping and Deliberative Democracy

Algorithmic filtering on social network sites like Facebook can prevent exposure to a diverse array of competing and contradicting views. Pariser, in *The Filter Bubble* (2010), puzzles over the fact that the political views of his conservative friends don't appear in his Facebook News Feed alongside the views of his liberal friends. In fact, conservative views are censored and made invisible to him. According to deliberative democracy theory (Dryzek, 2000), public deliberation is most likely to occur when citizens are exposed to diverse and antagonistic sources of information, not only views and information that merely confirm one's preexisting opinions and knowledge base. Access to a wide range of competing views can encourage an active and informed citizenry by creating the preconditions conducive to robust, wide open, and uninhibited dialog and debate (Bollinger, 2010). One potential benefit of algorithmic filtering is the censorship of incivility such as 'violence, racism, flagrant profanity, and hate speech' (Morozov, 2013, p. 164). However, first amendment protections in the US provide a high tolerance for incivility as a means to protect unpopular forms of political speech.

Algorithmic filtering can polarize debate by narrowing one's perspective and entrenching it through 'confirmation bias—the tendency to believe things that reinforce our existing views, to see what we want to see' (Mozorov, 2013,

p. 86). Vaidhythanan suggests that when 'using Facebook or Google, we're more likely to come across like-minded posts from like-minded people. A republic works better when we make the extra effort to engage with a variety of points of view' (2012). The impact of algorithmic gate-keeping can be far reaching in shaping how people think and come together to solve problems. Exposure to more diverse information, suggests Benkler (2001), can make us freer because we are presented with the options of what is possible. As our options become limited, so does our ability to shape our world and ourselves.

Algorithms, are not the only means to filter news and information. With the rise of audience fragmentation and selective exposure, people deliberately fine-tune their political and cultural information flows. A Pew survey revealed that users were likely to block, un-friend, and hide someone who posted political opinions and views that they disagree with or otherwise found offensive (2012b). Zuckerman, co-founder of citizen reporting network Global Voices, laments homophilic tendencies on the internet, and endorses global bridge-building and xenophilia to widen one's views online and to help solve global problems.

Homophily, Social Segmentation, and Intolerance

Facebook's personalization algorithms filter diverse views, including political ideology that can reinforce homophily or the tendency to seek similarity in one's friends. Homophilous online environments provide networks of mutual support and familiarity. But they can also discourage users from seeking diverse opinions and diversity in friends, which can reinforce sociological trends offline as 'physical communities are becoming more homogenous' (Pariser, 2010, p. 66). Personalized ads can deepen social divisions based on differences of race, ethnicity, class, age, education, location, and political ideology. Increased social segmentation is likely to result in a less tolerant society, where stereotypes, prejudice, suspicion, and hatred of the other can flourish. Stereotypes can also shape personal identity; people may feel pressure to filter out their own differences in order to assimilate within homogenous online communities. As the global internet expands the reach of dominant social network sites like Facebook, homophilous tendencies have far reaching implications for cross-cultural interaction and respect. Perhaps the increased emphasis on visual self expression (selfies, vine, video chat) within SNSs, may provide bodily engagement and experiential appreciation of irreducible differences, a precursor to mutual respect (Ess, 2009).

Discrimination and Coercion

Algorithmic guesses or inferences used to target people can reinforce traditional patterns of discrimination in the market place. Predictive analytics can make the same damaging correlations about demographic groups and reinforce cultural stereotypes used to discriminate against people as a result

(Nakamura, 2002). For example, studies have found 'statistically significant discrimination in ad delivery based on racially associated names,' including search results that associate names with criminal arrest records (Sweeney, 2013). Such predicted results can hurt one's ability to get a job, complete a rental application, apply for a loan, and make new friends. Personalization services can also result in price discrimination. For example, Orbitz guides Mac users to pricier hotels (Mattioli, 2012). Online stores such as Staples. com charge more for people who are browsing with zip codes that have fewer rival stores (Angwin, 2014). Calo (2011) suggests that in the future, companies will adjust prices according to when people are most vulnerable.

Racially targeting advertising can be used to guide media consumption that draws on feelings of in-group accountability and 'reinforce a consumer's identification with a commodity' (Gandy, 2003, p. 5). Market segmentation can reinforce boundaries between social groups—including macroscopic traditional identity categories (gender, race, class, nationality, and sexuality; McStay, 2013; Terranova, 2004), and reinforce disparities as a result. Consistent with a political economy critique, this serves the interests of advertisers; to interpolate subjects as distinctly segmented markets narrowly defined as 'consumers' rather than citizens, who assume power from consumption rather than from concrete political gains.

Discrimination can result when predictive algorithms infer inaccurate notions about who people are; online profiles can be flawed, incomplete, biased, and dead wrong, with harmful results. Predictive analytics might also overlook the relevancy of one's aspirational self, which entails one's dreams goals, ideals, and notions about the good life. Perhaps someone who is striving and aspiring to have a different life than their present demographic data and online browsing habits reveal. Can we trust algorithms to make the best decisions for who we want to be?

WEIGHING THE DISADVANTAGES AND ADVANTAGES OF PERSONALIZATION

Facebook has the algorithmic power to make decisions about people's online environments, to reinforce patterns of inclusion and exclusion, and to set social agendas. The social network has enough data on members' desires and interests to tailor online experiences in ways that can manage interactions and guide outcomes. Certainly personalization services, including personalized ads and News Feed analytics, can be framed as user empowerment—people are getting more of what they want, interacting more with who they want to interact with. Indeed, personalized services on social network sites can be incredibly efficient and convenient, saving one precious time weed-ing through irrelevant posts. People can also easily reach a focused social circle by creating a specialized group on Facebook. Rather than lessening political engagement, their 'Likes' on posts related to Network Neutrality, for example, ensures that the topic will likely continue to maintain high prioritization in their News Feed. Instead of being entrenched in one's viewpoint, they actually become more expert, engaged, and committed.

The convenience and familiarity of personalization services on social network sites should be weighed against their disadvantages, which includes ongoing surveillance, loss of informational privacy and self-determination (McStay, 2011). Certainly personalization services reflect people's choices and preferences, however these choices become structurally determined as the results of predictive algorithms can supercede the user's intentions.

CONCLUSION

This chapter discussed the implications of personalized services on Facebook, primarily the role of predictive algorithms and user data to personalize ads. The asymmetrical access to both one's data and the analytics for serving content, alters the relations of power between users, companies, and advertisers. I have suggested how the market values and business logic embedded in personalization services can mitigate against user autonomy, privacy, and freedom of expression. Moreover this analysis suggests that algorithmic filtering can prevent one's exposure to difference, undermine respect for diversity, discriminate against categories of historically vulnerable populations, and discourage deliberative democratic participation where people's exposure to differences of opinion can support a robust public sphere.

Research is inconclusive as to whether consumer attitudes toward personalized services are generally positive or negative. Perhaps if more people gain a greater understanding of the implications and constraints of personalized information services, they will reject them. Greater transparency of Facebook's tracking and filtering processes can help build critical awareness of the analytic mediation of 'human knowledge practices' (Gillespie, 2013, p. 2). People should have greater control over their data, a better understanding of how their information is used, and the choice to opt out of personalization altogether by default. The domestication of algorithms could prevent greater scrutiny as they grow commonplace, are naturalized and given neutral status as mere machine processes. Algorithms are human-machine hybridizations encoded with the values, interests, prerogatives, and priorities of programmers to produce desired outcomes; with ad-driven personalization outcomes oriented toward primarily commercial ends.

We must explore ways to restore and protect human agency to account for the power asymmetries between companies, advertisers and private citizens. Companies can embed human rights defaults into their sociotechnical systems, including the rights to privacy and informational self-determination.

Snowden's revelations about PRISM suggest that pervasive and systemic monitoring of private information by state-corporate cooperation requires strong privacy protections that are necessary and proportionate to the need for security. Consumer protection laws (such as HIPAA) should be passed to regulate internet and advertising industries to protect personal data. International principles on the application of human rights online, can also guide the design, use, and regulation of personalized services, including all facets of social media, advertising, and big data industries.

Because predictive algorithms are social shaping technologies, consisting of uses as well as the values and affordances embedded in the technology, they can be designed to reflect non-commercial outcomes that enhance intercultural collaboration, social movement building, diversity of information, and robust political discourse. It is yet to be seen if ethical algorithmists, 'new professionals in computer science, mathematics, and statistics' (Mayer-Schönberger & Cukier, 2013), can encode procedures that promote non-commercially based outcomes while respecting the digital rights of users. Perhaps the community design and architecture of the next global peer-to-peer distributed social network might opt out of algorithmic gatekeeping, filtering, and monitoring all together (Bodle, 2010). By restoring informational privacy, autonomy, and self-determination, people might be empowered to make their own decisions, to broaden their lives online rather than to narrow them.

REFERENCES

Angwin, J. (2014). *Dragnet nation: A quest for privacy, security, and freedom in a world of relentless surveillance*. New York: Times Books.

Beer, D. (2009). Power through the algorithm? Participatory Web cultures and the technological unconscious. *New Media and Society*, 11(6), 985–1002.

Benkler, Y. (2001). Siren songs and Amish children: Autonomy, information, and law. *New York University Law Review*, 76(23), 23–113.

Bettig, R. (1996). *Copyrighting culture: The political economy of intellectual property*. Boulder, CO: WestviewPress.

Bodle, R. (2010). Assessing social network sites as international platforms: Guiding principles. *Journal of International Communication*, 16(2), 9–24.

Bodle, R. (2011). Regimes of sharing: Open APIs, interoperability, and Facebook. *Information, Communication & Society*, 14(3), 320–337.

Bodle, R. (2013). The ethics of online anonymity or Zuckerberg vs. "moot". *Computers and Society*, 43(1), 22–35.

Bollinger, L. C. (2010). *Uninhibited, robust, and wide-open: A free press for a new century*. New York: Oxford University Press.

Bosker, B. (2013, May). Zuckerberg: Folks on Facebook are happy with all the ads we're showing them. *The Huffington Post*. Retrieved from http://www.huffingtonpost.com/2013/05/01/ zuckerberg-facebook-ads_n_3196195.html

Bucher, T. (2012). Want to be on the top? Algorithmic power and the threat of invisibility on Facebook. *New Media and Society*, 14(7), 1164–1180.

Calo, M. R. (2011). The boundaries of privacy harm. *Indiana Law Journal*, 86(3). Retrieved from http://papers.ssrn.com/sol3/papers.cfm?abstract_id=1641487

Cochran, T. (2013, May). Personal information is the currency of the 21st century. *All Things D.* Retrieved from http://allthingsd.com/20130507/personal-information-is-the-currency-of-the-21st-century/

Cohen, J. (2012). *Facebook's two new promos: Reach Generator, Logouts.* Retrieved from http://allfacebook.com/facebook-reach-logout_b79918

Constine, J. (2012, April). EdgeRank checker hustles, builds tool just five days after Facebook real-time insights API goes live. *TechCrunch.* Retrieved from http://techcrunch.com/2012/04/25/facebook-real-time-insights-api/

Delo, C. (2013, May). Facebook: 30% of our revenue now comes from mobile ads. *AdAge Digital.* Retrieved from http://adage.com/article/digital/facebook-30-revenue-mobile-ads/241240/

Dryzek, J.K. (2000). *Deliberative democracy and beyond: Liberals, critics, contestation.* Oxford, UK: Oxford University Press.

Electronic Frontier Foundation. (2013). The disconcerting details: How Facebook teams up with data brokers to show you targeted ads. Retrieved from https://www.eff.org/deeplinks/2013/04/disconcerting-details-how-facebook-teams-data-brokers-show-you-targeted-ads

Ess, C. (2009). *Digital media ethics.* Cambridge, UK: Polity Press.

Facebook. (2012a). Disabled—Fake names. *Facebook Help Center.* Retrieved from http://on.fb.me/vdj7JS

Facebook. (2012b). Targeting options. *Facebook Help Center.* Retrieved from http://on.fb.me/K00daT

Feuz, M., Fuller, M., & Stadler, F. (2011, February). Personal web searching in the age of semantic capitalism: Diagnosing the mechanisms of personalization. *First Monday, 16*(2). Retrieved from http://firstmonday.org/article/view/3344/2766

Fraley v. Facebook Inc., 11–1726 D.U.S. Northern California (2012).

Fuchs, C. (2012). Dallas Smyth today—The audience commodity, the digital labour debate, Marxist political economy and critical theory. Prolegomena to a digital labour theory of value. *triple, 10*(2), 692–740.

Gandy, Jr., O. (2003). *Privatization and identity: The formation of a racial class.* Retrieved from http://www.asc.upenn.edu/usr/ogandy/c53704read/privatization%20and%20identity%20i.pdf

Gillespie, T. (2013). Can an algorithm be wrong? *Limn* 2. Retrieved from http://limn.it/can-an-algorithm-be-wrong/

Greenstein, R. & Esterhuysen, A. (2006). The right to development in the information society. In R.K. Jørgensen (Ed.), *Human rights in the global information society* (pp. 281–302). Cambridge, MA: The MIT Press.

Introna, L., & Nissenbaum, H. (2000). Shaping the web: Why the politics of search engines matters. *The Information Society, 16*(3), 169–185.

Kitchen, R., & Dodge, M. (2011). Code/Space: Software and everyday life. Cambridge: The MIT Press.

La Rue, F. (2013, April). *Report of the special rapporteur on the promotion and protection of the right to freedom of opinion and expression.* New York: Human Rights Council, United Nations. Retrieved from http://bit.ly/10IqJna

Lyon, D. (2003). Surveillance as social sorting: Computer codes and mobile bodies. In David Lyon (Ed.), *Surveillance as social sorting: Privacy, risk, and digital discrimination.* New York: Routledge.

Mackenzie, A. (2005). The performativity of code: Software and cultures of circulation. *Theory, Culture and Society, 22*(1), 71–92.

Manjoo, F. (2012, April). The morning after: What's next for Facebook? Trying to make enough money to justify that $100 billion valuation. *Fast Company*, pp. 222–223.

Mattioli, D. (2012, August 23). On Orbitz, Mac users steered to pricier hotels. *The Wall Street Journal.* Retrieved from http://online.wsj.com/news/articles/SB10001424052702304458604577488822667325882

Mayer-Schönberger, V., & Cukier, K. (2013). *Big data: A revolution that will tansform how we live, work, and think.* Boston, MA: Houghton Mifflin Harcourt.

McChesney, R. (2013). *Digital disconnect.* New York: The New Press.

McGee, M. (2013, August). EdgeRank is dead: Facebook's news feed algorithm now has close to 100K weight factors. *Marketing Land.* Retrieved from http://marketingland.com/edgerank-is-dead-facebooks-news-feed-algorithm-now-has-close-to-100k-weight-factors-55908

McStay, A. (2011). *The mood of information: A critique of online behavioural advertising.* New York: Continuum.

McStay, A. (2013). *Creativity and advertising: Affect, events and process.* New York and Oxford: Routledge.

Morozov, E. (2013). *To save everything, click here: The folly of technological solutionism.* New York: PublicAffairs.

Mosco, V. (2009). *The political economy of communication* (2nd ed.). Thousand Oaks, CA: Sage Publications Ltd.

Nakamura, L. (2002). *Cybertypes: Race, ethnicity, and identity on the internet.* New York: Routledge.

Nichols, W. (2013, March). Advertising analytics 2.0. *Harvard Business Review.* Retrieved from http://hbr.org/2013/03/advertising-analytics-20/

Notess, G. R. (2012). Searching in disguise. *Online, 26*(1), 43–46.

Pariser, E. (2010). *The filter bubble: What the internet is hiding from you.* New York: Penguin Press.

Peterson, T. (2012, October). Another agency claims Facebook changes. *Adweek.* http://www.adweek.com/news/technology/another-agency-claims-facebook-algorithm-changes-144405

Pew Research Center's Internet & American Life Project. (2012a). *Search engine use 2012.* Retrieved from http://bit.ly/yj7QMP

Pew Research Center's Internet & American Life Project. (2012b). *Social network sites and politics.* Retrieved from http://bit.ly/zrzR0q

Simonite, T. (2012, June). What Facebook knows. *MIT Technology Review.* Retrieved from http://www.technologyreview.com/featuredstory/428150/what-facebook-knows/

Smythe, D. W. (1981). *Dependency road: Communications, capitalism, consciousness and Canada.* Norwood, NJ: Ablex Publishing.

Solove, D. (2002, July). Digital dossiers and the dissolution of fourth amendment privacy. *Southern California Law Review, 75,* 1083–1168.

Steiner, C. (2012). *Automate this: How algorithms came to rule our world.* New York: The Penguin Group.

Sunstein, C. (2009). *Republic.com 2.0.* Princeton, NJ: Princeton University.

Sweeney, L. (2013) Discrimination in online ads delivery study. *Data Privacy Lab.* Retrieved from http://dataprivacylab.org/projects/onlineads/1071–1.pdf

Tavani, H. T. (2010). *Ethics and technology: Controversies, questions, and strategies for ethical computing* (3rd ed.). Hoboken, NJ: John Wiley & Sons, Inc.

Terranova, T. (2000). Free labor: Producing culture for the digital economy. *Social Text, 18*(63), 33–58.

Terranova, T. (2004). *Network culture: Politics for the information age.* London: Pluto Press.

Tufekci, Z. (2014, Feburary 12). Is the internet good or bad? Yes: Its time to rethink our nightmares about surveillance. *Medium.* Retrieved from https://medium.com/matter/is-the-internet-good-or-bad-yes-76d9913c6011

Turow, J. (2011). *The daily you: How the new advertising industry is defining your identity and your worth.* New Haven, CT: Yale University Press.

Universal Declaration of Human Rights, The. (1948). Retrieved from http://www.un.org/en/documents/udhr

Vaidhyathanan, S. (2012, April 17). Voting against the algorithm. *Slate*. Retrieved from http://slate.me/IQpeF0.

Wasco, J., & Erickson, M. (2009). The political economy of YouTube. In P. Snickars & P. Vonderau (Eds.), *The YouTube reader* (pp. 372–386). Stockholm: National Library of Sweden.

Wasserman, T. (2011, January 31). Facebook ads perform about half as well as regular banner ads. *Mashable*. Retrieved from http://mashable.com/2011/01/31/facebook-half-click-throughs/

8 The Digital Transformation of Physical Retailing

Sellers, Customers, and the Ubiquitous Internet

Joseph Turow

The digital/physical and offline/online distinctions that have become part of many popular and academic discourses are anachronistic when it comes to shopping. That is not just because physical stores have websites but also because those stores increasingly use the internet to connect to customers while they are moving through physical aisles. The dominant reason for this development is retailers' desire for data. Sellers believe the right data about the right customers at the right time are required assets for their business, online and off. This perceived need is restructuring the architecture of physical and digital retailing, and the relationship between the two, in ways that make the physical selling environment increasingly personalized for the individual prospect.

The aim here is to elaborate this theme by exploring how and why physical retailing and the internet are coming together. The material presented here comes from ongoing research on social implications of the digital-media technologies employed by the retail institution. The work has thus far involved the wide reading of trade magazines, attendance of marketing-industry meetings, and examination of historical studies of merchandising. Based on this research, the following pages place the developments in historical context, sketch approaches retailers use and want to use, and consider their social consequences. An associated aim is to encourage work by communication researchers on the digital transformation of physical retailing. Although academics have begun to study the social implications of consumer surveillance, surveillance in the shopping aisle has received almost no attention. This neglect is unfortunate because the shopping aisle is becoming a crucial communication venue. Knowingly and unknowingly, people are circulating information about themselves to merchants via social, mobile, and location-aware media. Moreover, examining the retailing sector of the ubiquitous internet reveals interesting dynamics regarding a topic that academics have only recently begun to consider: how emerging technologies and elite discussions about them turn into taken-for-granted elements of people's worlds with profound implications that reinforce trends elsewhere in society.

SHOPPING AND THE UBIQUITOUS INTERNET

As the internet has become part of our daily lives, academics have been confronting topics that hardly, if ever, came up in previous writings on media industries. These include privacy (see Nissenbaum, 2009; Solove, 2010; Turow, 2011; Mayer-Schoenberger, 2011), the individual as both producer and consumer of media materials (Benkler, 2007; Jenkins, 2008), the increasing quantification of data about audiences (Turow, 2011; Turow & Draper, 2012; Mayer-Schonberger & Cukier, 2013), and changing brand strategies and media subsidies (Jenkins, Ford, & Green, 2013; Banet-Weiser, 2012). Academics have begun to study how these topics converge with digital tracking and to tease out their implications (Andrejevic, 2007; Lyon, 2007; Turow, 2011; MacKinnon, 2013; Mayer-Schoenberger & Cukier, 2013). Yet a major domain where individual interactions, new digital technologies, audience quantification, changing brand strategies, and surveillance mix—the shopping aisle—has received almost no attention from communication researchers. For example, an analysis of the titles of the approximately 2,500 papers presented at the annual conferences of the International Communication Association and the National Communication Association from 2008 to 2012 found only eighteen with the words *supermarket, mall, retail,* or *outdoor*—and only five papers with *GPS, geolocation* or *geo-location* in the title.

This lack of attention may reflect a general tendency of communication researchers to focus on industries that centrally aim to create and circulate media content, not industries that generate content as subsidiary to selling other products (Turow, 2014). It's also tempting to propose the seemingly pedestrian nature of shopping as another reason media studies scholars have paid this area little attention. Yet shopping is a fundamental human activity in twenty-first century societies. It is also the central area of commerce where organizations challenged by new competitive pressures are widely implementing suggestions for the tracking and quantification of individuals that marketing executives, futurists, inventors, device manufacturers, and consultants have offered for many years. This chapter will show, in fact, that twenty-first century merchants are making customer surveillance via digital media a strategic imperative in physical stores as well as online and on mobile. In the process, the increasing ubiquity of tracking devices as part of shopping is making surveillance a normalized—or 'habituated,' in van Dijck (2013) terminology—aspect of everyday life.

PHYSICAL STORES BEFORE THE INTERNET

Through much of human history person-to-person selling has been the norm. Whether via informal transactions or in more structured settings such as markets and stores, buyers and sellers have seemingly always haggled over the price and nature of merchandise. Records and stories going back to biblical times suggest that in their bargaining, buyers and sellers inevitably took characteristics and cues of their counterparts into account. The nature and price of merchandise was therefore often tailored to the particular transaction (see Fontaine, 1996; Friedman, 2004). When formal stores developed, they placed in public view items the merchants believed everyone could afford, but they also often invited relatively wealthy individuals to visit special areas where they could experience more expensive goods.

The rise of the department store in the nineteenth century represented an unusual break in this pattern. The historian Daniel Boorstin (1958) called department stores 'palaces of consumption.' Stewart's in New York, John Wanamaker in Philadelphia, Jordan Marsh in Boston, and Field, Leiter and Company in Chicago offered a wide range of merchandise at a variety of price points. Clearly, not all those who saw the goods could afford them. That anyone could gain free admission to see a wide range of expensive and cheap goods for sale was a novel idea built into the department store model. The stores also democratized prices. The policy of fixed fees, begun on a large scale by Stewart's in the US, was born partly of business necessity. Store owners could not trust their hundreds or even thousands of employees to haggle profitably with customers.

Despite the department store's ascent in the US, the traditional model of person-to-person selling continued. As late as 1954, sociologist Gregory P. Stone (1954) pointed out that widespread 'personalization and moralization of customer-clerk relationships' took place in the Chicago neighborhood he studied, particularly in 'independent' (that is, non-chain) stores. These sorts of tailored exchanges between sellers and buyers also appeared in homeowners' interactions with door-to-door sellers. The salespeople would often make unsolicited calls to homes to pitch products as varied as vacuum cleaners, brushes, cleaning products, storm windows, encyclopedias, cosmetics, and water softeners.

Discussions of traveling salespeople in comparison to local stores presage later dynamics around the internet. Neighborhood merchants worried about the price competition the itinerants posed because their fixed expenses were so much less than those of physical stores. Some localities outlawed door-to-door salespeople, ostensibly because they bothered people in their homes. And, in fact, analyses of home-selling dynamics brought out themes of extreme sales pressures and 'invasion of privacy,' which typically meant uninvited drop-ins (Jolson, 1972, p. 88). Yet many people seem to have appreciated at least some of the visits. One 1972 analysis of 200 Baltimore households found that 'nearly 65% of the consumer sample felt that a major advantage of direct selling is that all family members can inspect the product together so that a joint decision may be made.' (Sellers of expensive products tended to visit homes on weekends or evenings when family members were together.) The study also noted that 'approximately 45% of the consumers interviewed confirm the advantage of trying out the product under actual conditions of use'—for example, a vacuum cleaner in the home (Jolson, 1972, p. 88).

Behind discussions of sales tactics was a keen awareness of the data-gathering benefits the home environment brought to the seller. The in-home salesperson often picked up cues about the potential buyer and her family that helped the path toward persuasion. The home became both a place to exhibit products and collect information on consumers. Consider the Fuller Brush salesman as an example of this sort of interactive selling. Founded in 1906, the Fuller Brush firm created a sales force of thousands that called on nearly nine out of ten American homes through the 1950s. As late as 1985 all of the company's sales were still generated door-to-door (Lacitis, 2008). The Fuller Brush representative's interaction with and knowledge of clients is suggested in the memories of Art Pearson, who worked in the Seattle area. According to the *Seattle Times*, Pearson perfected the art of sizing up his customer to make a sale. 'When I go into a house,' he told a reporter, 'my eyes wander through the house quickly. I suggest, 'Maybe you need a wall brush for those cobwebs, or window cleaner" (Lacitis, 2008).

Fuller filed for bankruptcy in 2012, and the number of salespeople dwindled. Nicole Levy of the *Milwaukee Journal-Sentinel* telegraphed the changing forces at work: Many people now live in apartment houses where traveling salesmen are unwelcome. Many middle-class women now work outside the home and aren't inclined to salesmen when get home. And 'Consumers, more concerned with price than substance, are browsing discount store aisles or the internet to find the household items they need' (Levy, 2012).

SHIFT TO THE INTERNET

Note the mention of the internet. Levy astutely realized that for many people the internet at home has taken on functions door-to-door salespeople filled. Expenditures certainly support the idea that people's interactions with sellers via internet-connected devices drive purchases. eMarketer estimates these interactions spurred $351.8 billion of ecommerce spending during 2012 and projects the number will rise to $602.3 billion in 2017. What's more, eMarketer (2013) figures that people who buy on desktops, laptops, tablets, and/or smartphones now represent about 72% of the internet-using population, a percentage eMarketer expects will rise to 78% in 2017.

These expansions reflect a process that has been building for decades. A Wikipedia timeline charts the beginnings of electronic commerce back to the 1970s. The 1980s saw a number of key endeavors, including France Telecom's Minitel online ordering system (1982) and the first comprehensive electronic commerce service, CompuServe's Electronic Mall, in the United States and Canada (1984). It was during the 1990s that transformative developments ignited ecommerce along the lines we see today. A signpost of things to come was a 1993 *Adweek* essay urging the advertising industry to 'take note' of the internet. It has, the essay said, 'the potential to become the next great mass/personal medium' (Schrage, 1993).

One development encouraging this direction was the US government's allowance of commercial activities on the internet, which through the 1980s had primarily been a vehicle for university and military researchers. The real breakthrough for advertising and commerce turned out to be Tim Berners-Lee's turn-of-the-'90s creation of the World-Wide-Web system of hyperlinks. It led to the 1993 creation of the first popular graphical web browser, Mosaic, at the University of Illinois. Mosaic, and its commercial successor, Netscape, which appeared in 1994, allowed people to interact with photos of goods on websites as well as to purchase them directly on the sites.

Like the door-to-door sales organization, web-marketing firms marketers saw their strengths in interactivity and the associated possibility of collecting enormous amounts of information about the prospect. A crucial step in learning about the prospect was Netscape technicians' 1993 invention of the cookie. The aim was to allow a web merchant to store information about customer's interactions and purchases on the site. The cookie represented a first step in remembering the sales relationship online. Other developments around that time deepened the notion that the computer-driven environment was a place for both exhibiting products to prospects and collecting data on those people with the aim of using the information to persuade them toward purchase. Amazon.com launched in 1995, and it has since become an iconic electronic store with enormous capabilities for data gathering and analyses of customers. Google, the equally iconic venue for merchant advertisements, consumer product searches, and metrics indicating the value of the interactions, began its corporate life in 1998. It was around these fundamental building blocks for one-to-one selling that a digital marketing world emerged during the late 1990s and beyond (Turow, 2011, pp. 34–64).

TENSIONS BETWEEN THE INTERNET
AND PHYSICAL STORES

Through the 1990s and much of the 2000s shopping via the internet meant shopping from a desktop or laptop computer outside of a physical store. The emergence of what online merchants called Cyber Monday beginning 2005 as a major online shopping day after Thanksgiving recognized that people were using their high-speed work stations to buy Christmas gifts from web stores (Wikipedia, 2014a). Although Cyber Monday was evidence e-commerce was growing in the mid-2000s, it was still but a tiny part of the overall retail picture. Physical retailers did not worry about the competition, although many did field their own websites. In most cases (e.g., Miller, 2008) they treated these sites as separate businesses from the physical spaces; a bifurcation generally existed between the online and off.

By about 2010, though, US retailers in physical stores began to move urgently to connect digitally with customers in their physical spaces. Three related factors drove this development. The first was the spread of mobile devices, especially internet-connected smartphones. The second was retailers' concern shoppers were using the phones to purchase goods from the internet while in the stores. The third was physical retailers' perception that online competitors were posing threats that by 2010 had to be confronted directly. Together, these developments began to profoundly change the interactions between physical retailers and customers.

The spread of smartphones encouraged the other factors. According to the International Telecommunications Union (ITU, 2014a), in 2000 43% of Americans were internet users, although only 2.5% accessed it via wired broadband. By 2006 the proportion of American users had climbed to 68.9%, and 20% had wired broadband access. Around that time Verizon Wireless became the first US mobile provider of 'V-Cast' 3G wireless service that offered 'the equivalent of a broadband Internet connection delivered to the phone,' in the words of a 2005 *Adweek* article (*Adweek* staff, 2005). Still, mobile-cellular broadband was not yet a part of American life. A 2006 report on 'Home Broadband Adoption' by the Pew Internet and American Life Project did not mention mobile at all (Horrigan, 2006). Three years later the situation had changed substantially. According to the ITU, American internet users had climbed to 71%; 25.5% of those had 'fixed' or wired broadband subscriptions, whereas 46.9% now had 'wireless'—primarily mobile-cellular—broadband access to the internet (ITU, 2014a, 2014b).

Judging by the articles in *Advertising Age* and *Adweek*, the two major marketing trade papers of the era, it was only when American mobile phones came with internet connectivity that marketers began to publicly discuss links between the internet and in-store marketing. The 2005 Adweek article about V-Cast predicted that the mobile phone would be 'the device to bridge the multichannel retail customer experience.' It noted that 'The promise of mobile technology' is that shoppers would be able to learn about products as they walked through store aisles. '3G solves the speed barrier. Getting to ease of use will require good information design' (Adweek staff, 2005).

Insightful as this prediction was in the years before shopping-oriented mobile sites and apps, they proved to be overly optimistic in their vision of an informative web that would work harmoniously with the utility of the physical premises. The writer didn't anticipate the fierce competition that would arise between independent online sellers such as Amazon and Gilt and brick-and-mortar firms straining to compete with their lower overhead and therefore low and (often) tax-free prices. Such struggles developed rather quickly over the next few years, as the now-pervasive nature of the internet helped internet-only retailers to generate billions of dollars. The failure of the large Borders bookstore chain during 2011 in the wake of online competition raised the specter that internet merchants could one day marginalize brick-and-mortar locations. The tensions ratcheted higher and higher as online-only retailers adopted a variety of tracking and data-mining technologies to efficiently, and seemingly effectively, target and tailor their ads, sites and offers.

A good deal of retailers' angst from 2010 to 2013 crystalized around concerns that people go to stores to learn about products and then (often while in the stores) use their smartphones to find lower prices on an internet site and purchase from there via the phone or their home computers. The concerns reflect a realization of a potential power shift with the store. Prior to the digital age, the retail aisle was arranged through a negotiation between the goods manufacturer and the retailer. In the 21st century store that arrangement is potentially disrupted by the public's increasing use of digital media to subvert the prices and assortments that the retailers and manufacturers offer. They called the activity of store browsing and internet buying 'showrooming.' A Factiva search reveals that a *New York Times* reporter blog in December 2011 was the first mainstream source to use the term, and it was in connection with books. Reporter Julie Bosman (2011) wrote that 'Bookstore owners everywhere have a lurking suspicion: that the customers who type into their smartphones while browsing in the store, and then leave, are planning to buy the books online later—probably at a steep discount from the bookstores' archrival, Amazon.com.' Emphasizing industry concern, Bosman reported that bookstore showrooming's reality had now been verified through a survey by the Codex group.

The bookstores' fears, it turned out, were shared by a wide gamut of retailers. A month after the Bosman blog, the *Wall Street Journal* ran an article noting that Target was asking its suppliers to modify products with model numbers unique to Target. The goal, said the Journal, was to shield the retailer from the price comparisons that have become so easy for shoppers to perform on their computers and smartphones. Where special products aren't possible, Target asked the suppliers to help it match rivals' prices. The paper added that 'Showrooming is an increasing problem for chains ranging from Best Buy Co. to Barnes & Noble Inc., at the same time that it's a boon for Amazon.com Inc. and other online retailers. This year store sales overall edged up 4.1% during the holiday shopping season, whereas online sales jumped 15%. And although online sales represent only 8% of total sales, that is up from just 2% in 2000' (Zimmerman, 2012).

The article reported analysts' suggestions that Amazon could afford to price lower than most retailers on many goods because it was reaping profits from its cloud business and fees it charges independent merchants to sell on its website. Other online retailers have a step up because of significantly lower labor costs than brick and mortar stores and because they were not collecting sales tax in most states. If that weren't enough, 'consumer preferences are also moving to online.' The upshot, the *Journal* reported, was that analysts saw 'the old model' of retailing as broken. They didn't believe cosmetic product changes would fool customers and save the day. What seemed necessary was for brick-and-mortar retailers to compete well online.

In early 2012 that did not seem to be happening. 'Retailers like Target and industry giant Wal-Mart Stores Inc. have a lot of catching up to do, as analysts estimate their websites account for only 1% to 2% of their annual sales' (Zimmerman, 2012).

PHYSICAL RETAILERS' EMERGING INTERNET STRATEGIES

In the months that followed, some analysts and consultants questioned whether showrooming was the huge threat it initially seemed. In late 2013, for example, a joint study by the Columbia Business School and Aimia, a loyalty management company, concluded that 'only 6 percent of people using their smartphones in a store do so with the intent of purchasing a product online' (Clark, 2013). The Krillion shopping consultancy was more typical, however, in presenting evidence for substantial showrooming in 2013. Its report exhorted retailers to combat showrooming by providing 'consumers with more reasons and incentives to make the purchase while in the store' (Krillion, 2013). Other consultants more specifically stated that physical retailers needed to offer in-store internet to customers with the aim of learning information about them that could be leveraged to encourage or complete a sale. Biller Loller, a vice president of IBM's Smarter Commerce division, argued that a path to doing it involved making the internet ubiquitous in the store: '[R]ather than trying to stop customers from using their mobile phones while in store, retailers should offer them free wi-fi and alert them to it as soon as they walk into the store' (quoted in Clark 2013).

These suggestions reflect a wide discourse among retailers regarding responses to the challenges they see surrounding the shopper and the internet. The discussion centers on ways to use the internet to encourage repetitive visits and increased purchases in the face of competition from internet-only retailers. The core solution they have seized upon involves the internet's use for collection, analysis, and implementation of customer data. Retailers want to adopt virtual stores' ability to learn what products and prices will attract particular individuals and then present offers at opportune moments. They also want to enjoy their internet competitors' ability to identify customers with spending power in real time and, through personal messages, urge them toward reward programs with loyalty-status levels that will encourage purchases with profits retailers want. The brick-and-mortar retailers want to leverage all that with what they see as the still-unique position of physical stores as places where customers know they can hold, try, immediately buy, and easily return products. Exhaustive examination of the retailing trade press and attendance at marketing-industry meetings suggest three major strategies to do that are emerging. One is to identify and reach out to shoppers, and particularly 'best customers,' before they enter the store. A second is to call out to them with tailored offers while they are traveling through the store. And a third is to uses the check-out routine as a way to cement, extend, and refine digital relationships with customers. All three strategies involve use of the internet in conjunction with other digital technologies for the often-real-time collection, analysis, and implementation of customer data.

Reaching Shoppers Before They Enter the Store

Brick and mortar retailers believe they have to reach out to people digitally to lure them to the physical space. Catalina Marketing is a firm that helps supermarkets do that in the US, Europe, and Japan. In the US, it claims to understand 'the shopping preferences of 80 percent of U.S. households based on two years of purchase behavior' (Catalina Marketing, 2014a). Until a few years ago, Catalina's business centered on tracking people's purchases on 'reward' cards when they checked out of affiliated food, drug, and convenience stores and serving them coupons at checkout based on the previous fifty-two weeks of purchases. Although the firm successfully signed up advertisers interested in sponsoring the targeted coupons, the drawback was that offering customers discounts at the conclusion of a store visit led a substantial percentage of them to lose or forget to bring the coupons next time. Moreover, because 'the recent surge in digital coupon use over the last few years has consumers looking for value online even before they enter a retail store,' Catalina executives worked with their retail affiliates to distribute personalized coupons targeted to their customers (Catalina Marketing, 2014b). The goal was to yield higher in-store redemptions, learn additional information about customers by following their behavior online, and be able to reach two types of customers: those whose reward cards reflect particularly high purchases at a retailer ('your most loyal customers') and those who don't fit the most-loyal characterization but nevertheless 'pre-shop' the particular retailer by visiting its retailer's web, mobile, and social-media sites.

The online personalization Catalina is carrying out to help stores that sell consumer packaged goods is mirrored by a myriad of retailers and firms aiding all sorts of retailers. Department stores such as Macy's, big-box outlets such as Walmart, and supermarket chains such as Kroger's use personalized email, texting, and a gamut of social media from Facebook to Pinterest to connect with target audiences and their friends with tailored overtures. The Macy's department store chain has particularly been at the forefront of using online and offline data to personalize offers to customers and to more generally decide, based on the geographical footprint of products bought on its internet stores, what its physical stores in different locations should carry. Noting that seven of ten Americans visit a Macy's store at least annually, the firm's chief marketing officer in 2012 declared 'We saw we don't need more customers—we need the customers we have to spend more time with us' (Schiff, 2012). With the help of the Dunhunby retail-analytics consultancy, the chain instituted a program called MyMacy's. It gathers and analyzes Macy's customer data through three lenses. The *MyCustomerLoyalty* program quantifies the relationship between the frequency of individual customer visits and sales. *MyCustomerBehavior* monitors the style preferences and infers the purchase motivations of in-store and on the internet versions of Macy's. *MyCustomerEngagement* measures the extent to which the firm's optimization of activities covered by *MyCustomerLoyalty* and *MyCustomerEngagement* lead to profits (Schiff, 2012).

Both Macy's chief marketing officer (CMO) and its chief financial officer (CFO) have noted the importance of increasing the personalization of offers even before the customer sets foot in the store. The short version of Macy's privacy policy states bluntly that it collects information about 'you' from every interaction the individual has with the retailer, or with its vendors or undefined 'third parties' on the internet and off (Macy's, 2014). Those data can be linked to purchases via Macy's credit card and loyalty program. In a 2013 conversation with Citibank analysts, Macy's CFO noted that the firm uses the personal identification through Macy's credit card as an entry to 'communicating more closely with our customers and rewarding people who shop with us frequently. If you use our credit card we more quickly respond in terms of personalized emails, marketing, what have you' (Macy's, 2013). In 2012 tailored offers based on these data seemed to be behind what *DM Magazine* described as a 'hyper-personalized direct mail' effort: '500,000 unique versions of a single direct mail book in an effort to appeal to the individual' (Schiff, 2012). The next year, Macy's chief stores officer emphasized digital outreach as well as data-gathering; he stated that 'the whole digital realm allows us a lot more personalization' (Schiff, 2012).

Increasingly this digital outreach involves trying to lure people with personal offers as apps on their cell phones communicate proximity to deals. The activity is called geo-fencing; a geo-fence is 'a virtual perimeter for a real-world geographic area' (Wikipedia, 2014b). Supporters respond that mobile downloads for this purpose are becoming more common and shoppers will pick up the habit. At this point retailers see geo-fencing as an experiment. Venture capitalists are funding startups such as Retailmenot.com and Shopular with mobile apps that that track users' purchase interests. The firms aim to make money by selling retailers the ability to reach shoppers with personalized ads and discount coupons while they are nearby. Critics of the technology argue that individuals have not shown an inclination to load phone applications that badger them that way. Shopular tries to convince web users to download its app by arguing that the flood of retailers' emails can be overwhelming. 'Where do you begin,' its promotional video asks. 'Instead of hunting for deals, you're drowning in them. . . . With Shopular you will never miss your favorite deals. . . . Deals are handpicked and personalized. And the best part is, you don't even have to open the app.

Shopular will automatically pop up the hottest deals when you reach the mall' (Shopular, 2014).

In addition to these 'omnibus' geo-fencing apps that invite ads and discounts from a panoply of retailers, there are firms that aim to help individual firms invite and reinforce customers with personalized invitations in when they are in the vicinity. Catalina Marketing, for example, employs geo-fencing in apps it creates specifically for clients in order to augment the digital personalization aimed at whetting shoppers' appetites. In a press release clearly aimed at retailers, the company says geo-fencing, 'starts the conversation with the shopper the moment they arrive at the store' (Catalina Marketing 2013). Catalina adds 'Geo-fenced alerts and messages enable retailers to engage shoppers as they approach specific brick and mortar locations to remind them to use the retailer's app, giving them visibility into how much they can potentially save during that trip.' Similarly, Shopkick tells its over 6 million app downloads detects when shoppers are in or near partner stores Macy's, Old Navy, Best Buy, JCPenney, Crate & Barrel, Sports Authority, and Target, and offers rewards targeted to them. These are rewards, it tells its potential downloaders, 'for just walking in the store' (Shopkick, 2014).

In the emerging industrial logic of retailing, then, merchants reach out to potential customers even before they enter stores. Merchants moreover see the path near and around the physical sales emporium as a crucial data-transfer venue. Many also consider that the basic fact of surveillance is not hidden from the people to whom the merchants call out through their apps. The word spreading through the retailing ecosystem via consultants and the trade press is that people are willing to give up broad elements of their privacy if they receive relevant discounts and personalized service (see, for example, Forbes, 2013, p. 2). As Jose van Dijck (2013) notes, Facebook is changing the social meaning of words such as friends and sharing to match the marketing-and data-driven aims of the social media site. The activities describe here reflect a similar dynamic of habituating people to market-driven values. The physical retail industry's activities around stores embody the notion that information privacy is a path for exchanging a marketable asset rather than as a process for protecting personal identity shared with only cherished individuals. The same approach is suffusing retailers' two other major strategies for the ubiquitous internet in their physical realm.

Tailored Offers While Traveling Through the Store

Retailers have long used the word 'clienteling' to indicate an activity whereby desired customers walking in would be made to feel as if they were being treated particularly special. In high-end boutiques and expensive areas of department stores, sales associates greeted well-known frequent customers as they enter their departments, poured them coffee and even wine in special rooms, and even offered them unadvertised discounts at the point of purchase (Turow, 2006). Although salespeople in high-priced nooks might be able to do it regularly, high-traffic supermarkets, pharmacy, big box, and consumer electronic stores haven't had the ability to recognize people when they enter. Consequently, the idea of offering deals to customers coming into the store on the basis of what databases say about them is alluring. An obvious way to do this is to get customers to identify themselves electronically as they enter and move through the store.

Early forays in this direction involved supermarket kiosks that during the 1990s and 2000s invited customers walking into the stores to swipe their loyalty cards to receive customized coupons based on their purchase histories. In effect, it was the Catalina Marketing approach but at the beginning, not the end, of the shopping trip. Following those kiosk experiments were trials at Stop & Shop and other chains using hand-held devices presented personalized offers, including coupons, on the basis of how the supermarket had tagged the stopper. That paradigm has carried over to all sorts of stores because of the increased presence of the smartphone. In order to derail showrooming, stores encourage shoppers to access the stores' specific apps while in the aisles in order to access purchase lists they made before the visits, coupons they downloaded from home, new coupons as they enter the store, and maps of the location to help them find products.

From the retailer's standpoint, though, the internet is not an optimal technology to track someone inside a store because satellite signals that can specify a person's location do not typically penetrate buildings. It's therefore unrealistic to rely on the GPS signals of a smartphone to follow a person through the store and offer personalized discounts based on the products they are viewing, their shopping history, and a variety of life-cycle, behavioral, and social bits of information the retailer has collected or bought. To address that challenge a number of firms have been working with in-store radio signals or Bluetooth technologies to connect to people in the aisles. Shopkick is one of the firms expanding into this area with the help of Apple's iBeacon system. In November 2013 it touted trials at Macy's flagship store in Manhattan as well as its Union Square outlet in San Francisco. The technology involves inexpensive Bluetooth Low Energy (BLE) transmitters that Shopkick places around a store. When shoppers with Shopkick Apple phones with iOS7 pass the transmitters, Shopkick's 'shopBeacon' system can identify them and work with the retailer's information about them to assess their value and tailor offers. According to a Shopkick (2013) press release,

> shopBeacon can welcome shoppers when they enter a Macy's store and shows them location-specific deals, discounts, recommendations, and rewards, without having to remember to open the app. It can also tie at-home browsing behavior to in-store benefit; if the customer

'likes' a specific product online, if they so choose, shopBeacon can remind them when they enter the store that Macy's sells it. Even better, in the future it can also deliver department-specific offers throughout the store so favorite boots show up at the most useful time: in the shoe department.

(Shopkick, 2013)

One obstacle shopBeacon and rivals face is the need for the shopper to download the app. An alternative avenue toward customer recognition that doesn't require that step is automatic recognition of customers walking through the store. Retail consultant Karl Bjornson has suggested that in the future retailers will persuade their very good customers to unmask themselves coming in through instant biometrics—fingerprints, eye scanners—with the promise that they will have their identities protected from internet credit-card thieves and be rewarded as members of a community with special service and great deals. Retailers today seem to use biometrics only in check-cashing services. Moreover, retailers have so far not tried to implemented related biometric technology that doesn't require checking in: facial recognition. Part of the reason may be that it isn't perfected, but part of it may be a fear of alienating customers with passive cameras that learn who they are without permission and track their movements through the store. There are, however, several startups that help stores recognize customers' gender, age while they also provide 'real-time updates on where shoppers are browsing, how long they stay in store, what shoppers do at rival stores and how people window shop' (Rudarakanchana, 2013).

Euclid Analytics, one of the nascent recognition firms, deploys sensors in thousands of retail stores and fast food restaurants. Euclid chief managing officer Adam Wilson stated in 2013 that the data can help retailers develop a psychological profile of their broad shopping base. The data can also be matched with Census data to develop demographic profiles of a store's customers. All of the firm's images are anonymous to Euclid and reported in aggregate to the firm's clients. Although legal, a pilot Euclid project in stores of the luxury retailer Nordstrom attracted complaints from customers, concerns from lawmakers and regulators, and a call from privacy groups that retailers who track shoppers even anonymously should at least tell them Rukarakanchana, 2013).

Faced currently with the absence of socially acceptable ways to electronically track shoppers in stores without their permission, retailers are pursuing the approach of encouraging shoppers to see 'privacy' as a negotiating tool. They urge customers to download apps with the promise of maximizing their experiences and getting the best deals. So, for example, during the 2013 Christmas season the Famous Footware chain placed large 3D posters in mall walkways announcing that 'victory in the palm of your hand' would come to shoppers who down 'the Famous App.' The posters illustrated how a smartphone would deliver 'rewards points' and great offers 'anytime, on the go' if the shopper obeyed the bright-red exhortation to 'Download Now!' Some department stores, not inclined to trust their best customers will use apps, try a semi-automated avenue: stationing 'greeters' around the store whose goal is to ignite a data-driven exchange after asking the customer's name. As a South African marketing newsletter writing about European trends described it,

> Armed with roaming tablet or smartphone devices, in-store sales staff can tap into the central database of customer information—where profiles and preferences across channels are synched to create a full picture of a customer's entire history. Interactions are more informed, more personalised and therefore far more likely to result in a sale.
>
> (Marketing Update, 2013)

Using the Checkout to Cement, Extend, and Refine Digital Relationships

Retailers call the checkout area the point of service (POS), probably because it has traditionally been the one place where the customer and the store representative would surely meet—and where the representative could reinforce the image of the store. That role still exists, but the rising centrality of the internet in people's lives and the rising importance of digital interactions in the store are transforming the purpose and dynamics of the POS. The checkout is the place where customers redeem the coupons they printed off websites or loaded onto their smartphones before shopping, while entering the store, or in the store. It is also the place where the store can offer yet more personalized discounts, often through terminals provided by Catalina Marketing and sometimes from the retailer's own POS machine (which often alerts the sales associate) based its incentive algorithms.

From the retailer's standpoint, the standout utility of the new POS systems is for the collection of yet more data about individual customers that can be used for any number of decisions about interactions with them across desktops, laptops, feature phones, tablets, and smartphones. The aim is to be able to evaluate a customer's value efficiently and decide whether a customer should be a target of advertisements or discounts, and if so, which and when. Currently the main way of implementing this goal is by using the rewards card or store credit card to collect data about each basket of purchases; tracking the items, groupings, and prices paid over time; following customer's search activities online or in the store app; and linking all of that to other information about the customer and her/his family volunteered at loyalty-card signup and/or purchased from third-party brokers. Some analysts and technologists believe, however, that in the not-too-distant future these ways will be augmented at the POS using facial recognition (see Sullivan, 2013; Schuman, 2013).

A Russian technology firm, Synqera, conducted trials in late 2013 that suggest the utility of POS facial recognition for refining a Russian retail chain's understanding of a customer. The retailer's aim was to supplement loyalty-card information for customers who have one and stand in for a loyalty card for those who don't. Synqera's head of international marketing explained the approach to Evan Schuman of the StorefrontBacktalk retail news site. She noted that the POS camera-software combination will link shoppers with loyalty cards to their photos:

> If the customer has no loyalty card or doesn't want to identify himself with a loyalty card, then the system recognizes his general mood [by the presence or absence of a smile], gender and age in order to use this data for targeting of the content. . . . If the customer identified himself with a loyalty card, the system double checks the customer age and gender with data sourced through facial recognition. If the Synqera system sees that the loyalty card data differs from the camera data, then it evaluates the correctness of the camera data (probability defined for the particular user's gender and age) and, if it is high, gives it priority.
>
> (Schuman, 2013)

Theft might be one reason to be concerned with an unmatched photo and card. More commonly, though, the lack of correspondence relates to a card's use by friends or other family members. The facial recognition therefore helps the retailer to parse its data about the card. The POS systems and the backend analytics 'take into account that these few users are linked to one card and base the analysis and relevant content on the facial recognition data' (Schuman, 2013). As Schuman (2013) sees it, 'these biometrics help ensure that message or promotion being displayed are the right ones.' The Synqera executive noted (Schuman, 2013) that her firm's software can even note whether these are successful for each person at checkout. 'Users' smiles are used for the evaluation of the content effectiveness,' she said. She added smile recognition is also used in those stores as a way to get a prize of some kind. 'If the user smiles, he gets a virtual achievement badge or extra loyalty bonuses to his card,' she said.

CONCLUSIONS

Considering the future of facial-recognition systems such as Synqera, Storefrontbacktalk's Schuman (2013) noted two ways they can evolve beyond what Synqera is currently trying. The first is to link a checkout customer's features to a name by checking the internet and other sources. The second approach is to keep the person anonymous and 'instead merely captur[e] the facial data points and not[e] what purchases the person attached to that face makes. Then, when the cameras catch that same face again (say, perhaps four days later), the system will remember the prior purchases.' With either approach, once the system identifies the shopper and matches the person's face—or keeps track of an anonymous person's face—that that information can be tied to purchases via the smartphone and credit cards. In fact, as Schuman recognizes, the facial-recognition process might start outside the physical store. A merchant might present customers with financial incentives to download a free mobile app which as part of its terms and conditions gives the app the right to monitor peoples' faces as they walk into the store. The merchant could then offer entering shoppers service and deals personalized to their shopping histories and the retailer's calculation of their long-term value to the business. And although accuracy can be a problem today, says Schuman, 'look for this technology to get an order of magnitude more accurate over the next couple of years.'

This perspective is by no means unusual within the retail industry. Also not unusual is the related perspective that customers will come to accept surveillance during shopping if stores present them with incentives for doing it. As we have seen, data collection reflects the hope by merchants that programs built around knowledge of the customer are the solution to competition with online sellers along the abilities of many shoppers to check deals via an internet that is becoming accessible virtually everywhere in many societies. Public emporia increasingly imply to customers they are treated differently from one another based on information unknowable even by the customers themselves. Based on *customer-value* algorithms tied to scoring technologies, that mutability provides different shopping agendas, information, and prices to certain people rather than others. As early as 2005, retail consultant Karl Bjornson suggested (as quoted in Turow, 2006) that the trajectory of the business was to encourage people to accept recognition technology with the rhetoric of securing their identity and receiving relevant offers. Left unsaid, he noted, was that retailers will not treat all customers who offer their data equally. The best customers in the best niches will get the best deals. In contrast, 'people not in the right segments will be left behind. They will not have as rewarding an experience.'

As the twenty-first century moves forward, the technologies of personalization and the social-discrimination issues linked to them will become ever-central to the ways people shop for goods and services. The developments open a huge terrain of questions for media researchers. To what extent and in what ways are merchants transforming the architecture of physical and digital retailing, and the relationship between the two, in ways that make the selling environment increasingly dynamic and mutable for the individual shopper? How are stores dealing with quick-changing, often personalized, prices presented to customers by their competitors online and on mobile? To what extent and how do merchants derive new ways to define, identify, track, re-evaluate, and keep customers they define as more or less desirable from the standpoint of offering them special deals? How do shoppers respond to these changes? How, specifically, do they deal with uncertainty regarding what stores know about them and how stores score them? To what extent and how do the routines people adopt that enact privacy as a transactional process in the retail space carry over to their willingness to exchange data in other social institutions—for example, education, politics, and health care? The retailing industry's use of the internet is a fascinating, important topic that ought to engage communication researchers in the years ahead.

REFERENCES

Adweek staff. (2005, August 15). Interactive shopping: Art and commerce. *Adweek*.

Andrejevic, M. (2007). *Surveillance and power in the interactive era*. Lawrence, Kansas: University Press of Kansas.

Ball, K., Lyon, D., & Haggerty, K. (Eds.). *Routledge international handbook of surveillance studies*. London and New York: Routledge.

Banet-Weiser, S. (2012). *Authentic™*. New York: NYU Press.

Benkler, Y. (2007). *The wealth of networks: How social production transforms markets and freedom*. New Haven: Yale University Press.

Boorstin, D.J. (1958). *The Americans: The democratic experience*. New York: Random House.

Bosman, J. (2011, December 4). Book shopping in stores, then buying online. *New York Times Media Decoder*.

Catalina Marketing. (2013, October 7). Catalina modularizes its personalized mobile platform for CPG retailers. *Catalina Press Release*.

Catalina Marketing. (2014a, April 19). Insights. *Catalina Marketing Website*. Available at http://www.catalinamarketing.com/insights/

Catalina Marketing. (2014b, April 19). Digital rewards, *Catalina Marketing Website*. Available at http://www.catalinamarketing.com/media-networks/digital-rewards/

Clark, C. (2013, August 12). Showrooming: If you can't beat it, leverage it. *1to1 Media*. Retrieved from http://www.1to1media.com/view.aspx?docid=34416&utm_source=1to1weekly&utm_medium=email&utm_campaign=08122013

eMarketer. (2013). B2C ecommerce sales in North America, by Country, 2011–2017. *Emarketer*.

Fontaine, L. (1996). *History of peddlers in Europe* (V. Wittalker, Trans.). Durham, NC: Duke University Press.

Forbes. (2013, October). The privacy of privacy: Reflecting consumers' limits while realizing the marketing benefits of big data. *Forbes Insights*. Retrieved from http://www.forbes.com/forbesinsights/promise_of_privacy/

Friedman, W.A. (2004). *Birth of a salesman: The transformation of selling in America*. Cambridge, MA: Harvard University Press.

Horrigan, J.B. (2006, May 28). Home broadband adoption 2006, *Pew Internet and American Life*. Retrieved from http://www.pewinternet.org/~/media/Files/Reports/2006/PIP_Broadband_trends2006.pdf.pdf

International Telecommunication Union. (2014a). Welcome to ITU's ICT-eye. *International Telecommunication Union Website*. Retrieved from http://www.itu.int/net4/itu-d/icteye/

International Telecommunication Union. (2014b). ITU ICT dynamic reports wizard. *International Telecommunication Union Website*. Retrieved from http://www.itu.int/ITU-D/ICTEYE/Reporting/DynamicReportWizard.aspx

Jenkins, H. (2008). *Convergence culture*. New York: NYU Press.

Jenkins, H., Ford, S., & Green, J. (2013). *Spreadable media*. New York: NYU Press.

Jolson, M.A. (1972, October). Direct selling: Consumer vs. salesman. *Business Horizons*, p. 88.

Krillion. (2013, September). Mobile momentum: Spotlight on the mobile local shopper. *Krillion*. Retrieved from http://about.krillion.com/WhitePaperThankYou

Lacitis, E. (2008, April 20). Burien man is an American icon: Oldest active Fuller brush man. *The Seattle Times*. Retrieved from http://seattletimes.com/html/localnews/2004361380_fullerbrushman20m.html

Levy, N. (2012, August 27). Fuller brush salesman still pounding the pavement, *Milwaukee Journal Sentinel*. Retrieved from http://www.jsonline.com/news/milwaukee/fuller-brush-salesman- still-pounding-the-pavement-4d6k3ni-167629185.html

Lyon, D. (2007). *Surveillance studies*. London: Polity.

MacKinnon, R. (2013). *Consent of the networked*. New York: Basic Books.

Macy's. (2013, May 29). *Macy's management presents at Citi's 2013 Global Consumer Conference* (Transcript).

Macy's. (2014). Privacy policy. *Macy's Website*. Retrieved from https://customerservice.macys.com/app/answers/detail/a_id/40/

Marketing Update. (2013, December 17). Adobe believes omni-channel strategies will give local retailers the competitive edge. *Marketing Update Website*. Retrieved from http://www.marketingupdate.co.za/?IDStory=58650

Mayer-Schoenberger, V. (2011). *Delete*. Princeton: Princeton University Press.

Mayer-Schoenberger, V., & Cukier K. (2013). *Big data*. New York: Houghton Mifflin Harcourt.

Miller, C. C. (2008, December 4). An online boom that may not last. *New York Times*, p. B-3.

Nissenbaum, H. (2009). *Privacy in context*. Stanford, CA: Stanford Law Books.

Rudarakanchana, N. (2013, December 20). How big data companies are trying to win corporate clients. *International Business Times News*.

Schiff, A. (2012, January). Macy's CMO shares loyalty insights at NRF big show. *DMNews*. Retrieved from http://www.dmnews.com/macys-cmo-shares-loyalty-insights-at-nrf-big-show/article/223344/

Schrage, M. (1993, May 17). Out there: The ultimate network. *Adweek*. Retrieved from http://www.adweek.com/news/advertising/out-there-ultimate-network-bby-michael-schragbbr-clearnonebr-clearnonelooking-next-

Schuman, E. (2013, July 1). As chain trials facial recognition, channel assumptions flip. *StorefrontBackTalk*. Retrieved from http://storefrontbacktalk.com/print.php?ID=17510

Shopkick. (2013, November 20). Shopkick debuts shopBeacon. *PR Newswire*. Retrieved from http://www.prnewswire.com/news-releases/shopkick-debuts-shopbeacon-232652521.html

Shopkick. (2014, April 19). About. *Shopkick Website*. Retrieved from http://shopkick.com/about

Shopular (2014). Homepage. *Shopular Website*. Retrieved from http://www.shopular.com.

Solove, D. (2010). *Understanding privacy*. Cambridge, MA: Harvard University Press.

Stone, G. P. (1954). City shoppers and urban identification: Observations on the social psychology of city life. *American Journal of Sociology*, 60(1), 36–45.

Sullivan, L. (2013, August 23). Zoomkube introduces facial recognition in retail stores. *Online Media Daily*. Retrieved from http://www.mediapost.com/publications/article/207520/zoomkube-introduces-facial-recognition-in-retail-s.html

Turow, J. (2006). *Niche envy*. Cambridge, MA: MIT Press.

Turow, J. (2011). *The daily you*. New Haven: Yale University Press.

Turow, J. (2014). The case for studying in-store media. *Journal of Media Industries, 1*(1), 62–68. http://www.mediaindustriesjournal.org/index.php/mij/article/view/24/50

Turow, J., & Draper N. (2012). Advertising's new surveillance ecosystem. In K. Ball, D. Lyon, & K. Haggerty (Eds.), *Routledge international handbook of surveillance studies*. London and New York: Routledge.

Van Dijck, J. (Ed.). *The culture of connectivity*. Oxford, UK: Oxford University Press.

Wikipedia. (2014a). Cyber Monday. *Wikipedia*. Retrieved from http://en.wikipedia.org/wiki/Cyber_Monday

Wikipedia. (2014b). Geofencing. *Wikipedia*. Retrieved from http://en.wikipedia.org/wiki/Geofencing

Zimmerman, A. (2012, January 23). Showdown over 'showrooms, *The Wall Street Journal*.

Conclusion

Anja Bechmann and Stine Lomborg

In the introduction to this book, we provided a sketch of a conceptual framework for defining the ubiquitous internet as a multisided phenomenon characterized by accessibility, mobility, interoperability, and openness. The eight studies in this volume have expounded on these defining characteristics through analyses of how the ubiquitous internet is managed by users and the industry, respectively. Furthermore, in describing these characteristics and the associated practices the chapters all point to inherent tensions in the development and uses of ubiquitous internet.

Accessibility concerns the degree to which the internet is accessible across devices and platforms. Liu describes how the ubiquitous internet ought to be understood as seamlessly linking and encompassing not just networks and users but also an array of digital devices, each with (potential) embedded internet connectivity that facilitates decentralized usage in for instance public riots. Blank and Dutton show how the ubiquitous internet is increasingly taken for granted by the 'next generation of internet users,' defined as users accessing internet across mobile and multiple devices. At the same time, they suggest that ubiquitous internet creates new digital divides: Not all users adopt and benefit equally from the potential of constant, multiplatform access to the internet. Complementing these analyses of basic access patterns, Lomborg discusses how users regulate their accessibility once online. The users in her qualitative study appear to actively and reflexively redraw the boundaries of internet use that ubiquitous tethering to the internet tend to wash away, for instance, by turning off app notifications, and keeping their smartphones in silent mode as a way to control their accessibility. From an industry perspective, accessibility is thematized by Mosemghvdlishvili and Ibrus. Analyzing standardization processes at the level of internet governance and the politics of code, respectively, they suggests how access is negotiated between companies, governments, and organizations in in a constant battle. On the one hand, company business models rely on value creation through protection of services, codes, and standards (e.g., patents). On the other hand, collaboration and open standards, and by extension a more open internet, are for the greater good of society and foster the ability for industries to generate more user traffic.

Mobility refers to the idea of internet devices and platforms being portable, thus enabling users to be 'always on' (Baron, 2008), readily available for communication. Lomborg analyzes the lived experience of being always on and argues that it is chiefly manifested by users' sense of awareness of others and their continuous creation of personal bubbles with and for themselves (and not for communicating with others) in the course of everyday life. Expanding these insights with findings from analyses of behavioral data patterns on Facebook, Bechmann shows that even though mobile devices are used to access Facebook, an insignificant amount of the total posted status updates and links on Facebook derives from the mobile apps. This suggests that the mobility of the internet does not necessarily lead users to communicate more on social media despite the potential to communicate incessantly. Beyond everyday uses, Liu shows how mobility enables political protesters to organize and mobilize protests, thus emphasizing the empowering potential of the ubiquitous internet. From an industry perspective, Turow describes how mobile sensors and devices allow for (retail) business to create a precise profile of the customer feeding into more personalized services. Hence the mobility implied in the ubiquitous internet may both empower and commodify users.

Interoperability in this volume is described as the way in which internet services enable integration and data exchange with other services. Despite Facebook being one of the leading interoperable services on the internet, Bechmann shows how users choose not to share content across services to keep control of the self-portraying towards their network of friends. The users in her study clearly distinguish between different services and social arenas connected to these services. Based on the integrated character of internet services and the fine-grained user data generated from such integration Bodle illustrates how advertising through algorithms personalize user presentations. At the same time, advertising target only interested customers and thereby creates another ubiquitous internet divide. This calls for a societal need to focus on ethical algorithms.

Last but not least *openness* comes into play as the way in which the ubiquitous internet and its interwoven character expose data and thereby identities such as the behavioral patterns, filed and self-reported data of human subjects, organizations, and companies. The datafied society (Mayer-Schonberger & Cukier, 2013) makes openness both an opportunity and a threat. Liu analyzes how political activists can both be visible and hidden in the services of Facebook, Twitter, and YouTube. Transparent for the world to see the political regime of China and the riots, still hiding the data in international companies where political powers in China are not able to execute effective censorship. In response to the openness of the ubiquitous internet in terms of data-sharing and consolidation across services Bechmann exemplifies how high school students use more private forums such as Facebook groups to hide content and filter communicative exposure among the larger network of friends. Bodle points to the threats of openness as the (involuntary and voluntary) exposure of too much data about an individual as human subject, but also a need for openness on the level of the algorithms that control visibility on the ubiquitous internet in order to understand the filtering of information that is taking place. Turow proposes that businesses benefit from the ability to collect and consolidate user data, as this creates readily available knowledge and insights about customers. Yet openness is also a threat to the retail industry, as it comes with the risk that customers use the internet to find the most favorable price of a product elsewhere, thereby turning physical stores into showrooms.

The overall contribution of this edited volume is the identification and development of the four defining characteristics of the ubiquitous internet, each highlighted in different degrees and combinations in the eight studies presented. The characteristics are closely intertwined. Specifically, mobility is a part of the general accessibility of the internet and service interoperability provides potential for data exchange and data/code openness.

Despite a clear separation of user and industry studies in this volume, and in the media and communication studies literature at large, the user and industry perspectives converge in thematizing accessibility, mobility, interoperability, and openness. Each perspective highlights different aspects of these four characteristics, but together create a 360-degree perspective that shows how the ubiquitous internet consists of negotiations and ambivalence towards the communicative infrastructure and designs that we as society, industry, and users to a larger extend agree to as common standards in our lives and businesses (Bechmann & Lomborg, 2013). Still, this edited volume, along with other contributions (e.g., Ling, 2012), are only the first wave of interpreting the ubiquitous internet within media and communication studies. In terms of theory development, future research should refine the conceptual lens on ubiquitous internet along and beyond the interwoven dimensions of accessibility, mobility, interoperability, and openness launched in this volume. Further empirical work should explore new access platforms and the accelerations in sensorial devices, more bodily and mentally integrated internet and the connected practices and politics of users and industry stakeholders.

Against the background of the conceptual framework and studies in this volume, it is clear that the internet is not always ubiquitous. In critically thematizing the ubiquitous internet the studies have shown tensions in ubiquitous internet solutions and negotiations. For instance; the need of industry players to control and protect own standards and patents thereby creating divergence instead of convergence or interoperability, and the need of users to hide identities and information or control access to information through censorship. We have also seen how users shut off notifications and integration of app data. Instead of only using the potentials for ubiquity the users try to manually control their availability according to context. In the same way the digital divides (elderly, low income) accounted for in the concept of Next Generation Users (Blank & Dutton, this volume) suggest usage patterns that have more traditional character despite the promised benefits of ubiquity. This underscores the need in future research to address the ubiquitous internet not only in terms of the technological developments of integrating the internet in a wide array of products and devices, a development that implicitly assumes an all-encompassing internet. Rather, ubiquitous internet is an outcome of technological properties and social processes through which these properties are negotiated and adjusted in individual users' practices (e.g., their uptake or rejection of multiple access devices, and their strategies for managing the constant tethering), as well as by companies, policy makers, and other stakeholders.

REFERENCES

Baron, N. S. (2008). *Always on. Language in an online and mobile world*. Oxford, UK: Oxford University Press.

Bechmann, A., & Lomborg, S. (2013). Mapping actor roles in social media: Different perspectives on value creation in theories of user participation. *New Media & Society*, *15*(5), 765–781.

Ling, R. (2012). *Taken for grantedness: The embedding of mobile communication into society*. Cambridge, MA: MIT Press.

Mayer-Schonberger, V., & Cukier, K. (2013). *Big data: A revolution that will transform how we live, work, and think*. New York: Houghton Mifflin Hardback Publishing.

Contributors

Anja Bechmann is Associate Professor, Head of Digital Footprints Research Group at Aarhus University and board member of the National Council for Digital Security in Denmark. She is the initiator and co-developer of the Digital Footprints software and has published extensively on cross-media, internet economy, privacy regulation, and social media.

Grant Blank is Survey Research Fellow at the Oxford Internet Institute, University of Oxford, United Kingdom. He has published extensively on the digital divide and related topics. He manages the Oxford Internet Survey (http://oxis.oii.ox.ac.uk). He is currently working on a project linking census data with survey data to generate small area estimates of internet use and other internet variables for Great Britain.

Robert Bodle (Ph.D., University of Southern California) is Associate Professor of Communication and New Media Studies at Mount St. Joseph University and Adjunct Professor in the Department of Media, Journalism, and Film at Miami University. He has published extensively on the ethical and human rights implications of social media design, governance, and use, focusing primarily on privacy and freedom of expression. He is also Co-Chair of the Internet Rights and Principles Dynamic Coalition at the UN Internet Governance Forum.

William H. Dutton is the Quello Professor of Media and Information Policy in the Department of Media and Information of the College of Communication Arts and Sciences at MSU, where he is Director of the Quello Center. Prior to holding this chair, Bill was founding Director and Professor of Internet Studies at the Oxford Internet Institute, University of Oxford, and a Fellow of Balliol College.

Indrek Ibrus is Associate Professor at Tallinn University and an advisor on audiovisual affairs at the Ministry of Culture, Estonia. He has published extensively on mobile media, media innovation/evolution, and cross-media production. He is a co-editor of *Crossmedia Innovations: Texts, Markets, Institutions* (Peter Lang, 2012).

Jun Liu is Assistant Professor of Communication and IT at the University of Copenhagen in Denmark. His research on digital activism and social theory and political communication in China has been published in *Modern Asian Studies* and *Asiascape: Digital Asia*, among others.

Stine Lomborg is Associate Professor of Communication and IT at the University of Copenhagen in Denmark. She has published extensively on user studies, focusing on the role of social media in everyday life. She is the author of *Social Media—Social Genres: Making sense of the ordinary*.

Lela Mosemghvdlishvili (MSc) is a Ph.D. candidate and a lecturer in the Department of Media and Communication (Erasmus University, Rotterdam). Her current research interests include development of mobile technologies, the Critical Theory of Technology, Post-Marxist Critique, Political Economy, and Free/Libre Software Movement.

Joseph Turow is the Robert Lewis Shayon Professor of Communication at the University of Pennsylvania's Annenberg School for Communication. He is an elected Fellow of the International Communication Association and was presented with a Distinguished Scholar Award by the National Communication Association. His most recent book, from Yale University Press, is *The Daily You: How the New Advertising Industry is Defining Your Identity and Your Worth*.

Index

Printed and bound by CPI Group (UK) Ltd, Croydon, CR0 4YY

22/10/2024

01777626-0014